Social Science Theory.
Structure and Application

Social Science Theory, Structure and Application

by

Herbert I. London

Professor Social Studies Education
New York University

With Frederick A. Rodgers, H.H. Giles,
George G. Dawson, Leon Clark, Donald
Johnson, Durwood Pruden, Elazur J. Pedhazur

NEW YORK: NEW YORK UNIVERSITY PRESS   1975

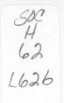
"Life Is Just a Bowl of Cherries," copyright © 1931 by DeSylva, Brown and Henderson, Inc. Copyright renewed, assigned to Chappell and Co., Inc. Used by permission of Chappell and Co., Inc.

"Brother Can You Spare a Dime," reprinted by permission of Warner Brothers, Inc.

"First Fig," reprinted from *Collected Poems* of Edna St. Vincent Millay by permission of Harper & Row. Copyright © 1922, 1950 by Edna St. Vincent Millay.

Chart of skills and concepts and Map Skills for Today reprinted by permission of American Education Publications, A Xerox Co.

The section entitled "Historical Conflict Analysis" in Chapter V, "Analysis of Social Conflict," is reprinted by permission of the author.

Manufactured in the United States of America

To a man who was gentle, loving,
kind and devoted to his family—
my dad.

PREFACE

With the post-sputnik age in America came what was tantamount to a revolution in teaching. Not only were academics encouraged to question their assumptions, they were asked to devise "new," presumably more effective ways of learning. The response of educational psychologists was, as one might expect, virtually instantaneous. From Harvard Yard and Berkeley's hills came a clarion call for "structure" and methodology and a somewhat hasty renunciation of most of the former educational practices. School administrators delighted in discussing with their constituents the "new math" and the "new science." And solicitous parents took courses in "teaching your child the new math." If the word "new" was not included in an education manuscript, most publishers either rejected it or included the word. To be opposed to this educational phenomenon was to be reactionary or, worse yet, old-fashioned. Since this irresistible movement captivated educators in all the disciplines, the social sciences were obviously involved.

For a decade now the "new social studies" have dominated the field. Most of the credit for this can go the Edwin Fenton and his practitioners who have maintained that learning the skills of the social scientist is as important as information itself. Surely this position has validity. But in the minds of many it has become all medium and no message. Moreover, an approach which was based on induction, on an inquiry with unknown goals, has often become as orthodox and rigid as the approaches it replaced. Perhaps this is the ultimate fate of any revolutionary change. But it seems to the authors of this book that a time for reexamination and possibly sunthesis is here.

This book is by no means critique of Fenton's work, nor is it intended to criticize the "new social studies." What it does do, however, is refer to those areas in which the "new social studies" can be appropriately applied, as well as other techniques which appear to have equal applicability. There is, therefore, no one approach that is endorsed by the authors, a feature which may be both the strength and the failing of this source. If anything, this book is eclectic; it represents the predilections of different men responding to different perceptions of the world with a combined teaching experience at every level of close to two-hundred years. Although most of the contributors are in the same department at New York University, every effort was taken to avoid parochialism and shared biases. If that goal was achieved, most of the authors would probably accept the book's flaws somewhat philosophically.

The organization of this text is designed to offer a theoretical and practical guide to the teaching of the major social studies components in the present high school curriculum. Additionally, there are chapters on specific teaching approaches, recommendations for designated students, and practical advice for evaluation.

During the actual writings of this book there were periods of consultation and review that very often led to chapter revisions. These were not particularly easy times, but on reflection they do seem profitable. Similarly, my pessimism about completing this text now seems like so much water under the proverbial bridge. For this I am indebteded to the contributors of this source and to the diligence of the departmental secretaries. Likewise, my devotion to various teaching approaches was continually challenged by those wedded to "the soundest method." I can attribute the diversity of recommendations in this text to the integrity and dedication of my colleagues at New York University.

Contents

Social Science Theory.
Structure and Application

CHAPTER I

Introduction

by Herbert I. London

If, as is implied in Gilbert Highet's *The Art of Teaching,* one cannot learn *how* to teach, then this project is quite irrelevant. If the reader believes that a man learned in his field, with a likable disposition and a concern for his students, is ipso facto an effective teacher, he should put this book aside. If one accepts the proposition that any benevolent adult with patience and understanding can efficaciously teach his subject, this study will provide no new insights into teaching. This book presumes that there are skills and techniques to be mastered before one can teach his subject well. It likewise presumes that while teachers must be concerned about their students, knowledgeable in their field of study, and possessed with pleasant personalities, these qualities singularly or in combination are not necessarily tantamount to successful teaching.

As a result of this rapidly changing society, the teaching of social studies has been dramatically altered, depending, as at no time in the past, on the mastery of certain skills and techniques rather than on "static" or historical facts. Teachers are becoming concerned not only with the obvious reinterpretations of data but also with the variegated teaching methods that will be most suitable in this time of educational ferment. At least two factors are responsible for changing these attitudes, programs, and methods in the social studies: increasing technological change, particularly cybernation; and the urgency of social problems which require trained practitioners for their solution.

1

TECHNOLOGY

Cybernation, or the condition in which machines run machines and even create machines, has uprooted education's conventional wisdom. Computers have accelerated the need to reevaluate not only what is to be learned but how it is to be learned. More than ever before flexibility must be built into the educative process for all students regardless of their knowledge of skills, ability to memorize facts, or predilection for certain subjects. There is now less sense in memorizing subject matter that computers can efficiently process and repeat at one's command, or in learning skills that computers make anachronistic overnight and can use more efficiently than the brightest of homo sapiens. In an age of computers, it is becoming more important to be able to ask questions than to answer them.

It does not follow, however, that factual information has *no* role in the school; but in a computer age information must be shaped to organize the student's existence by aiding him in the formulation of questions and in the ultimate evaluation of alternative solutions. But the information is not an end in itself (and this is the essential difference with the past); it is a tool that develops a capacity to inquire, to criticize, and to evaluate. With computers that store data and solve problems, in an environment where universal truths are ephemeral, it is what the information leads to that counts, not its identification.

For social studies teachers the implications of this argument are obvious. A conventional lecture-question approach to teaching in which facts are supposedly imbibed and recalled for examination purposes is fast becoming incongruous with contemporary needs. Yet the conventional approach continues to play a prominent role in American classrooms. Many students of American history study the Constitution by memorizing the articles and sections of the document and their historic implementation. They rarely have an opportunity to frame their study as an individual inquiry, e.g.: How would the government be different without a Constitution? Is the Constitution an aid or impediment to the forces of social change? How does one go about creating a Constitution? What values need be implied in a document of this kind? In all of these examples, and this is by no means an exclusive list, a student would have to shape the problem and find data applicable to its solution. And in all of the examples cited a knowledge of the Constitution, while indispensable, would still be subordinate to the development of the problem, the criticism of the data, and the evaluation of the solution.

A computerized society that is capable of solving more questions more efficiently undoubtedly has the capacity to be more inventive; but teachers must encourage this inventiveness in their teaching approaches. This involves several thoroughly discussed but virtually unexplored possibilities.

One approach which may complement the student's inquiry orientation is systems analysis. By postulating about future contingencies, describing assumptions, and using cross-disciplinary modes of thought, the analyst can be in a better position to examine existing and hypothetical issues. Using this kind of analysis, students may be forced to state objectives and solutions in operational terms instead of vapid generalizations, e.g., "We need more and better education." They should become, as a function of the methodological strictures, more proficient at using, discarding, and evaluating data. Likewise, the students can come to grips with the links between disciplines and the cross-fertilization within their culture. The wall between disciplines, artificially created and perpetuated by the school, has often acted as an impediment to learning, an impediment that is thoroughly inconsistent with systems analysis. Knowledge is not compartmentalized.

Can an inquirer of the American character (to whatever extent there is a distinct American character) find solutions to his questions by investigating one discipline? And if he does investigate one discipline, which should it be? Should he begin with language, slang expressions, Americanisms? Or should he perhaps commence with religious attitudes and even Max Weber's theory of the Protestant ethic? Or should he rely on David Riesman's sociological analysis of the "other-directed" personality? Can he ignore the economic issue in David Potter's *People of Plenty* or the geographic issue implied in Frederick Jackson Turner's frontier thesis? Or is the best explanation provided by American technological advances from the covered wagon to the computer? Or is the solution to be found in the lives of political heroes? Perhaps the romanticism portrayed by James Fenimore Cooper and Henry Thoreau and manifested more recently by the hippies can provide the greatest understanding. To be sure, any one of these questions and any one discipline cannot satisfactorily provide complete insights about the American character. Unless one considers the many ways of looking at and asking a question, answers will remain partial and remote under most conditions.

Another technique which can enliven social studies classes and encourage inventiveness is game simulation. An old barn, not far from the school grounds, could be the focus for an anthropology game as students search, touch, listen for clues about another generation. A geography lesson could be fashioned from the study of the local community if students were asked to give directions to an uninformed visitor. Game simulation has the potential to involve students in reflective problem-solving questions and to challenge historical "truths," e.g.: What would you have done had you been Czar Nicholas before the beginning of the Russian Revolution? Or, what route would you have taken to find the way to the East had you been a sixteenth-century explorer?

Still another requisite, and perhaps the most important in an environment where the accumulation of knowledge is subordinate to investigative processes, is the teacher's ability to heighten the sense of curiosity and to assist in the student's investigation. This is partially achieved by recognizing the dimensions of the teacher's role: He is not an answerman or a questioner; he should be a creative manager who provides those activities or offers counsel that encourages students to investigate problems of their own choosing.

Assume, for the sake of example, that one student curious about the electoral system decided, after preliminary study, to investigate the proposition: "Should the electoral system be abolished?" The first step in this teaching-learning process would be the framing of the question, an obvious indication of the student's curiosity about the problem. A question also lets the teacher and student perceive the purpose of the study. Had the example read, "Why should the electoral system be abolished?" a polemical argument could be deduced. In subsequent stages of the inquiry and depending on the student's ability, the teacher can guide, determine the degree of involvement, and assist the student to: formulate an hypothesis; clarify and delimit the problem; define all the necessary terms, e.g., electoral system; gather data; refine the available information; criticize the evidence; compute statistics when applicable; submit the data to a computer, if available; and evaluate the conclusions. These steps are interwoven into the investigative process. And most of the activities will probably occur outside the school confines. Ideally, these could take the student to libraries, congressmen, lobbyists, political meetings, and, depending on the liberality of the school board, rallies of every political persuasion. If inventiveness is to be the goal of schools and teachers, the school program and organization will have to be designed to encourage inquiry; teachers may have to guide students and reorient their goals; and both teachers and administrators will have to admit that the investigative process is at least as important as the knowledge imbibed in its implementation.

If this argument has validity for teachers and administrators, as most professional literature confirms, it is necessary to consider the argument's corollary: In what ways should instructional goals be prepared? Time-honored social studies topics such as the names of the presidents and the dates of their elections and the leading products of Latin American neighbors have less place in a computer age in which any subject-matter question relying on empirical evidence for an answer can be programmed. As Jerome Bruner has already noted, although his prescriptions for social studies teachers are not always clear, instructional goals should be seen in terms of process. "How does a description of products aid in the determination of life-style?" has more legitimacy as an aim than "What are the leading products in Latin America?" Likewise, the relationship of men and their views to their zeitgeist will provide more historical insights for the students than the name and election date for each president. The organization of the social studies curriculum in an increasingly technological society can no longer be predicated solely on chronological, topical, or sequential units; it should incorporate investigative processes into its design. In so doing it would no longer be necessary to teach what one thinks the student should know or what one thinks might interest him. Students could plan their own adventures. In fact, a curriculum guide which conspicuously omitted the mention of specific social studies topics might be more appropriate in schools that seek to arouse inquiry.

URBAN PROBLEMS

In addition to preparing students for the age of cybernation, inquiry skills can help students cope with the resolution of complex social problems in this contemporary society. With almost every American recognizing the cities as battlegrounds where the greatest challenge will be confronted and where the most humiliating defeat may be envisioned, the social studies program can serve as the avant-garde for creative change, as the defender of the status quo, or as a neutral force subservient to the course of history. The choice of goals for the social studies program is with the teachers, notwithstanding the preordained rulings of school board, administrators, and curriculum advisers. But the choice depends on the *ability* to choose.

Once again this analysis leads back to the need for inquiry processes. But this time the context is the city, and the intended audience is urban students (by the year 2000 futurists have predicted that over 90 percent of all students will be educated in large urban centers and their satellites). The solution to urban dilemmas, an enigma for experts, is not likely to be found in junior and senior high schools. However, a willingness to confront the problems, to gather data from the city population and its agencies, to state goals in operational terms, and to discuss solutions in relation to financial resources affords ways in which future voters can make reasonable decisions about municipal governments and budding urbanologists can begin their training.

Perhaps a research example will demonstrate the uses of inquiry processes for the tentative solution of urban problems. It has been recognized for several years that a substantial portion of the middle-class population wealthy enough to leave the city's epicenter migrates to suburbia. With the departure of this population goes a disproportionately large part of the taxable base. This migrant population continues to use city services, to earn its money in the city center, and to gravitate to the urban core for entertainment. Those who remain in the city, those too poor to make their exodus, and the very wealthy who often live in high-rise, high-rental apartments where proximity to the filth below is distant do not constitute an adequate financial base to pay for the increasing need for social services. To compound the malaise: State legislators have maintained, despite the *Baker* v. *Carr* decision, an historical devotion to malapportionment; federal funds to city governments are usually given with proscriptive strings and in amounts too small even to begin urban redevelopment (this includes the Model Cities Program); Vietnam spending channeled some federal funds abroad and, more importantly, has focused priorities away from the city; and the shrinking middle class in the urban setting is being forced to bear the brunt of taxation, causing resentment which is sometimes manifested as racism and which usually accelerates the move to suburbia. While solutions are discussed by political scientists and city planners, city residents are asked to endure garbage and transportation strikes, pollutants that poison the air, traffic woes that increase the workday by several hours, rentals that are highly restrictive, slum conditions that would shock Jacob Riis, antiquated public schools, and violence or alienation that has made the city a paradise for psychoanalysts.

After identifying the problem in this way, students can begin to isolate the variables responsible for the situation, the numerous solutions that have been proffered by experts, and the plethora of answers they will undoubtedly unearth. If they are well rooted in the process of investigation, they will culminate the exercise by testing their solutions.

Several alternative solutions, all with some merit as well as with obvious drawbacks, will arise in the initial stages of any investigation, e.g., the Walter Heller plan in which federal funds would be channeled directly to needy urban areas, the redefinition of boundary lines to coopt large parts of suburbia into the city, a metropolitan planning board for the redistribution of resources, a negative income tax or guaranteed annual wage that might alleviate the condition of the poor in the city center, "instant" housing projects that require limited investment and offer almost no displacement woes, a commuter tax (a moderate commuter tax is already being employed in some urban centers), local planning agencies that have money and responsibility for neighborhood programs, and so forth.

After these solutions are analyzed in respect to empirical evidence, those with limited potential for implementation or success can be eliminated. Other, more original, suggestions can be entertained, tested, and possibly evaluated once again. The process involves continual group discussions, individual inquiries, and outside consultations. Tentative solutions can even be tested within other government setups, for example, in an experimental student-dominated school administration, or by tendering the ideas to city officials. And an evaluation may even be based on the reception experts accord the student propositions or the viability of the propositions when implemented in the local school setting.

RACIAL PROBLEMS

At a time when racial separation has gained widespread currency, the social studies program seems a likely area for a discussion of presumed racial differences. Black leaders, from Booker T. Washington to Malcolm X, once neglected in the social studies program, should become an integral part of American studies. And this is not a suggestion for black students exclusively. White students can share a historical heritage with black counterparts that may make them all "soul brothers." If it can be adduced, as seems likely, that ignorance is a primary reason for racial misunderstanding, then shared learning experiences and some emphasis on black heroes may assist in closing the racial gap.

A southern worker for the Friends Society illustrated this point by relating a story from his own experience as an "integration coordinator." Immediately after the Supreme Court's 1954 desegregation order a school district in North Carolina demanded the public schools to admit black students. On the fateful day when blacks and whites were to share a classroom for the first time, a young white mother admonished her daughter to avoid any "niggers." "Keep your distance from those animals," she shouted at the frightened child. Two miles away on the other side of town a black mother warned her little girl to be on her best behavior since she was "part of an epic historical experience." The little girl's knees buckled with tremors as she tried to digest all those big words. Nervously she went to school, and even more nervously she entered her assigned class. As fate would have it the black child and the white one were seated next to one another, each attracted by their shared tension. After the school day the white child went home to report the day's events to her mother.

"Yes, it was fine, Mom," she said in response to the first question.

"Weren't there a lot of blackies, and weren't you scared?" asked Mom, with gestures that made the questions rhetorical.

The little girl pondered a bit, and then she said, "There were quite a few darkies and I was sure scared, but they seemed scared, too. Why, that little black girl next to me. . . ."

Before she could finish, Mom shrieked, "What black girl next to you? Why, you must have been frightened sick! What did you do, child? What did you do?"

In the ingenuous way in which children respond to such questions, the little girl remarked, "Well, I noticed how scared the black girl was and she noticed how scared I was, so we just sat and held hands all day."

If schools, and particularly social studies programs, can begin to teach the moral of this story, the anxiety experienced by the two little girls may not be repeated.

Perhaps the best way to investigate racial questions is to by means of inquiry. For example, the following questions could be employed to initiate a discussion of contemporary racial controversies: What does America mean to this community's black population? or How can black people develop racial pride without racial separation?

COMMUNITY ISSUES

A social studies course can serve as a melting pot for the exchange of various views; it can also serve as a catalyst for the solution of community problems. By using local issues as a focus for the program, students can learn how to poll, canvas, interview, persuade—skills that can be transferred to many learning experiences. The chore of finding out how local residents feel about the construction of a new government building in their area could be the central activity in a unit involving democratic processes. Students might learn how decisions, of the kind cited, are made and how, if a majority disapproves, redress of grievances is legitimately expressed. In a unit of this kind every cognitive and affective goal on Benjamin Bloom's glorified taxonomy could easily be included. Attitudes and understandings and values might all be affected by this experience with democratic (and perhaps not so democratic) decision-makers, although the teacher's role would be infinitely more arduous, and evaluation by conventional standards would be virtually impossible. An interaction between the social studies class and the community might be permanently established so that the former acts as a gadfly and informer and the latter as a respondent and evaluator. What were once distinctly community concerns—crime, divorce, social planning, and so forth—could, after the consummation of the new relationship, be joint class-community concerns.

INTERNATIONAL RELATIONS

Just as the social studies program should be a reflection of changing urban and community needs, so, too, should the program recognize the protean character of world conditions. The Jeffersonian maxim that "we should avoid entangling alliances" has been and, to an extent, continues to be, a plea for American isolation. But the events of the last four decades have obscured the parameters of national concerns. In a sense, Americans are willy-nilly existentialists establishing a new, and not always effective, code for world order. Problems of overpopulation, starvation, nuclear-weapons proliferation, and aggression across national boundaries, no matter where they occur, have become part of their concern, if not within their control. To complicate this analysis, America's concerns have increased at the same time her affluence has spiraled upward. With the majority of the world's population earning less than $200 annually and with the per capita annual income of Asians only $50, it has become increasingly difficult to empathize with those in developing societies and to avoid a patronizing attitude in international dealings. In fact, much of the foreign resentment of the United States stems from these factors. "How can you *tell us* how to run things when you, the most affluent people in the world, cannot eliminate your own poverty and racial distinctions?" is a recurring refrain from visiting diplomats to this country. To an extent, the social studies program has implicitly encouraged attitudes of superiority and, by acts of omission, has perpetuated a Copernican theory about America—a theory which suggests that all states revolve around the United States.

In view of this condition, the social studies program should be internationalized so that "I" and "mine" can be redefined as "we" and "ours." The study of foreign areas, particularly of the developing states, should encourage an appreciation for cultural uniqueness by using anthropological skills. Student role-playing that compares Thai, Arabic, Ibo, Indian, and American marriage rituals might serve as an introduction to the idea of cultural diversity. Likewise, family behavior patterns, relationships, and expectations in various cultures can illuminate significant historical and cultural parallels and differences among societies. The Westernization of so much of the globe has subtly promoted a myopia toward foreign contributions. A recognition of this condition can, at the very least, inspire courses and individual inquiries relating to cultural pluralism.

IDEOLOGIES

Another area of neglect in the social studies has been the matter of ideological confrontation. This subject is not posed as the hackneyed democracy versus communism conflict but as an effort to bridge alleged ideological incompatibilities. Can there be developed an attitude of modus vivendi, or is an international climate of disequilibrium and possibly "limited" war inevitable? If the main preoccupation of each of the major powers is domination, and this seems a dubious conclusion, can the resolution of competing arguments occur without bloodshed? And if it is necessary to shed blood to maintain a balance of power or the principle of self-determination, how does a state decide when or how to engage the presumed transgressor? How does one, in the complex world of artificially divided states, even determine the transgressor? Edgar Snow, in *The Other Side of the River,* suggests that the Chinese leaders are "legitimately" possessed with the right to free Asian states dominated by "Western imperialism." Does this abstract right exist? And does the assertion legitimate American action as a countervailing and, supposedly, democratic force in Asia? These rather complex questions open a Pandora's box of even more complex questions. But it is hoped, in the study of ideological and strategic issues students can begin to grasp the problems of this era, and probably the international problems of the age they will inherit.

The question of peace has been beclouded by issues such as patriotism, rising aspirations, ideological dedication, elitism, interest articulation, and many other factors carefully catalogued by political scientists. However, the prospect of nuclear incineration has obscured the importance of any other issue. At a time when thermonuclear warfare is an omnipresent death wish and simultaneously the stabilizer in the "balance of terror" between the superpowers, it has become essential to study the ways in which uniform disarmament can be conducted and peaceful uses of atomic energy can be exploited. This kind of information study, regardless of the obvious need for technical information, is primarily dependent on man's ability to create a climate for global stability and to reorder his priorities. The corollary argument to this panegyric is the reevaluation of social studies offerings so that inquiries about international order, the national role, and man's instinctual characteristics are emphasized. If it is necessary to understand one's self before one can understand his state, it is obviously necessary to understand man before one can understand the international condition. Social studies courses that recognize their own potential will countenance an individual as well as a national catharsis. A recognition of one's own assumptions will not create an immediate peace, but it is the beginning of a more resourceful approach toward the solution of international differences.

MEDIA

Perhaps the one area of American life that manifests the technological change and, at the same time, foments social change is communications media. Television in particular has changed the essence of learning. Teachers now are forced to compete with the Walter Mitty world created by "Underdog." And in almost every way television has the advantage. It provides an involvement teachers rarely achieve. It draws from every field of knowledge and does not rely on discreet disciplines. It is designed to interest, titillate, and excite. It is attuned to, and has helped to assist, the acculturation process of the "war baby" generation. And it can be controlled; with just a flick of one finger even a child can turn off that which is unpleasant and boring and turn on to a world of joy. Is it any wonder under these circumstances that students refer to boring teachers as "those who turn us off"?

Inquiry investigations can meet the challenge of television. If students can choose areas of interest to investigate—and this is the essence of student inquiry—teacher motivation and artificially induced involvement are unnecessary. Compartmentalized learning—for example, history as opposed to economics—will also evanesce as students doing their own research increasingly seek answers that are not available in one discipline. Lastly, inquiry assumes student control; students can, with teachers' guidance, decide what research routes to travel. Ultimately, learning is a student responsibility, and this is most clearly recognized by an inquiry approach to the teaching-learning process.

As an agent for social change, television can, through its delivery, manipulate millions of viewers. It is a tool and, in part, it is the creator of the young radicals. War has been brought into the living room, and reality has become an existential dilemma. Style, for some, has become meaning, and knowledge, has become an irrelevancy as television gives "all" the answers and creates so many of our "socially acceptable" attitudes.

By encouraging students to investigate issues of their own choosing, individuality may be sustained, complex ideas may be examined without reliance on clichés, and answers to social questions may arise from clearly thought-out, well-formulated ideas instead of from the "most vociferous voices."

In a recapitulation of this general view of social studies teaching, several goals, not stated in order of their presentation, are apparent:

1. At this time, when the memorization of facts is rapidly losing validity, inquiry processes should be the focus of the social studies.
2. An interdisciplinary approach to social studies will serve as the most fruitful way of investigating problems.
3. Simulation of events in the classroom is necessary in order to elucidate ideas.
4. Opportunities must be provided for students to leave the school confines in order to explore and test hypotheses.
5. The social studies curriculum can act as the avant garde for social change.
6. Emphasis in the program should be in those areas of existential ferment: the urban milieu, racial problems, international relations, and distribution of income.
7. Hypotheses related to urban and international affairs should be formulated and tested in relation to principles and generalizations about man and his environment.
8. The conventional wisdom in the social studies should be tested by each generation, and opportunities should be afforded for creative suggestions and revisions of existing truths.
9. Social studies programs should be internationalized so that parochial views can be identified and group consciousness can be encouraged.
10. Social studies teaching should inspire students to inquire about themselves and their world.

These idealistic goals in the social studies have been stated before. Almost every social scientist, despite individual disagreements on minor points, would accept the general formulation set forth here.

Nonetheless, much social studies teaching does not reflect these aims. In the interpretation of goals something occurs which obscures their meaning. It is probably true that the goals lack specificity and that the agents for the achievement of these goals lack direction. Many social studies textbooks cite the goals, admonish against the pitfalls, and outline general steps to be taken in order to achieve cognitive and affective objectives, but they rarely give specific illustrations of how to do it. Perhaps the tale of the tiger and grasshopper illustrates the current dilemma in the field of social studies education.

An obviously hungry and weary grasshopper approached a healthy, vigorous tiger and asked, "How can I be as healthy as you?"

The tiger, without any hesitation, described the reasons for his good health: "When I see a lame deer or a stray unsuspecting antelope, I attack my prey and devour it."

"But," asked the grasshopper incredulously, "how can I hunt and devour such large animals?"

The tiger stared at him for several seconds and replied, "What do you want? I gave you the idea. Now you fill in the details."

Most "experts" in the social studies appear to prospective teachers as "tigers." They have ideas, but often those ideas do not have practical application. What follows in this volume will be an effort to define the aforementioned platitudes in operational terms, to make the idea of inquiry processes a viable teaching concept. In addition, the contributors to the volume will attempt to construct a paradigmatic structure of what the social studies courses can be and how curricula can treat current issues related to social change. If in this analysis the contributors can assist prospective teachers in developing teaching skills and answering the question, How do you do it? their purpose will have been achieved.

CHAPTER II

The Class as a Teaching Resource

by Herbert I. London

If there is some validity to the scientific assertion that ontogeny recapitulates phylogeny (the development of an individual organism is in some ways related to the development of the race), then the social studies teacher should be able to make some parallels between individual experiences of class members and the evolution of human history. This does not mean that a student in the class is likely to be another Napoleon or Descartes or that any student has the potential to be either of these figures; nor does it mean that history inevitably repeats itself, so that contemporary events can be interpreted as duplications of past events. On the contrary, the scientific assertion assumes individual uniqueness, a uniqueness that is indubitably translated into societal actions at a particular moment in history. However, since men of every age have been motivated to some extent by glory, love, power, and security—or by all of these—and in groups have acted in response to these callings, all men share certain archetypal motivations. At times, due in no small part to social mores, man's passions are repressed or sublimated into socially acceptable channels, but they do not necessarily disappear. Konrad Lorenz argues that contemporary man still manifests a "hunting drive" in his business and family roles even though he may not be a hunter. Similarly, Freud noted that the sublimation of libidinal drives takes different forms, but the drives themselves are always present. The drives identified by Lorenz and Freud may not exist at all or may not have the influence over human action suggested by these men. But the notion that men share certain characteristics and have been motivated by similar passions is undeniable. Attila and Hitler were very different men responding to different situations, but their lust for power through expansion was curiously similar. Likewise, Newton and Einstein had different temperaments and lived in very different environments, but they asked questions about the forces of energy in the universe that were in many respects the same. Will and Ariel Durant, in *The Lessons of History,* made the same point differently by noting that "History repeats itself in the large because human nature changes with geological leisureliness."

If students, notwithstanding the limitations of their experience, share certain passions with their ancestors, there is the possibility that ideas related to human experience are within the ken of every student. More important, the recognition of this possibility can provide the teacher with a general strategy for the conduct of most classes. Students can attempt to relive human experiences. Obviously, this does not mean refighting World War II or reenacting the Watts riots in the classroom, but it may mean discussing the reasons why men fight, why contentiousness has been endemic to history, and why many students express a combativeness toward their peers. By perceiving the general character of conflict in human behavior, students may begin to ask questions about all conflict-producing situations. Perhaps this investigation could lead to the development of a typology of different kinds of conflict or even to an analysis of group interaction in the class, although the emotional states of individuals and communities are not always the same.

When the class is the stage for the unfolding of historical events, sociological principles, economic concepts, and political generalizations, students are better prepared to challenge some conventional wisdom and arrive at some self-deduced conclusions. In this setting, students will likely respond with more assuredness to questions involving human behavior. The very act of participation provides them with this security. Asking questions about leadership will produce little response from students who have not been leaders, have not recognized leadership roles, and have not consciously noticed their positions in a social system. But one simple exercise can sometimes dramatically create an awareness that was lacking beforehand.

In a class of more than twenty-five students a young teacher wanting
to illustrate the dynamics of leadership asked his students to seat
themselves in alphabetical order. Since this was the beginning of the
semester and the students were unfamiliar with surnames, they quiz-
zically looked at one another for direction. After several chaotic and
futile steps, including exuberant name identifications, a definite stra-
tum of group organization and leadership emerged. Groups of five and
six were organized and lined up alphabetically by those who assumed
leadership positions. Eventually, the class organization was orches-
trated by one of the group leaders, who managed the seating arrangement by calling out the letters of the alphabet and assigning seats.
The entire experience was recorded by the teacher and later discussed
with his students. Questions were asked about organization, reactions,
leadership, and social systems; and the class was pressed into arriving
at conclusions about its activities. In the subsequent discussion,
revealing student statements indicated not only enjoyment with the
exercise but a more precise understanding of the notion of leadership.

It is through this kind of exercise that intuitive student views can be
defined and challenged and intellectualized. And it is through direct
participation that students avoid a total reliance on the expert's opinion. In fact, there are numerous residual merits in using the class as a
teaching resource.

If one assumes that many social science and historical ideas can be
transmitted through class participation, then there need not be an
undue reliance on the homework assignment as the foundation of the
lesson. Many teachers can recall, to their horror, those days when the
lesson was abruptly terminated because scarcely anyone had completed his homework. This almost universally experienced phenomenon can be avoided. By attempting to teach through class situations,
the teacher may be able to broach new topics and may even be able to
inspire "outside reading," a term only the most experienced teachers
really comprehend. Students may want to compare conclusions arrived at in class with historical parallels. But even if this is not the case,
one can still assume that the student can learn more through observation and participation than in imbibing the homework assignment and
recalling the facts the following day. By comparing events in class with

historical events, hypotheses and investigations by an individual or the class can be initiated.. Shibboleths can be challenged and accepted truths tested. If, as was indicated in the experiment already mentioned, leadership is a response to the solution of a problem facing a social system, students might readily ask, "Why do many societies with pressing problems remain leaderless?" The question depends on a degree of historical knowledge, but the experiment's conclusion begs a question of this kind. A commitment to the development of inquiry in the class may mean creating class situations which engender hypothetical and empirical questions.

The question usually raised by teachers at this point is, "How do I create a continuing store of classroom situations?" Obviously, there are no pat solutions to this dilemma. Those most successful in answering this question are usually described as "master teachers." However, there are ways of approaching the problem which may be of assistance to the novice.

If what is important in the social studies, including history, involves relationships, theories, universal principles, concepts, and motivations, then the aim of the lesson as well as the unit should emphasize these points. For example, "What features are included in the Republican platform?" is less appropriate as an aim than "How will these objectives be implemented?" In answering the second question students would be forced to develop the relationship between acts and attitude. More important, if the teacher emphasizes this association in his own plan, he can develop class activities relating student acts and attitudes.

One activity which might serve as an example would be the announcement, in mock honesty, of a surprise examination. This will usually elicit a variety of student attitudes. Some will probably regard the lack of notice as an unconscionable act. Others, perhaps less success oriented, might be apathetic. Still others, usually those who are bright but rarely study, might openly favor the idea. In all cases, their actions will probably betray certain basic attitudes, attitudes that may determine their interpretation of world affairs, their future roles, and even their political preferences. If students can, through their own actions, be made to understand the relationship between their acts and their attitudes, it may facilitate their understanding of the Republican party's role as well as the essential correlation of acts and attitudes as it applies to other political movements in American history.

Having students compare their own feelings with historical figures is one way to demonstrate the universality of ideas, but it is by no means the only effective way of inviting active participation. A reliance on debate as a teaching strategy most often fails because it degenerates into an unreflective bull session. It therefore becomes essential for the teacher to vary instructional techniques so that class involvement is not routine. Surprise, contrived accident, organized chaos, and unconventional action should be part of a teacher's repertoire in order to heighten the sense of curiosity and to inspire questions, challenges, and generalizations.

In attempting to illustrate the subjectivity of historians, a lesson that could initiate a unit on the historical method, an instructor could invite a visitor to his unsuspecting class in order to arouse curiosity. Upon his entrance, the visitor, with considerable pomp and indignation, could argue with the instructor and, with a vigorous protest, storm out of the room. After the tumult had subsided, the class would be asked to describe the events in as much detail as possible, including remarks, clothes, actions, and emotions. Invariably, an exercise of this kind, as Walter Lippmann indicated in *Public Opinion,* brings to the fore "mental blindspots," errors in judgment based on stereotypes. These errors in description could be pointed out by reinviting the guest into the class and describing the scene. If reinforced by historical illustrations, the event can be a constant reminder that history is interpretation and as such is subject to criticism. This lesson is the *sine qua non* of the social studies. By recognizing man's fallibility, students will be inclined to test arguments for their reliability. For example, "Was Franklin D. Roosevelt a national savior?" as is sometimes implied by liberal historians; "Was he an irresponsible socialist?" as has been averred by many conservatives; or "Was he a basically conservative individual that history cast in the role of progressive?" as is suggested by Frank Freidel? Obviously, answers to these questions depend partly on evidence and, more important, on personal predilections. And it is from the recognition of these biases that historical understanding emerges.

In some respects these classroom events duplicate epic historical interpretations that involve subjective evaluations. In his description of the Sacco and Vanzetti case, Felix Frankfurter recalls the stereotypical testimony of Miss Blaine, who alleged she could identify "those Italian types" anywhere.

Associated Press and United Press International reporters listening to Castro's explanation of his Communist associations came to very different conclusions in their reports: In the one case it was noted that Castro had had Communist leanings since his university days; in the other report it was claimed that Castro became a Communist as a matter of political expediency, after a refusal by the American government to recognize his legitimacy.

In *American Foreign Policy 1932-1940* and *President Roosevelt and the Coming of the War* Charles Beard argued that President Roosevelt and his aides deliberately misled public opinion into thinking he meant to avoid war while the administration deliberately provoked Japan into attacking America, presumably so that public resistance to the war effort would crumble. Tracy Kittredge in an article published in *U.S. News & World Report* and Forrest Pogue, in *George C. Marshall: The War Years,* take a very different view of the events immediately prior to the Pearl Harbor attack. In both cases they reject a presidential conspiracy as the factor responsible for the attack, and Pogue demonstrates that General Marshall and his aides were convinced of Pearl Harbor's impregnability (based on optimism, not on fact) and the probability of a Japanese invasion in Southeast Asia, not in the mid-Pacific.

Whether it is because of stereotyping, "temporary deafness," or difference of opinion, it is notable that objectivity is a goal of, but not always a reality in, history and the social studies. In all of the cases cited the jury is still undecided, and if historical attitudes change toward such problems, they sometimes more clearly reflect the times in which they are written rather than the times with which they are allegedly concerned.

Since exactitude in history and the social studies is an impossibility, the student has to become discriminating in his handling of what is possible and what is probable. These nuances, regardless of the sources provided, are difficult to teach. For most students the printed word, despite McLuhan's claim to the contrary, is incontrovertible. And this is why a teacher must stress subjectivity, the personal dimension. In doing so, student critical faculties should be honed. The techniques of internal and external criticism, if thoroughly imbibed, can be the source for more inquisitiveness.

Teaching historical and social science techniques in the class depends on the assumption that the resources available can parallel conceptual designs. In some cases the class microcosm does indeed reflect the macrocosm; but the teacher's problems usually arise from an inability to find the universal thread that illustrates this parallel.

Illustrating the relative reliability of primary as opposed to secondary, or tertiary, historical sources, for example, could involve the graphic use of a student "chain message"—in the student lexicon it is called "telephone." By whispering a message to one student and having him pass it on, a garbled or somewhat revised version will generally result. Students should readily perceive without much analysis that reliability is inversely proportional to the number of message exchanges. And if this is true of their own experience, they will probably note that primary sources will be more reliable than secondary sources and secondary sources more reliable than tertiary sources.

In the cases cited, an effort has been made to make the past real, an overworked cliché used in every book of this kind; but just as necessary is the effort to make the present real. At a time when television has allegedly brought the world into our living rooms, it is assumed that students understand events, treat them as realities, and are concerned about the human condition. But in all too many cases the contrary is true: Many students are perplexed by events; they see tragedies and world-shaking episodes as a phantasmagoria and have not the slightest concern for events that do not affect them personally, although current pressures often force students to appear concerned. The electronic age that has made news more accessible has also made it increasingly difficult to dissociate the real from the contrived. For some, the assassination of King and Kennedy were only better staged "Avenger" programs.

Making the present real for the pseudo-sophisticated young who have "seen it all" via Telstar involves competition with the media. A class must be more real than a television program. Notwithstanding the obvious handicaps in a classroom, the teacher has one advantage over a television set: the possibility of actual participation.

Perhaps the most inexplicable lesson in the social studies is one dealing with international relations. The jargon of diplomats—balance of power, sphere of influence, status quo ante bellum—are difficult even for sophisticated adults to comprehend. Questions of credibility and sincerity only make the enigma more complex. "Why don't our leaders sit down with theirs and just make peace?" asked one student. Surely this is a question asked in thousands of classrooms all over this land, and just as surely the answers are unsatisfactory. Part of the reason for unsatisfactory responses is the failure to grasp the realpolitik, the power and interests that overshadow absolute principles. International relations, at their best, is the balanced use of carrot and stick that avoids confrontation, sustains moral reason, and promotes national security.

To appreciate this notion students can confront the dilemma of resolving a basic difference of view among competing class factions by using and discussing various tactics—namely, conciliation, militancy, negotiation, arbitration, mediation—in the context of a simulated United Nations. In the act of defending national states and developing diplomatic tactics, students may come to recognize the nations that threaten international stability, those that maintain the status quo in order to assure their own superiority, those that seek more leverage by relying on moral neutralism in place of power, and those that ally themselves with the superpowers in order to preserve their domestic tranquility. Debate in this class can be predicated on United Nations procedures and on the operating agreement that all student participants will attempt, as accurately as possible, to duplicate the views of the nations they represent. Records of all the statements, as well as individual logs, should be kept, since they are data essential for the ultimate evaluation and analysis of the sessions.

Despite the value of this rhetorical exercise, it sometimes creates the false impression that states are willing to accommodate their views to international opinion. In most cases, however, the United Nations is viewed as only one arm of foreign policy even by the alleged defenders of that international body, and all too often the United Nations has proved itself powerless to control the superpowers. Consequently, bilateral talks (usually secretive) should be simulated, along with the deployment of forces and possible alliances. This can be done by playing Diplomacy, a game in which the unfolding of international struggles is conducted through the movement of game pieces and the consummation of secret agreements (not always kept) "behind closed doors." The use of the game where power can be displayed, and where diplomacy can be conducted along with simulated United Nations sessions, accurately duplicates the manner in which foreign affairs are actually conducted. It is through these experiences that students can realistically discuss international relations and suggest paradigmatic models for the resolution of tension and hostility. Even a perplexing notion as widely discussed and abused as One Worldism can be rationally criticized using the theories of international affairs stemming from these lessons.

As has been stated differently several times in this chapter, the class can reproduce much of the past and some of the present when the attitudes and events in the classroom present some semblance of the mental state that existed when the historical events occurred. Perhaps this explains why field trips and museum excursions are so often unsuccessful: They very often fail to re-create the mental state of the past even when the artifacts are authentic. An activity that involves living rather than observing the past is generally more enlightening for students. But this does not mean that a class should spend three months constructing the traditional Indian tepee while it neglects every other phase of Indian culture. It does mean that models, paintings, pictures, and behavior patterns that represent the past should be emphasized so that the history can have meaning, the unfamiliar customs a raison d'être.

Can the scholar learn as much about Sparta's civilization from a book as he can from investing the unusual happenings of ancient Sparta with plausibility? Will the student learn more from the expert's opinion of a Spartan school than he will from the reproduction of the milieu in a Spartan class? For those who cynically ask whether Johnny can read after these "playful exercises," let it be noted that Johnny will read when he wants to know about something, and Johnny will adopt more sophisticated approaches to problem-solving when he stops relying totally on the expert's opinion.

The dramatic technique can lead to a new sense of reality. But it is only one technique that, unless varied, can be a superficial device justifiably rejected by students as fatuous. It can also be used improperly, as is so often the case. A student-teacher, convinced that something dramatic had to be enacted in his class, began a lesson by asking his students to "Imagine yourselves on the moon." Another teacher, more concerned with the past, asked her class prior to any reading assignment, "What would you have done if you were at the Constitutional Convention?" In both cases there was no student response. The classes did not know how to respond. When drama is completely dependent on imagination, it obscures reality. The possibilities of life on the moon and the conditions prevalent there, as well as the decisions and representatives at the Constitutional Convention are appropriate preludes for questions involving hypothetical situations. It also seems likely that illusions within the parameters of accumulated knowledge will stir the imagination more than random thoughts about unfamiliar settings. For example, a comparison of political organizations in school and nation with an ideal conception proposed for the first moon settlement might provide insight about the essential prerequisites, as well as about the possible flaws, in existing political systems.

Regardless of the approach emphasized, it is unlikely any will be successful unless the class recognizes a classroom atmosphere that is open. All points of view and any proposition should be subject to scrutiny. And the criteria for evaluation of any issue should be the same despite ideological differences of opinion. But the shibboleths for a democratic classroom espoused by every educator this side of the John Birch Society are empty proposals unless the class has an opportunity to propose conditions in the classroom and assume the responsibility for its actions. In spite of the teacher's potential fear and insecurity in a class he does not actively lead, it is essential for the development of reflective students that they have confidence that their decisions will be enacted.

If the teacher is willing to accept the proposition that all affected by decisions should participate in their formulation, then the class can be a democratic instrument for experimentation and for the discussion of numerous problems with indeterminate solutions. At least one way to engender this reflective state is to consider the class a quasi-constitutional convention in which expectations and modes of behavior are determined. Students, viewed as equal members of a convention and responsible for their own decisions, can prepare a code of class behavior. Discipline could be a class-dominated social control; learning, an inductive experience, at least partly influenced by student predilections. In the evolution of consensus, groups could caucus, competing interests could be discussed, expectations could be recognized. Obviously, the class convention does not duplicate historical illustrations, but its very existence makes the study of parallels more credible.

The class as a microcosm of the society has many more possibilities as a teaching resource than has been indicated here. But it is the purpose of this chapter to encourage the use of the class itself as a teaching resource. If it is realized that intellectual skills are more easily learned and retained when their value is demonstrated in the solution of problems, as was suggested by John Dewey, the teacher's responsibility to and in his class will be apparent.

CHAPTER III

Inquiry in the Social Studies

by Herbert I. London

At a time when there is increasing interest in, and reliance on, the social sciences, their character remains quite obscure. There is not even unanimity among experts as to the disciplines that constitute the social sciences. And despite claims to the contrary, there is little evidence to substantiate the claim that there are discrete research methods for each social science discipline. In fact, there is no consensus on what is fact as opposed to opinion in the field. To compensate for these ambiguities social scientists often embrace their theories as contemporary "defenders of the faith." But this loyalty often conspires to elicit pseudosciences, quasi-religions, and opposing schools of thought that compound the confusion—for example, the ideological struggle between Jean Paul Sartre and Levi-Strauss *—and point out the limited parameters of an empirical base in the social sciences.

In addition to these problems, there has also arisen a polarization of attitudes over the issue of emulating natural science methodology or discarding it as inappropriate for the social sciences. "Inter-disciplinarians" are willing to borrow any methodological tool or idea from any discipline. In their view, preempting research techniques from other fields is not only necessary but desirable. Purists, on the other hand, are trying to discover and, in some cases, retain that which is unique to their disciplines. But even they would have to admit that

* Sartre, as a Marxist accepting deterministic logic, presupposes "societal progress," while Levi-Strauss asserts that each culture has to be examined as a unique adaptation without regard to an ideological bias associated with "progress."

while it was once relatively easy to dissociate disciplines, recent research has made it virtually impossible. Is Richard Hofstadter, author
of *The Paranoid Style in American Politics,* more accurately described as
historian or social psychologist? Is C. Wright Mills a sociologist, an
anthropologist, a psychologist, or an historian? And once assured of the
answers, is there any relevance to the questions?

Inquiries into human behavior belie strict classifications and pure
disciplines. Franz Alexander noted the interdependence of disciplines
when he wrote:

> No individual can be understood without knowing the social scene
> in which he lives and which has molded his personality, but no
> historical event can be understood without knowing the fundamen-
> tal principles of human motivation, which are the dynamic driving
> force behind the ever shifting scenes of history.[1]

Statements of this kind, as well as the work of C. Wright Mills, Hans
Gerth, Goodwin Watson, John Dewey, David Potter, Margaret Mead,
to mention just a few, have elevated the stature of interdisciplinary
studies and, analogously, may even be responsible for the loose usage of
the term "social sciences" to connote any field outside the "natural
sciences."

The result of research in this field, notwithstanding the many significant breakthroughs, have generally not kept pace with the ambitious claims of the researchers. So-called laws of social phenomena
which have evolved from social science experiments are in themselves
proscribed; they have applicability only to the extent that all the
variables are identified, tacit qualifications and exceptions are enu-
merated, and a consensual methodology is employed. But even when
the researcher follows the demands of his discipline, there is no assurance that his conclusion will be accepted. His generalization may be
incompatible with similar studies, or his selection of data and methodology may be condemned as partisan. These hazards confront the
social scientist at each stage of his research and are constant reminders
that investigations in the social sciences are not as easily controlled as
are those in the natural sciences.

This difference between the two fields does not necessarily lead to the conclusion that natural science is more reliable. One can conclude only that it is easier to control variables in most natural science experiments, and in this sense they tend to be more objective. Since objectivity and accuracy are goals in the social sciences as well, it is easy to understand why scientific methodology is being used and expanded by social researchers. So widespread is this emphasis that "behaviorists" have put "empiricists" on the defensive. The narrative technique as a method of analysis, despite its widely recognized virtues, is presumably not as research (read: science) oriented as its analytical competitor. In the frantic effort to be more precise, empiricists, with few exceptions, have either capitulated or have accommodated themselves to the rising star of behaviorism.*

Accordingly, inquiries in the social sciences, including history, are coming to resemble those in natural science, in spite of the circumstances that interfere with controlled experimentation. The very term "experimental procedure" now usually evokes a universal meaning that can be applied to any discipline. Social laboratory and field experiments, experiments relating to social change and cultural characteristics, satisfy in most respects the requirements for any kind of research.

For the student engaged in an investigation there should be an understanding of this discernible experimental procedure, a sequence of related research methods. Since this understanding is the essence of the social sciences, the research method should be both a means and an end of the teacher's objectives. A focus on human affairs presupposes a knowledge of, and skill in, using the research techniques (inquiry method), so that decisions may be reached which ameliorate or, at the very least, mitigate and control existing problems.

The term "inquiry method," as has already been indicated, implies certain intellectual operations which ultimately lead to a decision

* This controversy between "empiricists" and "behaviorists" has been the central issue at American political science conventions in recent years. Although the lines are still drawn, most observers would agree the behaviorists have won the major debates. Empiricists have relied on political experiences for the creation of models and theories, while behaviorists have relied on accessible facts of human behavior for their theories.

involving some problem. However, in this process the student, not the teacher, is the inquirer. What the student does is the focus of the process. The teacher's role, which will be explained below, is preparatory; during the investigation itself he is generally passive.

Inquiry commences when the student confronts a question, dilemma, or problem to which there is no easily identifiable solution. For example, a question such as the number of posts in the president's cabinet is unacceptable. An answer depends on one source, and the knowledge obtained is quite limited. However, another kind of question involving numbers could lead to a rather sophisticated inquiry. Attempting to explain the discrepancies in the number of people employed by the Works Projects Administration during various years in the 1930s would be a very profitable research question. In this case the student will find notable differences in the government statistics. Several explanations, none of them completely satisfactory, could be explored: the rapid rate of employment; poor statistical measures; Harry Hopkins's possible effort to exaggerate the figures so that more funds might be allocated for public projects; President Roosevelt's possible desire to use the WPA for political capital; cabinet and other advisers seeking assurance that their economic approach to the depression was producing satisfactory results; advisers opposed to the economic measures of their colleagues who were intent on illustrating the failure of government-assistance programs; and corrupt practices that permitted fictitious candidates to receive jobs while administrators pocketed the salaries.

The second stage in the inquiry is the delimitation of the problem. This is easier to point out than to accept. Students are often unaware of their precise area of interest even when their general concern is defined. "Egyptians" or "Greeks" are unacceptable research topics because almost any exposition could, by virtue of the lack of limitation, be puerile. In order to enable students to define more clearly an area of interest, they should be permitted to grope on their own, ideally at their own pace, among the available literature. John Dewey called this approach "leaps in the dark"; it is these "leaps" that can often produce the most startling learning experiences.

After delimiting the question, the student must ask himself, "What is it I am trying to ascertain?" Deciding that he will investigate the domestic legislation of Theodore Roosevelt's presidency can be an unproductive exercise. One could conceivably get this information from the *Congressional Record* or, if the researcher is less diligent, by perusing George Mowry's *The Era of Theodore Roosevelt and the Birth of Modern America.* But of what use are these data? Without a hypothesis, inquiry is fruitless. Compare, for the sake of illustration, these two questions: "What were the significant bills endorsed by President T. Roosevelt?" and "How did President T. Roosevelt's endorsement of certain bills indicate his political philosophy?" In the first case, the researcher will have to determine the criteria for judging "significant bills," but the rest of his research is clerical, involving very little reflective thought. In the second case, relationship and theory have to be analyzed and an eventual judgment considered. Not only is the thinking infinitely more sophisticated than in the former case, but each additional piece of information has to be tested against the tentative conclusion implicit in the problem: for example, Roosevelt's endorsement of certain kind of bills was indicative of his political philosophy. A hypothesis is, therefore, an unproved thesis, or a tentative answer, that requires testing before a more definite answer is obtained.

If the inquirer is trying to prove or disprove his hypothesis, which precludes the use of some standard recipe for obtaining an answer,* he should then select those methods and obtain the necessary skills most appropriate for his particular hypothesis. In the case of a historical question, certain of the historiographer's skills must be grasped. But very often these are not easily discerned. In most cases, students will rely on reading and selecting information from secondary printed sources and occasionally from primary sources. However, historians may use any method of inquiry in the social sciences and on occasion even those outside the social sciences. Traces of the past take different forms, requiring of an ambitious investigator a chameleonic quality. He may on occasion be philatelist, numismatist, anthropologist, philologist, and geologist, just to name a few of the host of roles he

---

* The scientific method which establishes a general research methodology is considered, by this author, to be different from a recipe which establishes specific steps a researcher *must* follow to arrive at an answer.

might assume. Undoubtedly, it is difficult to obtain considerable expertise in each role, but ignoring different approaches may vitiate ultimate conclusions. Champollion not only deciphered hieroglyphics through an examination of the Rosetta stone, he also provided historians with clues about ancient Egyptian civilization. An analysis of words such as "laconic," "draconic," "philippic," "ostracize" not only offers an understanding of their social derivatives for philologists; it also furnishes insights for historians about modes of behavior and major figures in Greek civilization. Similarly, the study of family relationships in Tikopia is not solely the concern of anthropologists, it probably remains the sine qua non for any researcher trying to comprehend Melanesian culture.

Selecting an appropriate methodology for a social science question is equally complex. In this case, the researcher is usually dealing with contemporary problems whose very character is undecipherable from the spirit of the times. For example, data obtained about racial attitudes immediately after the Watts riots would be different from data obtained during a period of relative quiescence. In addition, the social scientist relies on techniques such as the interview, poll, canvass, and the like, that often require personal responses dependent on personal interpretations. If a question is carelessly constructed so that it could have a double meaning or if it is purposely designed to embody the questioner's bias, the results can be thoroughly misleading and of little scholarly use. It should be noted, however, that the illusion rather than an actual conscientious concern for methodological strictures is sometimes the standard procedure for the popularizers of the social sciences.

Despite arguments to the contrary, social scientists claim to have adopted several "controlled" methods for the study of their discipline. These include: the artificial situation (social laboratory environment) that resembles "actual" conditions and in which variables related to the social phenomena are manipulated while other relevant variables are held relatively constant, for example, determining racial attitudes by having a random sample discuss prejudice scales designed by a group of researchers; conducting a field experiment which depends on the selection of a limited community that meets the experimental criteria, as in the Lynds' study of Middletown; and undertaking the "correlational study," which attempts to ascertain causal events for social change or societal characteristics, such as the use of contraceptive advances, the currency of lay Freudian psychology, the liberalization of sexual mores and their relationship to variations in the birth rate.

The difficulties associated with these methodologies are similar in many respects to those usually confronting the historian. However, all social scientists must recognize the problems of causal imputations. In the case of the historian the *post hoc, ergo propter hoc* (after this, therefore because of it) fallacy has served as a reminder, somewhat remote for some, of the complexities involved in dealing with causality. The *post hoc* reasoning infers that the time sequence determines causation. Therefore, a chance conversation between the president and a mystic occurring immediately before the president's decision to sponsor a bill may be viewed as responsible for the decision. Hence, the two unconnected events are characterized as integrally related. There is also the crucial problem concerning the evidence necessary for attributing validity to a study's conclusions. In far too many cases evidence is accepted as an assertion without proof *(ipse dixit)* because it is articulated by the so-called expert. Thus, some of Arthur Schlesinger, Jr's, comments, even some of those casually expressed, may be accepted and probably repeated authoritatively by disciples of his historical stripe.

Procedural techniques are obviously critical to the eventual credibility of a study's conclusion. They are also influential in, and related to, a subsequent step in the inquiry method: the collection, classification, and verification of data. Collection of data, as has already been noted, can take different forms. It can, and usually does, imply reading materials, but this is by no means the only desirable way of obtaining evidence. Statistical measures, listening to sounds, interpreting drawings, smelling distinctive cultural odors, tasting foods, and touching artifacts are all techniques that can be of assistance to the social scientist, despite the usual subordination of these means of collecting data to the more conventional scholarly approaches.

The arranging of data accumulated, or its classification, permits the researcher to compare events or phenomena and describe models of action and "rules" of social systems. To conduct research without classifying, or to classify using an arbitrary criterion such as alphabetical order, is to reduce all research to manifestly inconclusive results. One cannot seek data and then simply report findings; an intermediate step in the process which allows for the transferability of ideas and the construction of theories and paradigmatic models is crucial to the eventual conclusion.

Using classes or categories is a fundamental research procedure. But this may not necessarily reduce the possible invalidity of one's findings. "General" and "limited" standards, two extremes of the same problem, can make classification a research hazard. In the former case, categories may not be exclusive enough; for example, using the term "modernization" to account for all social, political, and economic change in underdeveloped states is misleading. Conversely in the latter case, categories may be too exclusive, thereby inhibiting generalizations; for example, using illustrations in Ecuador and Zambia to report on conditions in developing states.

Classifying data is a process closely related to the verification of the evidence. Student faith in the veracity of the printed word often makes verification an extremely arduous research chore, but if carefully pursued it inevitably becomes the most interesting aspect of his investigation. To verify, the student must be a historical detective, clever enough to find the flaws in a document and to excoriate its inaccuracies and, at the same time, a plaintiff's lawyer, able to recognize errors in verisimilitude and logical exposition.

Establishing authenticity of the evidence (external criticism) depends on having sufficient skill and awareness to detect fabrications. A researcher must ask himself if the evidence is genuine or a forgery; and he must remain open to the possibility that any document can be a fake. This detachment, suspicion possibly, must be part of the student's research repertoire. Without it, he and the so-called experts are lost. Perhaps an example will demonstrate this point.

Immediately after World War II an embittered Dutch painter, van Meegeren, "discovered" and sold several paintings that were widely accepted as genuine Vermeers. No question of their authenticity was raised until van Meegeren claimed to have painted them himself. His admission was extracted when he was accused of collaborating with the Nazis after having sold Marshal Goering the national art treasures for £160,000. Van Meegeren, rather than be condemned for collaboration, pleaded guilty to the lesser charge of forgery. But his detractors, including many Vermeer experts, did not believe him until he painted another "Vermeer" under the court's supervision. Despite his moral triumph, he was convicted of forgery, and he subsequently died in jail. But the story of the forgery did not end there.

M. Jean Decoen, an art critic, maintained and proved to the satisfaction of many art critics that van Meegeren "not only fooled the critics into accepting several van Meegerens as Vermeers but double bluffed them into accepting two Vermeers as van Meegerens." [2] A completely satisfactory judgment may never be made in this case. Perhaps the best one can say is that the authenticity of very few great works has been firmly established.

With all evidence it is necessary for a researcher to ask: Is it forged? Are the materials authentic? Is the handwriting, seal, letterhead consistent with the author's other work? Was the document restored? Are words and spellings consistent with the time in which they were used? Can other sciences be used to confirm the authenticity of the source?

Internal criticism of a source involves the determination of credibility. In other words: Could the event described in a source have occurred? The social scientist, once he has established the authenticity of the document, has to ask whether the information itself is accurate and whether its author is reliable. In this sense every inquirer is at least part social psychologist. If the researcher knows enough about the author of a source, he may conclude, among other things, that this author: did not want to reveal the "truth"; wanted to reveal the "truth" but was unable to do so; thought he was revealing the "truth" that was relevant to only one era and subsequently lost its universality. As is apparent, credibility is largely a function of the author's or creator's proximity to the event and his competence in relating it, as well as of independent corroboration that may justify his claims.

Without the slightest regard for corroboration and with very little or no evidence about the authors, a series of myths, some with a degree of truth, have gradually become incorporated into the national histories of almost every state on the globe. Through continuous repetition they are accepted as accurate and are even used to glorify a national character or particular historical figures. Several historical questions illustrating this phenomenon are cited below. Could, or would Louis XIV have used the expression *"L'état, c'est moi"* ("The state, it is I") which is often attributed to him? Is it likely Marie Antoinette said, "let them eat cake?" Is it reasonable to assume that Paul Revere warned the Massachusetts populace that the British were coming? Should one necessarily associate the authorship of the Monroe Doctrine to James Monroe merely because it bears his name? Is there any document that substantiates the claim that Dutch traders paid Indians twenty-four dollars for Manhattan? The possible list of these assertions is endless; all are more or less so integrally woven into the national fabric that they are rarely, if ever, subject to the scrutiny of the student researcher.

Once the inquirer has compiled, classified, and verified his data, he is ready at last to test his hypothesis and reach some conclusions. This is the stage when interpretation is required, when the researcher selects those ideas and theories that he thinks are suggested by the data. It is the time when caution is demanded. Regardless of the inquirer's scrupulousness, he will in all likelihood have omitted some sources. In fact, as has already been mentioned, his inability to control all the variables in his inquiry inevitably leads to a series of "unknown" characteristics which, although not apparent in the data, may actually have been responsible for an event. A mood, a whim, an irrational response by a thoroughly rational man, or mere chance, are but a few of the forces impeding certitude. They are the "dark" motives submerged in the subterranean depths of one's psyche that are rarely articulated but often recognized by the perceptive social scientist. They sometimes proscribe conclusions, and they are responsible for the social scientist's repeated reference to the words "probability" and "possibility."

A second obstacle subtly influencing social science generalizations is the "culturally determined" character of social phenomena. Since nearly all behavior is dependent on culturally imposed habits and attitudes, it is likely that data amassed will consequently reflect this cultural imposition. This in effect makes the scope of all social science results restricted, confined within the limits of the research epoch, the institutional milieu, and the cultural interpretations. For example, reporting information on the calorie consumption of various nations is inextricably limited to time, class, and national values, all of which are in flux and may in another period reflect different results. In fact, recent scientific advances have demonstrated the misconception in counting calories at all. It is now believed that it is not total calorie consumption but the kind of food consumed that is the primary indicator of nutrition. Many inhabitants of the Occident have learned to their dismay that fats, usually high in calorie content, also have deleterious effects on the circulatory system.

This cultural intrusion imposes a significant degree of moral relativism on the social scientist. Yet relativism is not always his goal or rationale. And the extent of its adoption varies from researcher to researcher. One relativist, Herbert Butterfield, has admonished researchers to avoid moral judgments. But another, George Barraclough, has decried the loss of moral absolutes, which he attributes to the currency of "relativism." Max Weber, the eminent social scientist, was a vigorous proponent of "value-free" investigations. But still others in the existential school of thought argue for a radically different approach to the social sciences: an approach that emphasizes moral judgments and contends that it is more important to establish goals for the future than be influenced by the traditions of the past. Inherent in all investigations is a value orientation; and the investigator, despite his alleged "value-free" predilections, is still affected by values, however marginally that may be. This explains in part the difficulty of obtaining the unbiased conclusions widely regarded as the goal of the social scientist. It also illustrates that the social sciences do not always establish their purported goals even when their contribution is praiseworthy and widely accepted. Furthermore, the value orientation often invalidates the predictability of the social sciences. It is little wonder that Karl Marx's predictions based on the values of a nineteenth-century model of capitalism have not materialized in the way he suggested. With his nineteenth-century attitudes, it was virtually impossible for him to predict the adaptability of Western Capitalism, labor unions acquiring as much power as many industrialists, and the widespread practice of profit-sharing. However, it is worth noting parenthetically that the existentialists would argue Marx's contribution was not his predictions but his moral fervor. It is this fervor, they claim, that provided revolutionaries with the wherewithal to "adjust" the forces of history to Marx's "determinism."

These limitations in the use of social science methodology do not reduce its utility; they serve mainly to restrain the social scientist from making hasty generalizations that might be of little value. In this sense, the guidelines of research help to make conceptual designs and new insights more meaningful in man's search to find out about man.

This emphasis on inquiry methods has relegated traditional teaching to a more passive, but still important, role in the classroom. Instead of continually relating information, the teacher may, at various stages in the inquiry process, advise, question, direct research, criticize, and, at times, instruct. Despite the emphasis placed on inquiry in this chapter, as well as by advocates of "inductive approaches" such as Edwin Fenton, Maurice Hunt, Laurence Metcalf, and Benjamin Cox, there still is a definite need for instruction. Teachers cannot assume that students can always choose a problem to research without being exposed to a wide range of ideas and experiences. Similarly, not all problems accommodate themselves to student inquiries and might better be served through a reading-discussion-lecture methodology. But teachers should perceive this instruction as a way of introducing, perhaps even of guiding, inquiries so that students will ultimately be able to concern themselves with their own research problems.

If the inquiry approach is employed, it should be noted that each of the inquiry stages, after the choice of a problem, is susceptible to individualized counsel. Delimiting the problem; extracting an hypothesis; selecting research methods; acquiring research skills; collecting, classifying, and verifying data; and testing the hypothesis are techniques and skills that students should learn only after mastering each step that requires the use of the next. This could call for whole-class instruction if, under unlikely circumstances, every student mastered a technique at the same time. But even if this should be the case, students, during the inquiry, should rely on their own initiative. A teacher moving about from one student to another can encourage this attitude of self-reliance and still provide the needed assistance to mitigate frustration of others in the class.

To teachers with experience, these suggestions may seem quite impractical. Libraries are often not sufficiently equipped to handle major research projects; administrators are sometimes unwilling to permit the flexible scheduling which inquiry may necessitate; parents are unwilling at times to allow their progeny to conduct research off the school grounds; and teachers themselves are occasionally untutored in research methodology. The major indictment of the approach, though, is the teacher's lament that "There is so much to do . . . so much of the ground in the school curriculum to be covered." Why this ground is to be covered is rarely questioned. Presumably, it has some inherent value all its own. And why inquiry appears to some as incompatible with imbibing data is another unanswered query. Presumably, inquiry for the uninitiated implies "process," not "facts." Inquiry, in the sense used here, is no more than an instrument for learning. As an instrument it demands skills to function well; but the skills are needed to work with and on data. It is absurd to think that there is only *a way* to learn. Yet this assumption persists, and it is at least partly responsible for the restricted student initiative characteristic of so many classes.

In the final analysis, the teacher is the jury; he must, using class opinion it is hoped, evaluate and guide the research conclusions and the methodology pursued. As a critic he should not only illustrate possible flaws in the research but also the limitations implicit in any cultural investigation. He must weigh, judge, and compare. This can truly be the most profitable experience for the student, for he is getting the guidance necessary to approach all future research problems satisfactorily. If his perception of problems in the past, present, or future is more keen as a result of the inquiry and the consequent criticism, then the inquiry process has fulfilled the most optimistic affirmations of its supporters.

NOTES

1. Franz Alexander, "Psychology and the Interpretation of Historical Events" in Caroline Ware, *Cultural Approach To History,* New York: Columbia University Press, 1940, pp. 48-57.
2. "How Good Is An Old Master?" *Manchester Guardian,* September 13, 1951.

BIBLIOGRAPHY

Barzun, Jacques, and Graff, Henry. *Modern Researcher*. New York: Harcourt Brace & World, 1962.

Burton W., Kimball, R. B., and Wing, R. L. *Education for Effective Thinking*. New York: Appleton-Century-Crofts, 1960.

Dewey, John. *How We Think*. Boston: D. C. Heath, 1933.

Durkheim, Emile. *The Rules of Sociological Method*. New York: The Free Press, 1964.

Fenton, Edwin. *Teaching the New Social Studies*. New York: Holt, Rinehart & Winston, 1966.

Gottschalk, Louis. *Understanding History*. New York: Alfred Knopf, 1964.

Hunt, Maurice P., and Metcalf, Lawrence. *Teaching High School Social Studies*. New York: Harper & Row, 1955.

Johnson, Henry. *Teaching of History*. New York: Macmillan, 1960 (revised ed.).

Krug, Mark. *History and the Social Sciences*. Waltham, Mass.: Blaisdell, 1967.

Massialas, Byron, and Cox, C. Benjamin. *Inquiry in Social Studies*. New York: McGraw-Hill, 1966.

Mills, C. Wright. *The Sociological Imagination*. New York: Oxford University Press, 1959.

Rose, C. B. *Sociology: The Study of Man in Society*. Columbus, Ohio: Charles E. Merrill, 1965.

Sorauf, F. J. *Political Science: An Informal Overview*. Columbus, Ohio: Charles E. Merrill, 1965.

Weber, Max. *The Methodology of the Social Sciences*. New York: The Free Press, 1949.

CHAPTER IV

Teaching Social Studies to the Disadvantaged

by Frederick A. Rodgers

The teaching of social studies to disadvantaged students is beset with unique problems specifically related to the nature of the *learner*, of the *content*, and of the *instruction*. If the teacher intends to develop a balanced pedagogical approach for instructing disadvantaged students in the social studies area, it is necessary that he establish a rationale, a type of instructional procedure, and a content that relates to the particular characteristics of the learner and to the requirements of society now and in the future. A careful analysis of the facts as they relate to these three components and to developing trends in society is crucial if an appropriate teaching approach is to be formulated and pursued.

THE SETTING

The environmental setting of the disadvantaged student can be viewed from several different, though interrelated, vantage points. The environment of the disadvantaged student on the whole does not allow for the effective participation in, and integration into, the major institutions of the greater society. This situation fosters conditions that encourage segregation and discrimination and that create a fear, suspicion, and a sense of apathy. The life-style of the disadvantaged student is affected by the low wages, unemployment, underemployment, and a general lack of the resources that provide the structure necessary for a regular and stable existence.

41

In most instances disadvantaged students have crowded and other-wise poor housing conditions. They fail to come into contact with any viable organizational structure outside their nuclear and extended-family units. This lack of contact with viable organizational structures limits the disadvantaged student's opportunities to develop the effec-tive patterns required to operate in a highly complex and specialized society. He does not experience a childhood, a sense of privacy, a feeling of family solidarity—only a feeling of helplessness and inferior-ity. With this description of the environmental setting of the disad-vantaged student, we can now turn to specific instructional problems related to teaching social studies to this selected student.

THE LEARNER

During the 1960s many scholars and educators attempted to de-scribe the characteristics of disadvantaged youth[1] and to prescribe a pattern of teacher education [2] based on the qualities noted. This ap-proach tended to create, substantiate, and perpetuate myths about the disadvantaged that contributed little to our ability to improve in-struction. It should be further noted that most of the authors have provided little support for their conclusions through the use of reliable and well-validated research. This situation has led to the perpetuation of widespread beliefs that disadvantaged youth: (a) are slow in cogni-tive tasks, (b) learn most readily through a physical concrete approach, (c) are anti-intellectual, (d) are traditional and superstitious, (e) are inflexible and not open to reason, (f) feel alienated, (g) blame others for misfortunes, (h) are deficient in auditory skills, and (i) are not competitive.[3] If the disadvantaged student is characterized by the above factors, is it possible for a teacher to teach him the complex subject matter constituting the social studies area? On the other hand, the problem is somewhat different if the qualities of the disadvantaged do not parallel the characteristics outlined. In either case, we are faced with the problem of determining some of the characteristics of the disadvantaged student and his environment as they relate to effective teaching and learning.

Before an effective instructional approach can be devised for the disadvantaged, a realistic description of some of their personal attributes and of the typical environmental conditions they face must emerge. For the most part, disadvantaged youth: (a) are denied a choice in their careers, (b) lack a semblance of political power, (c) are denied opportunities to learn how democratic decision-making takes place, (d) are stigmatized by their cultural backgrounds, and (e) are denied an opportunity to attain inter- and intrapersonal competence.[4] It is possible to teach social studies to the disadvantaged if a teacher has a functional picture of the realities the disadvantaged face in society. In short, a teacher of social studies for the disadvantaged must respect the potential strengths of this group, "rather than be armed with a set of mythologies, masquerading as theories of social science, which only discourage the economically disadvantaged or minority youth from investing in education." [5]

It has become quite evident that keeping the disadvantaged student alive academically is the only way to ensure viable options for him. This student must be given knowledge and the experience requisite for intelligent choices in order to enable him to deal with real problems in his daily life. To accomplish this goal, teachers must convince disadvantaged students that they can learn to be important in a society that does not need their skills to produce the basic goods required by its members. In short, the teacher of the disadvantaged is faced with the problem of dealing with the unskilled in a humane manner even though they are no longer needed for the survival of society. On the other hand, the teacher can organize his instruction to provide disadvantaged students with the necessary skills required to deal with complex social organizations in terms of the students' ability to contribute to, and participate in, society and social change.

More specifically, teachers of the disadvantaged in social studies must make the material and the ideas relevant to the lives of the students. If teachers are to be effective, they must demonstrate that concepts and skills learned in school are directly applicable to the life-situation facing students as human beings. The teacher must deal with open and honest inquiry in his approach to the issues of the day and be willing to help his students formulate a course of action based on the conclusions of effective inquiry. It is absolutely essential that the disadvantaged student perceive and understand the relationship between knowledge (content and skills) and effective functioning in a society. As he attacks problems related both to effective inquiry and to so-called relevance, the real limitations of segregation, bureaucratization, racism, credentials, and nepotism should be approached realistically as problems to be resolved. What a student learns in the classroom must help him make choices as a learner, a worker, a citizen, and a human being. At this point, there is no separation between life and school for the disadvantaged student.

THE CONTENT

The content of the social studies is in part determined by one's definition of this area of study. For purposes of this discussion, the term "social studies" denotes that segment of the curriculum which deals specifically with man in his dynamic relation to his social and physical environments. The social studies are concerned with a knowledge of how man is influenced by his environment, how he in turn uses and alters his environment to satisfy individual and group needs, how customs and institutions have emerged, how man is attempting to solve current problems, and how he draws upon his experience to plan for the future. In a sense, the above description is only an outline of the ingredients required to formulate an operational definition of the social studies area. This is in part caused by the fact that man's dynamic relationship to his social and physical environments is constantly being altered by the discovery of knowledge in the social sciences and by a constant change in the basic structure of these environments. Therefore, any operational definition of social studies as it relates to teaching the disadvantaged must be considered for its temporal and situational qualities. Social studies content for the disadvantaged must be adapted to real-life situations as they exist for the learner.

Closely related to the content issue are the logical and methodological patterns used to select, collect, organize, and present the ideas and materials that become the social studies content. For the development of effective citizens, the clarity with which the logical and methodological patterns are communicated to the learner is more crucial than the facts themselves. In this sense, the content of the social studies should provoke effective thinking for the student; the content of the social studies represents both process and product.

In selecting social studies content, it is sometimes difficult to help students develop effective thinking skills related to the central issues involved in the subject being studied. The nature of this problem is directly related to how "settled" or how transitory a period of history or how reliable a social science theory being studied are. During a relatively "settled" period of human association, the patterns which characterize how man deals with his social and physical environments tend to be taken for granted because functional systems are perceived as being effective. The rationalizations used to justify social systems tend to go unchallenged and serve as evidence that effects are the results of known actions. Critical thinking about changing and improving social systems during such a period is not encouraged or supported. Both thinking and knowledge are used to maintain established patterns and institutions rather than to formulate plans and approaches to change and reconstruct.

It should be evident, then, that when social studies content is selected that is representative of a "settled" period, it is difficult to make the material appear relevant to the disadvantaged learner and to generalize the conclusions drawn for real-life situations known to him. At best, this kind of content can be used to develop basic skills needed to interpret information. Even though disadvantaged students can probably understand certain kinds of human relationships by using this approach, it may not hold their interest because of its seemingly static quality. This kind of content would probably hold much more appeal for the more capable students, who profit from the use of abstract examples, contrived situations, and representative models. For the disadvantaged student, effort would have to be expended to encourage him to seek data as a viable alternative to direct experience.

Since we are experiencing a period of rapid transition in every sphere of our existence, the content of the social studies for the disadvantaged should reflect the human associations that are in flux. In a period of rapid transition like our own, alternatives to established and traditional functional social systems are opened to public awareness. Conditions of human relationships in society become problematic rather than assumed. The traditional base of our common social relationships and personal commitments are exposed, and their irrational justifications are laid open to scrutiny. Arguments which were once viewed as rational explanations and justifications of our social arrangements come to appear as rhetorical rationalizations that serve to support special-interest groups and solidify entrenched powers. Careful and critical investigations of motives and activities must reflect the conditions that are representative of life-styles and thought during the period. It is possible that findings which result from this approach to the study of society can help man to shape aspects of his social system.

When content for the social studies is selected from a period of transition, the possibilities for developing effective thinkers is greatly expanded. However, the task is much more difficult because of the number of alternatives related to a myriad of problems for investigation and study. The problematical aspect of roles, institutions, and ideologies brings forth a wide range of issues and allows for the consideration of many contemporary topics of interest to learners. Social studies content which covers a period of transition is more likely to meet the alleged needs of disadvantaged students.

The aforementioned discussion deals with social studies content in general terms and not with the specific skills that are required to identify and digest information. The "operational content" of the social studies is the basic skills required for study. The purpose of these skills is to help students acquire the necessary tools to gain certain insights into their environmental setting and to develop intellectual and social habits compatible with their role as students. Since basic skills are the fundamental tools for learning and personal growth, the disadvantaged student must acquire a command of those skills during his school experience that allow him to adjust to other situations later in life.

Such skills as locating, organizing, and evaluating information are indispensable to the disadvantaged. This student must also be taught how to acquire information through reading, listening, and observing.

He should acquire skills in communicating orally and in written form; in interpreting charts, graphs, tables, and pictures; and in working with others in a task-related or social situation. Particular emphasis should be placed on reading social studies materials, applying problem-solving and critical-thinking skills to social issues; interpreting maps and globes; and understanding time and chronology. The teaching strategy employed to instruct the disadvantaged in social studies skills should allow for: (1) the introduction of specific information through a structured learning experience; (2) development of a skill in a systematic pattern; and (3) reteaching, reinforcing, maintaining, and extending the skill across a variety of experiences and activities. If disadvantaged students are exposed to skills in the social studies in this manner, they can be helped to acquire the means to interpret data independently.

A program in the social studies must include basic skills as part of the content. Systematic instruction in the use of these skills must parallel the approach to the content and the concepts to be learned. It is important for disadvantaged students to realize that the skills learned and used ultimately determine what the content of the social studies reveals and contributes to their understanding of their immediate world.

THE INSTRUCTION

An essential attribute of an effective teacher of the disadvantaged is his awareness of the realities of the society in which both he and his students function. This awareness must be the focal point guiding the formulation of instructional activities. The curriculum program for the disadvantaged must be responsive to instructional clarity and to the functional levels of the students. Every attempt must be made to ensure a setting that enables every learner to gain knowledge that is useful to him as a member of the society. This outcome is the special responsibility of the teacher, and it should be achieved through manipulating the instructional program.

Regardless of the teaching style and content to be learned, the teaching act can be effectively divided into a number of distinct phases. Each of these phases affect the possible outcomes and the nature of the concepts that can be developed. Below is a list of these phases and a discussion of how they can contribute to teaching the disadvantaged student.

1. *Preparation.* A teacher of the disadvantaged must pay particular attention to his preparation for instruction. This is the "practice" phase of the teaching act. It is also a critical phase in determining how content, process, and concept will be operationalized for a given group of students. This is the time when the teacher explores and gathers appropriate materials, organizes the ideas to be learned, designs a teaching strategy, reviews this knowledge for understanding of the content, and decides on an introductory activity. Every attempt should be made to adjust instructional preparation to the type of teaching strategies suggested by the selected content.

2. *Motivation.* Any approach to instruction of the disadvantaged must capture the attention of the learner. This phase of the teaching act is important because the student's interests should coincide with his notion of what is being learned. Formally, this is the "motivation" phase of the teaching act. When teaching the disadvantaged the stimulus for a lesson can determine the effect of the instructional impact. For the most part, attempts to motivate this group of students must take into account the relationship between what is to be learned and the daily experience of the learner. As the content becomes more remote from life-experience, motivational techniques become less useful. Therefore, it is the teacher's responsibility to ensure the development of a motivational strategy that parallels the interests and background of each student.

3. *Presentation.* The act of presenting the learning task to disadvantaged students is probably the most critical phase of the teaching activity. Since this segment of the teaching act is the interactive phase, it is at this point that the preparational and the motivational phases are combined with the teaching strategy. It is at this stage when teachers receive their initial feedback—both cognitive and affective—regarding the impact of the approach selected. As the teacher confronts his students with learning tasks to be performed, he is operationalizing his notion of how students should approach the

problems outlined and what content students should be learning. During this phase, a teacher demonstrates the response expected, the means for achieving it, and some of the consequences when alternative means are selected for solving a problem. Ordinarily, the teaching strategy to be employed is determined prior to initiating the presentation phase. Depending upon the strategy selected, a decision is made regarding the elements of presentation that are to be replicated, memorized, interpreted, and applied by the students. At this point, the teacher acts both as an artist and as a skillful technician. Even though a teacher's effectiveness is partly dependent upon the technical skills he possesses, he must base many of his procedural moves on an intuitive analysis of the situational requirements confronting him. The presentation phase of the teaching act heavily taxes a teacher's sensitivity and experience as he plots his course with a given body of students.

The most troublesome area related to teaching the disadvantaged is the presentation phase. At this point the teacher confronts his students directly and is forced to deal with unpredictable problems. These problems are often related to discipline, home background, personality, achievement, and social issues. If the teacher is not equipped to deal with situational variables which commonly characterize classrooms with disadvantaged students, the presentation phase is likely to be adversely affected. Any attempt to improve instruction received by disadvantaged students must deal with how they make teachers more effective in their presentation efforts.

4. *Student Response.* The student response is the most important criterion of the presentation's effectiveness. This is the point where the observable impact of the teaching act on individual students is initially noted and assessed. Students must demonstrate their mastery of, and facility with selected prototypical tasks that are related to present standards in the social sciences. Since the trial student response occurs early during the presentation phase, it serves as a guide to both the learner and the teacher because it suggests the pattern of the next step in the teaching strategy to be employed and outlines what is to be learned. The trial response of learners is an indispensable segment of the teaching act.

When the response of students is good or acceptable, no further instruction may be required and the learners can proceed. When the opposite results are evident, the teacher must either correct or help the student to correct his trial response before moving on to the next level of intellectual involvement. This is basically the operational pattern that is evident between learners and teacher during the teaching act.

5. *Perpetuating the Response.* Only in rare instances is the material to be learned by students considered temporary and restricted to a specified period of time. Most of the information and processes that are learned by students are "future oriented" because learners are expected to apply what is learned to other situations at other times. But whether a subject or skill is learned is often determined by how much time and repetition are given the learner during the teaching act. This obvious emphasis on concentration and repetition in learning skills is so patently important and so under-valued by so many teachers. Helping students to learn appropriate responses for social studies problems is critical in aiding their facility for interpreting complex social ideas. It must be remembered that a student's ability to process and use social data is a function of the quantity and quality of the social studies skills he possesses.

6. *Evaluation.* Because evaluation involves making certain judgments about performance, care must be exercised to ensure that the purpose for evaluation justifies the approach. Since evaluation can be used (1) to chart the course of instruction with a class or an individual, (2) to determine the extent to which students have mastered a concept or specific knowledge, and (3) to judge the effectiveness of an instructional approach, the teacher must always differentiate between how and why the evaluation technique is being employed. Social studies teachers must also consider the evaluation of social studies in terms of the skills needed to process and understand information.

Evaluation in the social studies can be structured to deal with basic knowledge, thinking skills, attitudes, and intellectual skills together or separately. Therefore, the evaluation technique employed in the social studies is dependent both on the teacher's purpose and on the subject considered. When judgments are to be made about the adequacy of learning in the social studies, the approach to, and the method of, evaluation should contribute to a better understanding by the learner and the teacher of the results of the learning and teaching act, respectively.

SOME EFFECTIVE APPROACHES
TO TEACHING THE DISADVANTAGED

What is an effective approach to teaching the disadvantaged social studies? In order to respond to this question, one must specify the content, the population, and the teaching situation. Since the content of the social studies covers a wide range of materials and concepts and the disadvantaged population encompasses an inexhaustible number of characteristics, it is probably most helpful (and far less risky) to focus on the teaching situation as a basis for formulating effective instructional approaches. The teaching situation determines the system of instructional techniques and concepts selected to influence the teaching act. In a classroom of the disadvantaged teachers should deal with (1) instructional sequencing, and (2) management and control. There is an obvious but often unstated need for teachers of the disadvantaged to be well versed in the nature of social studies content and in the logical structure of the concepts it includes. When the social studies teacher fails to understand the concepts, causes, and values associated with the content, he probably lacks the intellectual and linguistic skill required to inspire his students. Too often this situation causes teachers to attribute ineffective teaching to students' deficiencies in comprehension rather than to their lack of sophistication with the subject.

Another area of concern involving the teaching situation for the disadvantaged student is related to management and control. For the most part, the teacher's management skills determine the nature of disciplinary problems. Classroom management involves such factors as preparing lesson plans; arranging the classroom environment; planning teaching strategies, motivation techniques, modes of presentation; and students' responses. In order to determine the classroom management pattern to be employed by teachers of the disadvantaged, a consideration of the following selected program features should be considered:

1. *Content Selection.* The content of the social studies for the disad-

vantaged should be based on the student's environment and background experience. When social contacts between people or institutions are considered for study, they should resemble relationships in the students' experience. It is only after students have demonstrated their facility with the content of familiar social or institutional relationships that more esoteric areas can be considered and introduced.

2. *Selection of Study Problems.* Since disadvantaged students are faced with unusual and readily discernible personal problems, the social studies subjects selected for study should be real and offer possible solutions to known social problems. This approach can be effective because it enables students to see a relationship between school and living. When real problems are selected for study, a teacher increases his chances of correlating his instruction to the interests of students.

3. *Reinforcing Basic Academic Skills.* One of the critical problems facing disadvantaged students is their incompetence in basic academic and work-study skills. This deficiency is even more critical in the social studies because so much of a student's ability to handle material in this area is dependent upon his mastery of academic skills. Any approach to teaching the disadvantaged must formulate teaching strategies that allow for repetitive practice of basic academic skills.

4. *Multisensory Instructional Patterns.* Disadvantaged students must be afforded opportunities to learn content and concepts without reading. This can be done through the use of field trips, discussions, films, models, maps, charts, graphs, and demonstrations. Students should have an opportunity to handle materials and equipment so that they can relate the verbal concepts to application and vice versa. In this way, students who do not read can gain facility with many concepts which might escape them.

When the teachers of the disadvantaged make use of these factors to guide their approach to classroom management, they are likely to experience some success in effecting student attitudes toward social studies as a discipline.

CONCLUSION

The prospective social studies teacher of the disadvantaged student has many concerns which could be the focal point of his attention.

These concerns relate to both his own personality traits and his technical skills. The pattern for dealing with these concerns is a function of the subject matter, the teaching strategy, the learning environment, the characteristics of his students, and the expected outcomes. All of these factors interact with each other to determine what effect the teaching act will have on a selected group of students. More specifically, the prospective social studies teacher of the disadvantaged student must:

1. Respect the unique experiences and home backgrounds of his students.
2. Understand the way in which students learn and build on their strengths.
3. Know the language of students and how their language patterns affect intellectual functioning.
4. Tailor the materials and teaching procedures to the learning patterns of students.
5. Have extensive knowledge of the subject matter being taught.
6. Believe in students' ability to learn the subject matter being presented.
7. Structure a teaching strategy for fostering measurable progress within an atmosphere of planned and controlled flexibility.
8. Approach the teaching role with an open mind and a desire for measurable results.

If the prospective social studies teacher is not prepared to do these things then it is unlikely that he can be successful in teaching those who need his help most.

NOTES

1. Frank Riessman, *The Culturally Deprived Child*, New York: Harper & Row, 1962.
2. Miriam L. Goldberg, "Adapting Teacher Style to Pupil Differences: Teachers for Disadvantaged Children," *Merrill-Palmer Quarterly*, volume 10, April, 1964, pp. 161-78.
3. Riessman, op. cit.

4. Othanel B. Smith, *Teachers for the Real World,* Washington, D.C.: The American Association of Colleges for Teacher Education, 1969.
5. Ibid., p. 4.

BIBLIOGRAPHY

Berg, Harry D., ed. *Evaluation in the Social Studies.* Washington, D.C.: National Council for the Social Studies, 35th Yearbook, 1967.

Fair, Jean, and Shaftel, Fannie R., eds. *Effective Thinking in the Social Studies.* Washington, D.C.: National Council for the Social Studies, 37th Yearbook, 1967.

Frost, Joe L., and Hawkes, Glenn R., eds. *The Disadvantaged Child.* New York: Houghton Mifflin, 1966.

Kerber, August, and Bommarito, Barbara, eds. *The Schools and the Urban Crisis.* New York: Holt, Rinehart, and Winston, 1965.

Passow, A. Harry; Goldberg, Miriam; and Tannenbaum, Abraham J., eds. *Education of the Disadvantaged.* New York: Holt, Rinehart and Winston, 1967.

Passow, A. Harry, ed. *Education in Depressed Areas.* New York: Teachers College Press, Columbia University, 1963.

Smith, B. Othanel. *Teachers for the Real World.* Washington, D.C.: The American Association of Colleges for Teacher Education, 1969.

CHAPTER V

The Analysis of Social Conflict

by H. H. Giles

I
PROBLEM-SOLVING AND THE USE OF
CONFLICT EPISODE ANALYSIS

Everybody has problems! Students, families, teachers, governments, and even rock-and-roll bands. Not to mention racial and religious minorities, campus protesters, the Federal Reserve Bank, and pro football players.

When you have a problem how do you solve it? Do you do what most of us do—either evade it or try something someone else tells you to do? If so, you may never realize that most exciting and lasting of human joys—the experience of true learning.

At the turn of the century—way back in the 1890s and early 1900s—a great American named John Dewey began to publish books and articles that explained how we learn. Essentially, he said, we learn through encountering problems and trying to solve them. In order to do this, we first have to recognize and define the problem (not as easy as it sounds, sometimes); then we have to figure out all possible reasons why the problem exists; figure out ways to test our ideas of why, and what to do about it; and then test our notions by putting one after another into practice. The results tell us what works and what doesn't.

Of course, in order to do all that you have to have a purpose—a real desire to deal with the problem. Most of us don't desire to breathe clean air or drink clean water enough to analyze and do something about the pollution of our sky and our streams. So it gets worse all the

55

time. Maybe George will take care of it for us. George Wallace, George Washington—or, perhaps, some dictator who knows all the answers.

As a matter of fact, the whole idea of social studies as part of the school curriculum grew out of the great discovery that our society has many problems that keep us from coming closer to that happiness Thomas Jefferson guaranteed us the pursuit of. And so, to the study of drum-and-trumpet history, the memorizing of maps and place names, the recital of the list of presidents and other sundries, the daring innovators of the 1920s and 1930s began to add teaching about people, about you and me and the relationship of history and geography and government to each other and to us little people.

A lot of the teaching, unfortunately for this splendid idea, was of the same type as still goes on in those parts of the world where the students sit on the ground in front of the teacher on his rug and repeat after him what he utters. This type of approach to schooling is known as the Swallow and Regurgitate method (two famous names in the entire story of the great battle between the weak and the strong).

Opposed to Swallow and Regurgitate, rote "learning" (memorizing), and the general operation of school systems and classes by petty dictators is the idea that teaching actually is a reflexive verb. That is to say, we teach ourselves when we truly learn. This, by the way, is one reason for the old educational adage, "If you want to really find out about a subject, teach it!" As it has turned out, although a few real teachers (facilitators of self-teaching) have always practiced the encouragement of pupil initiative and have always been concerned about individual capacities and interests, it is likely that modern technology, rather than a great educational philosopher, will speed self-teaching. Whatever brings it about, let us now assume that problem-solving is the true road to learning. How do you make use of it in the classroom?

There are as many ways as there are minds to conceive of them. But the rest of this chapter will be devoted to two specific step-by-step procedures: Conflict Episode Analysis and Problem-Solving, Short Method. The former is richer in some potentials, so it will be presented at greater length.

II
CEA METHOD

The CEA method (Conflict Episode Analysis) was originated in a sociology class at New York University many years ago and since then has been employed in many core and social studies classes. It is called "A Tool for Training in Social Understanding." It has been used ever since its inception as a method for stretching the minds of students concerned with the problems of our society and their effect on human development. It has been used with graduate students, with college undergraduates, as a form of problem analysis—all social conflicts present problems—and it has been used in high school classes.

It is a clinical method. It requires the analyst to diagnose and prescribe. It requires him to use every bit of his knowledge of factors that cause social conflict, and to recognize the difference between such causal factors and the surface symptoms. As this is being written a new president is recommending a large increase in the number of policemen, prosecutors, and judges in Washington, D.C. The president feels he must speed up the legal system to counter crime on the streets in our nation's capital. But while he does this, he himself recognizes that the police and the legal system will be dealing with symptoms, not causes. And the use of police power and punishment by the courts will be a repressive type of treatment. It is unlikely to "cure" or to be very constructive. So in addition to treating symptoms, some more curative and longer-range methods must be found. These will have to deal with old wrongs done to the poor and to blacks, with family and educational failures, with many relationships and misunderstandings between human beings.

A major purpose, then, in analyzing social conflicts by the CEA method is to find the greatest possible range of likely alternatives in the treatment of symptoms and causal factors.

And this method is distinct from that of Machiavelli's in that it has the overall aim of finding ways of treating conflict so that the greatest possible number of those involved are aided, not destroyed or threatened; aided to develop, to survive, to belong, to grow as all human beings want to do.

The method has some kinship to the work of a detective. In order to carry out a good analysis we have to find out what the facts are. We have to discover the feelings and opinions of those involved and estimate their depth and strength. The method requires a combination of science and art: science for objective research; art for the creative imagination that has to be unleashed to replace old, worn, and useless ways of dealing with social conflict by better ones. We see an example of how urgent this is in the case of war and international anarchy. The late General Douglas MacArthur, a rather well-known national figure, summed up our need in this instance with the statement: "War is no longer a feasible instrument of national policy."

In outline, the CEA analysis must employ the following guidelines or categorical headings. There are seven of these:

Conflict Episode Analysis Outline

    I. Title.
   II. Presenting incident.
  III. History.
  IV. Diagnosis: (A) Symptoms; (B) Hypothesis; (C) Prognosis.
   V. Treatment: (A) What has been done? (B) Other possibilities.
  VI. Results to Date.
 VII. Conclusions: (A) Dynamics; (B) Principals re method; (C) Unsolved questions.

Looks simple—or does it?

If it does, just go ahead, pick a conflict, and try it, by yourself or with a class.

If it doesn't, or if you run into difficulty, you may want to refer to the commentary which follows, and to the case example of the use of CEA as a unit in the teaching of history by a high school social studies teacher.

SUBJECTS FOR ANALYSIS

It must be clear that the CEA analysis is designed for a clinical look, by social clinicians-in-training, who really care about figuring out some better ways to deal with the world's problems.

It is desirable, then, that the choice of conflict areas be made in such a way that each student is rarin' to go. There are three ways that the choice can be made: (a) it can be completely free and open to each student; (b) it can be made by a group; (c) or it can be made by the teacher. If the teacher makes the choice, he will need to spend enough time explaining his reasons and answering questions so that the class members are in real agreement. And whatever the choice, it is usually best to begin by identifying conflict areas and then choose and define the specific conflict(s) to be analyzed.

Conflict areas might be: family conflict, or generation-gap conflict, neighborhood conflict, race or minority vs. power-group conflict, strikes of public employees, historical conflict, international conflict, and so on, ad infinitum. Specific conflicts in these areas might be: child vs. parents over dating; gang vs. gang over territorial rights; black-power community-control advocates vs. teachers' union overhiring and transfer of teachers; police vs. budget director over salaries; Socrates vs. the archons of Athens over academic freedom; U.S.A. vs. Castro's Cuba over communism and expropriation.

Whatever you choose, the analysis always has the same major purposes: to understand, and to find the fullest possible range of symptoms, causal factors, and treatment.

Here is the way one social studies teacher reports his experience in using this method in a history class:

HISTORICAL CONFLICT ANALYSIS
A UNIT METHOD FOR THE NEW SOCIAL STUDIES
BY PATRICK M. BIESTY

The search for a "new social studies" comparable to the "new math" has presented the classroom teacher with the feelings of anticipation and frustration that accompany a period of exploration and discovery. Yet methods and answers to the question "What works?" have been only partially forthcoming, for as in subject matter, the methods of teaching the social studies are more dependent on human factors, imprecision, and variance than are the physical and mathematical sciences.

We agree with Bruner's statement that "The first object of any act of learning, over and beyond the pleasure it may give, is that it should serve us in the future."[1] It is felt, however, that students will need a method by which they can analyze the world in which they will live, a method which can unite the concepts of the social sciences in a useful way. Structure must serve students in the future when they are faced with social conflicts and seek possible alternative actions. In the natural sciences concepts share emphasis with a valuable skill, the scientific method. In the social sciences there is not an accepted method, but rather at times an emulation of the method of the natural sciences. It is to fill this need that the method of "historical conflict analysis" is offered as a suggestion. It is hoped that the method will serve students in achieving conceptual learning and further serve them as a skill in analyzing the social problems that will face them in the future.

The method serves to fulfill both the cognitive and the affective goals of the "new social studies," combining the problem-solving approach with use of original source material.[2] The search for concept development is handled inductively by the students, allowing the teacher to serve more fully as a resource person.

The method is an adaptation of "Conflict Episode Analysis" as developed under the guidance of Professor H. Harry Giles of New York University and used in the social conflict analysis seminars at the N.Y.U. Graduate School of Education, in which the author is enrolled.[3] The seminars have been held since 1945 and would be valuable for teachers who would attempt to use the approach.

Two points regarding the method need to be kept in mind. The method has been used in the secondary schools with average and above-average students with good results. The method is untried with slower and lower-level students. Use in these areas needs testing. Secondly, the similarity of this method to that of medical analysis did not result from conscious efforts in the development of the original method, but was recognized by the developers after it was devised. The similarity is accounted for by the presence of numerous clinical psychologists in the N.Y.U. seminars.

Historical Conflict Analysis

Following each item in the outline, examples used in the study of the Russian Revolution appear in parentheses.

1. Title
   (The power struggle in Russia: 1917)
2. Historical happening
   (The Russian revolutions of 1917 acted out in play form from original source material)
3. Student's view
   (a) Focus of the conflict: Party I vs. Party II
       Conflict for study chosen from the many conflicts present in the historical happening.
   (The Bolsheviks vs. the Socialists)
   (b) Student's participation, or association with the historical happening, including prejudices.
   (Parents lived under Chinese Communist rule)
4. Diagnosis of the conflict
   (a) Symptoms of the conflict
   (Bolshevik call for "all power to the Soviets")
   (b) Probable and immediate causes. Include what the student considers the most important cause.
   (Differences in interpretation of Marx's writings; failure of the July offensive against the Germans)
   (c) Prognosis
   (The Bolsheviks will triumph)
5. History
   (a) Early symptoms of the conflict
   (Formation of separate Socialist parties)

(b) Situational factors at the time of the conflict other than those presented in the historical happening (2).

(Formation of Soviets in Moscow and other Russian cities)

6. Treatment

(a) Of symptoms

(Kerensky attacks Bolshevik war policy as "naïve")

(b) Of causal factors

(Failure of provisional government to enact a meaningful land-reform law)

7. Results to date

(Bolshevik arrest and imprisonment of opposition)

8. Conclusions

(a) Dynamics (deepest causes): environmental, social, and individual forces.

(In periods of insecurity people seek strong leaders)

(b) Other treatment possibilities

(1) Of symptoms

(If elections for a Constituent Assembly had been held in June, democratic forces would have had a greater chance of survival)

(2) Of causal factors

(If the provisional government had given land to the peasants, chances for stability would have improved)

(c) Questions for research and student's hypotheses regarding each

(Question: Did the Bolsheviks ever intend to share power?)

(Hypothesis: The Bolsheviks wanted all the power for themselves)

The outline serves as a guide for in-class presentation and discussion and also as a guide in writing a report on the conflict studied. The final report, in my experience, is an impressive student achievement, unmatched by the collection of question-and-answer homework assignments they have been used to. As used so far, the analysis has been a group effort, with all members of the class contributing to one analysis, but writing separate reports. At a future time it is hoped that committees will work on different conflicts, report to the group on their findings, and stand the test of group questioning. The final goal is the use of the method by each student on his own, gaining from the experience a mastery of the method which will aid him in understanding his and our world.

The outline deserves explanation and comment for a fuller understanding of its use. Under each section of the outline I have included comments and examples from the classroom analysis of the Russian revolutions of 1917.

Historical Conflict Analysis. History is used in this method as a stage, or perhaps, in keeping with the medical metaphor, as the operating table for an autopsy. The chronology of history is handled in two separate sections of the analysis, although no pretension is made that the continuous flow of history is accomplished. The method resembles, in this aspect, the post-holing approach. History is neither "thrown out the window" nor able to make teacher and class the prisoner of its discipline. At the same time, however, the importance of having relevant and accurate historical facts is emphasized.

Title. The title is left open until after the presentation of the historical happening and is chosen by the students as the title of the written reports. The title may be descriptive or connotative: for example, "The Power Struggle in Russia in 1917," or "The Socialists vs. the Bolsheviks."

Historical Happening. To make the study lively and dynamic, and to involve the students in the process, the historical happening was presented in play form using original source material for the roles. In this case the play carried the action from the March Revolution through the Bolshevik Revolution in November, with a radio commentator providing the transitional material in a "You Are There" format. The dramatic use of source material overcomes one of the major criticisms lodged by students, that source material is often dull.

Putting together a dramatization takes effort and time, but the rewards are great. Publishers hopefully will find that this format is useful and may provide the needed material in play form in the future. Movies of historical events, recordings, eight-millimeter single-concept films, and transparencies also can be used to provide verisimilitude.

However, the author feels the participation of students in a dramatization has multiple rewards far exceeding those obtained by electronic presentations.

Student's View. (a) Focus of the conflict: Party I vs. Party II. In this
section the students are asked to discover as many conflicts as possible
in the dramatized historical happening. The complexity of any period
of history is a concept discovered by this exercise in critical thinking.
Among the intriguing ideas students learn are the existence of conflicts
within groups that are themselves in conflict, and the crossing over and
combining of participants in different conflicts. This discovery on the
students' part deserves attention in the initial use of the method, for
this very complexity can intimidate. After discussion of the diverse
conflicts, the students are asked to select the conflict which was most
important and to support their contention by referring to the historical
happening and its results.

By avoiding the possibility of having committees study separate
conflicts, the teacher emphasizes the method. When the method is
better known, committees can be used to good advantage. In the study
of the Russian Revolution the conflict finally chosen for analysis was
the Bolsheviks vs. the Socialists.

The method is not meant to establish a dialectical determinist view
of history. By admitting the existence of many conflicts and establishing multitudinous causal factors, a broad understanding of historical
developments is achieved. The singling out of one conflict provides the
opportunity for in-depth study.

(b) Student's participation with the historical happening, including
prejudices. In the attempt to gain objectivity and to train students to
be aware of possible biases in material they read, the outline calls for
students to state any relationship or bias they have. Students are often
unaware of their biases even when asked to state them. However, they
soon become aware that they view historical events from a distinctly
American point of view. One Chinese boy wrote, "My parents lived
under a Communist government, but that won't bias me in favor of the
Bolsheviks." The student, of course, should be aware that his parents'
experience might bias him against the Bolsheviks. This training in

objectivity also prepares students to critically analyze original source material.

Diagnosis of the Conflict. (a) Symptoms of the conflict. Selecting symptoms is a difficult task for students trained to look at history as little more than causes and results of great events, or as a narrative of man's progress through the ages. The experience is often painful for the glib student who has generalized his way through the study of history in secondary school courses, and who studied only when he had to memorize specific facts. Superior students find a new challenge in the social studies when meaningful thought and reflective thinking are required.

Time should be taken to train students in perceiving society as the scientist perceives phenomena. When Kerensky, at the first meeting of the All-Russia Soviets, attacks the Bolshevik war policy as "naïve," and Lenin rises to object, the student is alert. Is this a symptom or a cause? Can a symptom also be a cause? The painful yet urgently inquisitive expression on the student's face is evidence of his growing conceptual · thinking.

Students must become accurate observers and reporters if their conclusions are to be valid. The lesson of accurate observation has application to the way newspapers are read and understood. How important is accuracy? What responsibilities do newspapers and television companies have to the public in reporting the news? Does a government ever have the right to manipulate the news? Emerging from the practice of precise observation and reporting is a discipline that students will carry with them beyond their school years.

(b) Probable and immediate causes. The aim here is to go beyond the simple differentiation of immediate and underlying causes of historical events. If we push students, we can establish many more causes than textbooks list. How can we go beyond the usual listing of social, economic, and political causes?

The study of the period from March 1917 to November 1917 in Russia gives symptomatic evidence of other causes. Twenty or more possible causes may be listed and discussed, including the effect on Lenin of his brother's execution for plotting against the czar. Students should choose which cause they believe to be the most important. Where there is difference of opinion, the opposing sides can debate their positions.

In addition, the teacher must introduce psychological and sociological explanations for men's actions. Students react positively to the deeper thoughts the behavioral sciences attempt. In arguing for the study of group and individual values, Donald W. Oliver states:

> We feel that one of the essential requirements of this task is that the individual student be liberated from his own narrow value system to the point where he can see the relationship between his personal value judgments and those of other groups within society; to the point where he can see and feel sources of conflict within himself, and between himself and others; and to the point where he can handle these conflicts by predicting courses of action which will maximize the possibility of individual or group fulfillment as individuals and groups may define this fulfillment." [4]

Students should recognize that differing values can cause conflicts between groups, but we must also understand the forces that generate value formations. It is here that psychological and sociological concepts serve to illuminate our understanding of conflicts.

(c) Prognosis. Although in the study of history the outcome is known, training to predict the future course of events is an important goal for individual fulfillment, as Oliver points out. By studying the past and the factors which resulted in the ultimate outcome, students are encouraged to apply their knowledge to current conflicts and to hypothesize outcomes.

History. To make the study of man fully rounded, we seek to discover early signs that a conflict with vast destructive potential was developing. The attempt is not merely to establish the organic relationship of the conflict to the history of the nation involved; it is also to train the students to look for symptoms which may develop into destructive behavior in the future.

In addition, since the historical happening (2), which set the stage for the analysis, may give a limited view of the conflicts and causes, relevant material is added to round out the historical background. Hopefully, this section will overcome any bias inherent in the selection of material presented in the historical happening.

Treatment. The political apathy of our citizenry is, perhaps, a product of the approach to social studies in our schools. Have we directly or indirectly taught our students that it is best to sit passively by while events unfold? It is a possibility. Often treatment of social ills is nothing more than sitting passively by, that is, doing nothing. To do nothing is, in fact, to do something. This is sometimes a new concept to students.

When we have isolated the symptoms and causes of a conflict, we can then proceed to determine exactly what was done to effect change. Treating symptoms and causes separately is of the utmost importance in the analysis, for in our daily lives we hear recommendations for symptomatic treatment that is mistaken for treatment of causes. Often in history we find that little was done to treat the causes of destructive conflicts. Later in the analysis students are asked to consider what else might have been done within the range of realistic possibilities.

Results to Date. The conflict is developed as far as possible into the present times. The possibility of the reappearance of the conflict on a confrontation level is also considered. In this way students are made aware that conflicts do not usually disappear—that they merely subside.

Conclusions. (a) Dynamics (deepest causes). To quote Professor Giles, "Dynamics here is taken to mean the most fundamental drives or motive forces operating to cause the behavior of individuals or groups." [5] It is an amusing but worthwhile exercise to continually ask a student the question "Why?" until no further answer can be given. To prepare students to delve more deeply into causes, I asked a student volunteer why he was late coming to school that morning. The final answer we reached was that "Man needs friends." (In this case, the friend the student regularly came to school with was late.)

By seeking dynamics we draw more and more upon the behavioral sciences and draw further away from the textbook. The dynamics thought of by students are usually rough in wording, but lead to discussion and research into the findings of social scientists, which the teacher can introduce.

(b) Other treatment possibilities. If students are to become involved citizens, they must be trained to consider and suggest possible courses of action. The outline calls for a distinction between treatment of symptoms and treatment of causes in order to reinforce an under-standing of the complexity of the conflict. As an aid in selecting treatment possibilities, the students were urged to keep in mind the goal of treatment, which we established as "the greatest good for the greater number." The form, "If *a*, then *b* . . ." was suggested as the wording for treatment possibilities.

(c) Questions for research and students' hypotheses regarding each. The questions which linger in many students' minds are here asked for in print, along with the hypotheses, or guesses, the students have come up with in answer to the questions. Questions can deal with the conflict, with the dynamics, or with the method of analysis. Thus, we admit that our understanding may be incomplete; but we can direct our attention toward seeking answers.

CONCLUSIONS

The method of "historical conflict analysis" can be effectively used to attain the goals of the "new social studies," for it includes a problems approach, inductive learning, emphasis on social studies concepts, and the use of original source material. In addition, the method itself will aid the student in placing the phenomena of future conflicts within a frame of reference they can understand. Justification for use of the method lies in its use as an aid to our students in the future.

IV
A SIMPLER FORM THAT SOME PREFER

Problem Analysis

All conflicts present problems, but not all problems have become overt conflicts.

A type of problem analysis which has been applied to many social conflicts by many generations of students, consists of the following:

I. Selection of the problem area and definition of the specific aspect or problem to be studied.

II. Presentation of opposing views as to what should be done about the problem.

III. Analysis of the data and weight of opinion supporting each competing view.

IV. Conclusions: The problem analyst's personal decision as to the best course of action (who should do what, when, and how) and what he personally will do to help achieve that course of action.

One of the most lively classes in the experience of the present writer was a group of forty-one teen-agers who initiated their study of the social conflicts in our time by brain-storming—listing on the board every conflict and conflict area that anyone in the class considered interesting and important for any reason. No criticisms of the choices were raised by the teacher or allowed by him during this process.

When the board was filled with the designated conflicts and conflict areas, the teacher asked which were areas, and which were specific conflicts. One by one, each was labeled.

Then the class was asked to divide into buzz groups of six members each, to come up with three areas, ranked in the order of importance for study during the term.

Each buzz group reported its recommendations. There was some agreement, some hot argument (but reasons had to be stated), and a final vote which selected not three but six areas, with the understanding that the class would go as far as it could in the fifteen weeks it had available for the study.

The class was then designated (by the teacher) as the United States Governing Assembly with elected officers. Members were asked to consider how they stood on the issue or conflict chosen as No. 1. They were also asked to reseat themselves in the classroom according to whether they considered themselves generally Conservatives (to the right), Middle-of-the-Roaders, or Leftists.

Anyone who wished could submit in writing a resolution (what to do) regarding Conflict No. 1. A Governing Body Committee scheduled the hearings, and the order for presentations and debate on the resolutions.

At the same time every member of the class turned in his choice of problem within the area of Conflict No. 1 and began the process of preparing a written Problem Analysis (Steps I-IV) with a list of sources (books, articles, interviews, observations).

An exciting and lively time was had by all! The two concurrent procedures—preparation of what amounted to position papers, and debate in the U.S. Governing Assembly—complemented each other.

This form of study, requiring real research, doing away with lectures, and stressing personal participation in planning, in doing, and in analytical decision-making, led to considerable reading and searching for ideas and proposals. These were tested by the sharpest of evaluators—the students—but at each day's meeting the teacher took ten minutes at the end for a summing up, and some time to raise his own questions.

The papers—problem analyses—were graded twice. They were exchanged with classmates who rated them from 1 (outstanding) to 10 (lousy!) and wrote criticisms on them. They were handed back to the writer. Then the teacher collected them and repeated the rating and written-criticism process.

V
CONCLUSION

Two similar but distinct forms of social conflict analysis have been presented in this chapter. Each has been classroom tested and refined over a long period of time. Each has its own raison d'être, but the common elements are of most importance. These are the following:

1. Use of social conflict analysis as a technique for stretching minds to go beyond prejudiced or unexamined opinion to substantial examination and conclusion.
2. Recognition of the importance of involving each student in each step of a process of planning, analyzing, and deciding.
3. Recognition of the value of using hot issues and real (to the students) problems as the focus of study.

NOTES

1. Jerome Bruner, *The Process of Education*, Cambridge, Mass.: Harvard University Press, 1960.
2. For an extended treatment of these goals, see chs. 2 and 3 in Edwin Fenton. *Teaching the New Social Studies in Secondary Schools: An Inductive Approach* New York: Holt, Rinehart, and Winston, 1966.
3. H. Harry Giles, "Conflict Episode Analysis—A Tool for Education in Social Technology," *Journal of Educational Sociology*, XXVI, No. 9, May 1953, 418-433.
4. Donald W. Oliver, "The Selection of Content in the Social Studies," in Edwin Fenton, op. cit., p. 107.
5. H. Harry Giles, op. cit., p. 427.

CHAPTER VI

Teaching Economics

by George G. Dawson

WHY TEACH ECONOMICS?

Economics should be taught because it affects everyone. There is probably no problem, issue, or topic in economics which does not somehow relate to the individual, directly or indirectly. A teacher with a reasonably good understanding of economics should have little difficulty in relating every topic to some aspect of the lives of pupils. Because economic topics and principles do have a bearing on our personal lives, there should be little difficulty in motivating the students. For example, let us take the problem of inflation. Why should a teen-ager be interested in this issue? Because one's own level of living can diminish as a result of it. The average teen-ager has a voracious appetite for such things as popular recordings, clothes, hamburgers, drive-in movies, bicycles, and automobiles. Whether the young person earns spending money, has an allowance, or shares in the family budget in a general way, rising prices may mean that he or she will enjoy fewer of the things wanted.

Unfortunately, many social studies teachers express little or no interest in economics. A recent survey revealed that only 50 percent of all colleges with teacher-training programs require economics of their social studies majors; and that unless economics *is* required, usually fewer than 10 percent will elect to take it. Furthermore, only 22 percent of the nation's colleges provide the social studies major with any instruction in methods of teaching economics. This is indeed difficult to understand, for every subject in the social studies area has an economic dimension. Can a teacher adequately deal with the background of the American Revolution without considering the economic problems caused by Britain's mercantilistic policies? When over half of all major legislation before the Congress and the state legislatures in some way deals with economic issues, can a teacher leave economics out of government lessons? Does geography have much meaning if we fail to note the economic implications of geographic facts and concepts? Can we ignore the economics of poverty or the financial difficulties of urban areas in dealing with serious sociological problems? Obviously, the answer to all these questions is a resounding *no*. This means, then, that those social studies teachers who consider themselves to be strictly history instructors, specialists in government, geographers, or sociologists cannot perform competently in any of those areas without including economics in some of their lessons. This chapter will attempt to provide some guidance to these teachers, as well as to those who will teach a separate course in economics.

In recognition of the fact that economics has relevance to everyone, more and more secondary schools are including separate economics courses in their curricula. Some of the most recent curriculum revisions in leading states and cities reveal that many basic economic concepts are being included in history, government, geography, and other social studies courses. Those who have looked upon economics as being strictly a college-level subject may be amazed to learn that such "sophisticated" topics as scarcity, the factors of production, division of labor, taxation, money, the role of banks, supply and demand, opportunity cost, and diminishing marginal utility are even being taught in the elementary grades!

If economics can be taught to elementary school children in a meaningful way, certainly the secondary teacher can find the means to instruct students in this vitally important discipline. Probably every social studies teacher sees his or her purpose as preparing the youth of today for intelligent citizenship tomorrow. One should not forget, then, that every citizen must constantly make economic decisions. Economic issues pervade every political campaign, and candidates are often elected or defeated on the strength of their economic promises. Many voters make decisions on how they will cast their ballots on the basis of economic promises, although they have little understanding of the implications of their actions. Thus, people may support policies which are not only harmful to the public in general, but to themselves personally. Aside from the periodic casting of ballots, however, it must be forever remembered that every resident of this country is an *economic* citizen, whether or not he or she is old enough to vote or whether or not that privilege is ever exercised. As consumers, we all have something in common. It has almost become a cliché in economics to say that the consumer's dollar is a ballot, and that every time we spend or save a dollar we are helping to guide and direct the American economy.

In an economy which is still basically free from rigid government direction and control, the importance of an economically literate citizenship cannot be overemphasized. If a product or a service meets with the consumer's approval, he or she signals this by showing a willingness to spend dollars for that item. If we become tired of a good or a service, if we consider the quality to be too low, or if some substitute pleases us better, we refuse to spend dollars on it, and American industry soon gets the message. Whether one is making a decision regarding one's own family budget, or whether one is voting in an election involving important economic policies, one ought to have some understanding of what one is doing—and why.

This chapter cannot provide the reader with a short course in economics. We must assume that the basic concepts are familiar, or that the reader will take steps to acquire an understanding of basic principles. In addition to the formal college introductory courses, today there are many workshops, institutes, and in-service courses available for teachers. It is not impossible to learn a substantial amount of economics through self-study.[1] In discussing the teaching of economics, however, we shall touch upon some of the basic concepts that can and should be included in the secondary school curriculum.

Earlier, it was said that the basic economic topics and principles have a bearing on our personal lives. Let us examine a few more of these topics and show how they relate to the individual. In this writer's view, the relevance of economics to the life of the student is the key to motivation. This does not mean that we should encourage a narrow "what's in it for me?" attitude. On the contrary, we should see to it that our students place their own welfare in the context of the public good. The worker who demands a wage increase in excess of his productivity may be putting more money into his pocket today, but must also be helping to cause inflationary pressures that will erode his purchasing power (and lower his *real income*) tomorrow. The shortsighted employer who pays starvation wages may increase this year's profit margin, but may in the long run be destroying the market for his output by making it difficult for the consumers (a very large portion of whom are workers) to buy it. Those citizens who repeatedly refuse to vote for higher school taxes may hold their tax bills in check, but may be weakening their educational system to the point where the entire regional economy can be adversely affected. (In one actual case, the schools had to be closed, halfway through the academic year.) Since one of the most important elements in economic growth is education, the voters may be reducing their own incomes in the long run, in order to preserve their spending power today.

The most basic economic problem is the problem of *scarcity*. The sad fact is that human wants are usually greater than the resources available for satisfying those wants. Since we cannot have everything that we want, therefore, we must make choices from among alternative possibilities. This applies to the personal, national, and even the world situation. Suppose that a youngster has earned $5 by mowing lawns. He wants a baseball glove priced at $5, but he would also like to have a record album costing that amount. If he chooses the former, the *real cost* of the glove is the sacrifice of the record album. (We might also say that the cost of the glove was the labor he expended in mowing the lawns to earn the $5, and the sacrifice of his leisure time in so doing.)

Once the student understands the simple *real cost* (also called *opportunity cost*) principle, it can be applied to many other situations. On the family level, if the members of the household want a new car and also desire a trip to Europe, but have money enough only for one of these, they must realize that the real cost of the trip to Europe is the car that they sacrificed by choosing to take the trip. (Or the sacrifice could have been a down payment on a home, a portion of the cost of providing a college education for the children, and so on.) Let us extend this principle now to the community. The businessmen of the town are pressuring the town board to build a public parking lot in the business district, in the hope of attracting more customers. Many townspeople (including youngsters) want a playground, however. Resources are available for only one of these. If the parking lot is built, there can be no playground; if the playground is built, the town's parking and traffic problems will worsen. The real cost of one of these public facilities is the sacrifice of the other. Certainly, in any community (whatever its size) there must be similar problems in which the young people have an interest and which call for economic analysis. In this case, they might examine the problem by asking such questions as these: If we build the playground, will the town lose business because of the lack of the parking lot? Will traffic jams and parking problems create the need for more police, and thus raise our taxes? Would the parking lot bring more business into the town and perhaps make it possible for us to reduce property taxes or other town taxes? On the other hand, would the playground be an attraction that would bring people into the town and thus increase our tax base? In short, from which of these facilities will we derive the greatest total satisfaction for the least cost?

Nationally, economic choices must be made as well. If we are already fully employing our productive resources, we can increase the output of one thing only by decreasing our output of something else. Thus, if we increase our defense establishment, for example, we must decrease the production of nonmilitary goods and services. If we increase the production of capital goods (factories, machines, tools), we must shift resources away from the production of consumer goods (food, clothing, radios, etc.). We are not suggesting which choice *should* be made in these cases; we are simply pointing out that the economically literate citizen or politican will have a better understanding of the consequences of one choice as opposed to its alternative.

Economics can be taught by any of the accepted methods. It lends itself to the well-known problem-solving technique, to case studies, to inquiry methods, to inductive reasoning, to conflict analysis, and to games and simulation, as well as to the more "traditional" approaches. Some examples of these approaches will be given later in this chapter.

THE CONTENT OF SECONDARY SCHOOL ECONOMICS COURSES

The question of what topics, principles, problems, and issues to include in high school economics courses often arouses controversy. Recently, the NYU Center for Economic Education polled a number of educators on this point. A list containing forty topics commonly found in college and high school economics texts was sent to high school economics teachers and to college economists interested in the economic education movement. The high school teachers tended to favor topics having some immediate relevance to students, such as consumer problems, labor relations, welfare, and personal income distribution. The college economists placed greater stress on analytical principles, such as the law of supply and demand, national income accounting, principles of economic growth, and money and banking. Some leaders in the field of economic education feel that these two points of view can be merged.

In any event, as more teachers become trained in economics and thus feel more comfortable with theories and principles, it is probable that many high school courses will begin to resemble the typical introductory college course in principles of economics. Indeed, some of the more recent high school economics texts contain such things as supply and demand curves, the marginal productivity theory, national income analysis, the multiplier, and other concepts that high school teachers formerly shunned. Some schools have a two-track system, in which the college-bound student takes the course stressing analysis and theory, while the terminal student concentrates upon such things as family finance, labor, taxation (from the personal point of view), organization of business (stressing small business), and others relating directly to the individual and the household.

A course for the college-bound student might include some or all of the following topics, although not necessarily in the order presented here.

1. The basic problem of scarcity
2. Opportunity cost.
3. An introductory overview of the American economic system
4. Functional distribution of income
5. National income (GNP, etc.)
6. Economic growth and development
7. Money and banking
8. The business cycle—nature, causes, and controls
9. Fiscal and monetary policies
10. Taxation
11. Personal distribution of income
12. Labor and industrial relations
13. The market mechanism—supply and demand
14. Organization of business
15. Problems of business concentration
16. Urban economic problems
17. Principles of international trade
18. Tariffs and other trade barriers
19. Balance of trade and payments
20. Problems of the underdeveloped countries
21. The firm in perfect and in imperfect competition
22. Poverty, welfare, and social security
23. Alternative economic systems

Some of the above items could be combined into one topic, and others could be broken down into several. The securities market, a popular topic in secondary schools, could be related to the topic of organization of business. Inflation could be included in a study of money and banking, of the business cycle, of the national income, of fiscal and monetary policies—or all of these. There is no *one* way to organize an economics course. One thing should be clear, however; every one of the above topics can be meaningful to high school students, for every one of them affects them in some way or another. The teen-ager, even if he or she does not work and does not file a Form 1040 every year, *does* pay taxes. Excise taxes, sales taxes, real estate taxes, business levies, and others, will affect one's real purchasing power.

Unemployment occuring during a recession most immediately involves the person who has lost a job, but it also affects the nation as a whole. When unemployment exists, the national income is lower than it should be; for people who are out of work are not adding to the country's stock of goods and services. The national "pie" is not growing as rapidly as it could be growing, and many of us will end up by getting a smaller piece. The teen-ager, in particular, is affected by unemployment, because the rate is far above the national average for that age group.

How does the law of supply and demand have meaning to high school students? First, of course, they are consumers. They can save a considerable amount of money through an awareness of the effects of supply and demand on market prices. For example, one can buy next year's Christmas cards at half price if one will buy them *after* Christmas this year. Summer suits are much cheaper toward the end of summer, for many retailers have an unsold supply on their hands, while the demand has diminished. The same applies to bathing suits, surfboards, swimming pool supplies, airconditioners, and other seasonal goods. Second, high school students are usually giving serious thought to future work. They should be aware of the demand-and-supply conditions applying to the occupations of their choice. (This is not to suggest that demand and supply are the only factors accounting for wage rates, but they certainly play an important role.) The girl who aspires to be an actress should know that she will probably have to accept very low pay unless and until she becomes famous (the "big name" performer has a kind of personal monopoly, and thus commands a high price), for the supply of actresses is large, while the demand is relatively low. The person desiring to be an engineer, on the other hand, may have a better chance of commanding a high wage or salary.

A teaching unit on the subject of the students' chosen careers can be of great personal value, and at the same time include many of the analytical tools of economics. We have already seen how an understanding of demand and supply can be related. Even the business cycle can be brought into such a unit, for students should know how their chosen occupations may be affected by general trends in economic activity. Certain businesses usually go into a sharp decline during a recession or depression (firms producing luxury goods, for example) and ride high during a prosperity period. Others tend to ride out business slumps without too much damage. If the student contemplates becoming a business person, he or she should know something about the various forms of business enterprise—proprietorship, partnership, and corporation—and the advantages and disadvantages of each. He or she should be aware of the competitive situation in the industry, how stable the demand is for the product or service, what taxes and government regulations apply, how costs are determined, and what management may face in the way of labor relations. Each student can make a study of his or her own career choice, applying many economic facts and concepts. The practical value of such an assignment is obvious.

These examples have been included to demonstrate that the analytical economics course designed primarily for college-bound students need not be so abstract that it bears no relationship to the personal interests of the student. Many of the same economic principles which are taught to the college-bound student can be included in courses designed for the terminal student. The difference might be in emphasis and in degree. The terminal student ought to know something about the national income in order to be a more intelligent citizen, but might be spared the intense analysis (with the numerous $45°$ line graphs) that the other students would receive as part of their preparation for college economics.

The student who enters the labor force (or who attempts to establish a business) immediately upon leaving school should know about the role of unions in our economy, the basic laws affecting unions and workers, and the problems of labor-management relations. But he or she should also understand something about modern wage theories, particularly the relationship between worker productivity and wages. Students should be taught that there are four factors of production (natural resources, labor, capital, and enterprise) essential in all productive enterprises and that each is entitled to a return. They should be given a simple explanation of the way in which income is divided (the "functional distribution of income," in technical terms) among these four agents of production, so that they can see their own roles in the proper context.

As a taxpayer, one ought to know more than the mechanics of filing an income-tax form. People are entitled to know something about the federal, state, and local taxes they pay, and whether the taxes are progressive, regressive, or proportional. Every citizen should understand that federal taxes can be used not simply to raise revenue for the financing of government activities, but that they can also become tools for fighting inflation on the one hand, or stimulating economic growth on the other. On the local scene, one should know the implications of financing a public project or activity by borrowing (bond issues) as opposed to pay-as-you-go taxation.

Thus, the principles, theories, and analytical tools of economics *can* be applied to the personal problems of interest to the terminal student. Simpler materials can be used, and assignments can be less demanding than those employed with the bright, college-bound student; but there are many basic economic concepts which should be clear to everyone, regardless of his or her future role in society.[2]

SOME PRACTICAL IDEAS FOR TEACHING ECONOMICS

Just as there is no *one* right way to organize the content of an economics course, there is no one method or technique that is inherently superior to others. Some recent research suggests that programmed textbooks and/or television courses yield significantly greater results in conveying economic understanding than a conventional lecture approach, but one can also find similar studies claiming the opposite. There are many variables that are difficult to control in such experiments: the ability and personality of the teacher, the intelligence and motivation of the students, and even the time of day when the course is taught. In any event, the social studies teacher should be aware of the fact that there are many different ways of handling economics at the precollege level. The best that we can do here is to describe some of these methods. The teacher will have to decide in each situation which is best for *his* or *her* class. It should be remembered, too, that a method that works well with one class will not necessarily work well with another, and—in fact—a method that yields spectacular results today may fall flat tomorrow, even with the same class. In short, through trial and error, and through their own knowledge, understanding, and sensitivity, teachers will develop the approaches which produce the best results.

1. The Developmental Lesson

It is not easy to find agreement on a definition of "developmental lesson." According to Edward Prehn, who uses the term "developmental-discussion-type lesson," this is an experience

in which the students attempt cooperatively to find solutions to a problem which the class has accepted as worthy of study. As its name implies, its main and subordinate concepts are developed through a half-dozen stimulating, thought-provoking pivotal questions which serve as the basis for class discussion. Properly constructed, these key or pivotal questions, when they are analyzed by the students under the guidance of the teacher, will bring under discussion the essential concepts connected with the problem for the day.[3]

The author of this chapter is in general agreement with Prehn's definition. For our purposes, the developmental lesson is one in which a problem, concept, important idea, generalization, topic, or principle is introduced to the class and developed under the teacher's guidance through well-planned questions, discussion between the teacher and the class, or discussion between pupils.

The lesson may begin with an interesting statement, an anecdote, a quotation, a challenging question, a short audio or visual aid, or anything else which sets the stage for the ensuing development. The beginning should arouse student interest, relate directly to the topic of the lesson, and show the class that it is something of importance to them. The pivotal (main) questions should be designed to develop all major points of the topic. From time to time there should be summary questions (usually called *medial summaries*) which do not simply call for a parrotlike repetition of what has been discussed, but which will help to show whether or not the students understand the material. Then, there is a final summarizing question (final summary) which relates back to the beginning, ties the entire package neatly together, and drives home the major point.

A developmental lesson need not be confined entirely to questions and answers or to discussion. Short audiovisual aids may be used; material may be put on the chalkboard; references may be made to the text or to other readings; pictures may be displayed; and graphic materials may be employed. The teacher can (or should) be flexible, in that questions or subtopics not originally planned may be injected into the lesson as it progresses. However, the main theme is developed to some logical conclusion, generally under the skilled control or guidance of the teacher. Lessons which might not be classified as "developmental" would include experiences wherein the students spend the period working in groups, doing individual assignments, going on a field trip, planning the unit's work, viewing a long film (one too long to leave time for discussion and analysis), and the like.

Lesson plans may take many different forms, and the sample which follows is not being set forth as the one and only way of constructing a lesson plan. Some teachers jot down a few ideas on an index card; others write several pages. The former may serve the highly skilled and experienced teacher adequately but will probably not do for the beginner. The latter may provide comfort and security to the new teacher, but it also suggests a too rigid approach. One or two pages should be sufficient, but the plan should be so clear and logical that another teacher could pick it up and teach the lesson pretty much as it would have been done by the creator of the plan himself. (Remember that the day may come when some poor substitute must take over your class. He or she should be provided with a fairly precise idea of what you wanted to do.) The sample lesson plan below is *not* being put forward as a perfect model, nor as the only way in which the subject can be taught. Indeed, the reader is invited to examine it critically and to try to think of better questions and approaches.

SAMPLE LESSON PLAN ON INFLATION—
HIGH SCHOOL LEVEL

Unit topic: Money and Banking
Lesson topic: Inflation: How Does It Affect Us?
Key idea: Inflation should be controlled because it can have harmful
                     effects on the individual and the nation.
Specific aims: 1. Understanding what inflation is.
                     2. Understanding how inflation affects certain individuals.
                     3. Understanding how inflation can affect the nation.
                     4. Acquiring the attitude that all should take an interest in
                         dealing with the problem of inflation.
Motivation: Put on the chalkboard a table comparing today's prices of
                     certain goods and services with prices in the past. Use things
                     needed or wanted by the average teen-ager which have
                     undergone dramatic price increases—medical care, college
                     tuition, sports equipment, and the like. (The same data
                     could be mimeographed and distributed, either in the form
                     of a table or of a graph.)

Lesson Content	*Questions*
Table or graphs on price changes.	*Motivational question:* What problem is illustrated by the table (or graph)? How does this affect *you* personally? *
The students may be able to buy fewer of the items wanted in the future if prices rise. They may have to sacrifice one item, in order to obtain another.	*Subquestions:* What are some goods and services *you* plan to buy in the future? How will you be affected if their prices rise?
"Inflation."	*Subquestions:* What is the word used to describe this problem?

* Although two or more questions are listed together in parts of this plan, the
student must *not* assume that the teacher should present the questions to the class in
one breath. The second question should not be presented until the class has had an
opportunity to respond to the first. "Multiple questioning" is a bad habit which
causes confusion and wastes time.

Lesson Content	*Questions*
A general rise in prices.	How can we define "inflation"?
	Pivotal question no. 1: What are some of the ways in which inflation affects various people? Why?
Retired persons on fixed incomes suffer as prices rise but their incomes do not. Creditors lose, while debtors gain, for the money will buy *less* when it is returned to the lender.	*Subquestions:* Do you have grand-parents living on a fixed income? How are they affected? Suppose you had loaned me $100 ten years ago, and I repaid you the $100 today? Who would have gained on this transaction? How? Why?
If the amount of income fails to rise as much (or more) than prices, we can buy less with it; therefore, our real income (the goods and services that we can buy) declines.	*Medial summary no. 1:* Economists say that "money income" can rise, while *"real* income" can remain the same or fall. How would you explain this?
	Subquestions: Between 1967 and 1974 average prices rose by about 50 percent. What do we have to know about your family income to tell whether or not you are better off today than you were in 1967?
Rising prices can mean fewer sales of American goods to other countries. Americans might be inclined to buy more foreign goods. Our debt to others may rise. Jobs and profits in our export industries can be hurt. (This is treated simply here, on the assumption that the class has not yet studied the balance-of-payments concept.)	*Pivotal question no. 2:* Foreign trade is important to every nation. How might rising prices here affect our trade with other countries?

Lesson Content	*Questions*
	Subquestions: If foreign trade declines because of inflation here, how might this affect those who are involved in import-export industries? How might our debt to other countries be affected?
A nation "loses face" when it fails to control inflation. Its currency becomes less desirable, and its debt to foreign nations may rise.	*Medial summary no. 2:* Every nation wants to be respected, and wants to be solvent. How might inflation in the United States affect our reputation with other nations?
It concerns all, because it affects us both as individuals and as a nation.	*Final summary:* In the last presidential election, both major parties promised to control inflation. Why does nearly everyone seem concerned about this problem?
The average person can try to handle personal finances so as to guard against inflation, and he can support government policies designed to control it.	*Subquestions:* What can the average person do about it?

The above lesson is fairly simple and to the point, and should be covered easily in a period of 45 or 50 minutes. It is based upon the assumption that the students have done some reading on the subject. It sets the stage for the next lesson, which might deal with the possible means of controlling inflation. Now let us analyze this lesson, step by step.

At the start, we see that this topic is not an isolated one, but is part of a planned unit on money and banking. (The topic could also be placed in units on the business cycle, economic growth, personal financial management, and others.) We note that the topic is: "Inflation: How Does It Affect Us?" The basic idea ("key idea") that the teacher is trying to convey, however, is that inflation must be controlled. (One might argue that this is subject to debate. Some economists favor mild increases in average prices—2 or 3 percent a year—as helping to stimulate economic growth. It is doubtful that anyone favors a runaway inflation, however. As the students become more knowledgeable about the subject, they can perhaps begin to deal with such sophisticated topics as: "How much inflation should we tolerate?") The specific aims indicate precisely the knowledge that the teacher wants the students to gain from this particular lesson. In some cases, these will include skills and attitudes as well as understandings and the acquisition of facts. This sample lesson is designed to achieve the first three aims in one lesson (although further reinforcement may be needed later) and to start convincing the students (specific aim no. 4) that everyone should be interested in the problem. It often takes several lessons to change attitudes.

Notice that the *motivation* is directly related to the lesson topic. It also includes some information useful in achieving some of the other aims. It relates the topic to the needs and interests of the students as well. The subquestions give the students an opportunity to become involved immediately by stating some needs or interests which the teacher might have overlooked. Much of the material developed during the lesson can be put on the chalkboard as the period progresses. A clear definition of inflation should be written on the board, and the students should write this in their notebooks.

The first *pivotal question,* it will be noted, is directly related to one of the specific aims—understanding how inflation affects certain individuals. Note, too, that the pivotal question does not call for a simple yes or no answer. This first pivotal question does seem to call for a fact-oriented response, but as the student states that "inflation hurts retired people" the teacher asks for an explanation. The best pivotal questions stimulate thought and call for analysis. They are "how" and "why" questions, rather than simple "what" questions. Thus, the example given here would not be a very good question if it were not followed by the teacher asking: "Why?" If the teacher wants a detailed outline of the lesson to be written in pupil notebooks, at this point he or she might write a heading on the chalkboard: "People Hurt by Inflation." As student responses are given, he or she can write under the heading:

1. People living on fixed pensions.
2. Creditors.
3. Workers whose incomes do not rise. Etc.

Study the *medial summary* very carefully. This does *not* simply call for a repetition of the material developed thus far. Indeed, in this case it even introduces an important new concept—*real income*. The student is then expected to relate the concept of real income to the material which was brought out by the preceding pivotal question and sub-questions. In this way, the teacher finds out whether or not the previous material was understood, for it *has* to be understood to be applied to a new idea. The subquestions, obviously, provide further examples, re-finement, or development of the pivotal and medial summary questions.

Pivotal question no. 2 refers to specific aim no. 3, in this sample lesson. Here we assume that the class has not studied the principles of international trade and the balance of payments. This being the case, it is clear that the student must really think about the question to be able to answer correctly. Even if the class has not yet studied the law of demand, it should be able to see that increases in the prices of our goods will probably affect our exports. (The teacher should be prepared, however, to deal with unexpected or incorrect responses. Suppose that a student had said: "Inflation here will mean that we sell more goods to foreigners." The teacher might then ask the class: "Do you agree with that?" "Why?" "Why not?" Indeed, an impromptu debate might ensue before the "truth" finally emerges. If there is too little time for this, the teacher could ask the student: "If you were a French store owner wanting to handle American typewriters, and you saw that the price of American typewriters was rising while the price of Italian typewriters remained the same, what would you be inclined to do?")

Medial summary no. 2 calls for a re-examination of the material brought out by pivotal question no. 2, but also asks the students to see the implications of the facts. The final summary demands a review of all major points developed in the lesson, stresses the fact that the problem is one of great importance, shows again that it affects the individual and the nation as a whole, and helps to establish a base for the lessons to follow. In this sample, a subquestion goes beyond the planned aims for the lesson by asking "What can the average person do about it?" This is the type of question which can be held in reserve in the event that there is time for it. (Nothing is more horrifying to the new teacher than reaching the end of a planned lesson and having another five or ten minutes to "kill." Thus, it is always wise to plan for this possibility by having a few extra questions—just in case.) Of course, there will not be time for an adequate development of most questions, but it can be treated in a very general way and can thus provide a transition to the next day's lesson, when the topic might be "What can we do to protect ourselves from inflation?"

The above lesson plan was deliberately kept brief and simple. Many other items could have been included. For instance, in dealing with the effects of inflation on the creditor, we might have included the following little poem:

> D is for Dollar—a round silver piece.
> When loaned or invested it once could increase;
> But now it is shrinking so fast that to lend it
> May net you a loss—so you'd better go spend it!

The students could be asked to interpret the poem in general, or to interpret and comment on various parts. (For example, is this *really* good advice? What would happen if everyone took this advice and spent their money instead of investing it? Etc.) Some teachers put their homework assignments on their lesson plans, list the books and other materials that will be used in conjunction with them, and even include a few test questions based upon the content of the lessons. (The latter practice makes it easy to construct a unit test. If one waits until a month-long or six-week unit is over, there is a tendency to forget what has been covered and what might have been omitted.)

2. Using Community Resources

Every community, however small, contains many resources that can be used in teaching economics. The utilization of these resources can range from guest speakers in the classroom to intensive studies of the region's economy.[4]

A. *Guest Speakers.* Local bankers, business people, stockbrokers, labor leaders, and government officials are often happy to visit a class to present their views on a given economic issue. The teacher should plan very carefully for such a visit. The visit should be directly related to the material being studied in the classroom at the time. The guest should be informed in advance of the topics the teacher would like him or her to cover, the amount of time he or she is expected to speak, the amount of time to be used for questions or discussion, the general ability level of the pupils, and what the students have already learned about the topic. If a speaker plans to present only one side of a controversial issue, a speaker who would present the other side should also be invited, although not necessarily during the same period unless both speakers agree to this sort of arrangement. The teacher can learn about potential speakers simply by consulting a local telephone directory and noting the business firms, banks, labor unions, government agencies, or foundations having something to do with economic issues. The pupils should be prepared in advance for the guest's appearance. They should know what they are expected to get from the presentation, and they should formulate questions that they might wish to ask.

B. *Field Trips.* The field trip can be useful, but it is often mis-used by teachers and students. It should not be seen as simply a pleasant outing or as a means of breaking the classroom routine. It should supplement the work going on in the classroom and come at an appropriate point in the unit. There is little to be gained by visiting a bank while the class is in the midst of a unit on labor-management relations. Whether the trip is used to help initiate a unit, as part of the development of the unit, or as a culminating experience, it should be very carefully structured and planned. The host institution should understand what the teacher wants the class to gain, and the class should know the specific aims of the trip. Questions should be prepared in advance, and the students should know what to look for. For example, a visit to a bank might be interesting because it includes a look at the cash piled in the vault, or because the students can see various automated operations. But the real value comes from learning something about the function of the bank in the economy. More can be gained from the trip if the class has already had the rudiments of money and banking. Then they should be prepared to ask such questions as these.

1. Is your bank operating under a federal or a state charter? Why do you consider this type of charter to be best for you?
2. How are your interest rates established for various loans?
3. How do actions of the Federal Reserve affect your loan interest rates?
4. In what ways do you serve the local community?
5. How do you relate to other banks in the community? Nationally?
6. Are there any international aspects of your operations?
7. How do commercial banks help to create part of the nation's money supply?

C. *Exploring Local Economic Problems.* Every locality has some sort of economic problem that can be studied by a secondary school class. In such cases, the well-known *problem-solving approach* can be used. Although there are many variations, the following steps can be applied to most economic problems.

1. Clearly identify and define the problem. ("How can we eliminate poverty in Stone County?")
2. Objectively describe the current situation. (Facts and figures on incomes, poverty, unemployment, etc., in Stone County.)
3. Trace the historical development of the situation, stressing possible causes of the problem.
4. Objectively gather all existing views on how the problem should be handled.
5. Learn how similar problems are handled elsewhere, and add some of these to the solutions set forth in number 4.
6. Analyze each of the proposed solutions in terms of feasibility, cost, and the extent to which each would help achieve the accepted goal. (The goal, in this case, is elimination of poverty in Stone County.)

7. Select the proposed solution which seems best.
8. Take action to solve the problem. (Present your proposal to political authorities, try to convince others to support you, etc.)

Note that the problem must be a manageable one. Such idealistic questions as "How can we make everyone in the world happy?" are too vague and too vast. The wording of the problem should suggest something other than a simple one-word answer. "Should we try to end poverty in Stone County?" suggests a yes or a no reply. Admittedly, "How can we eliminate poverty in Stone County?" assumes that indeed we should, but it is a fairly safe bet that almost everyone will agree to it, and the question leads to thoughtful study and analysis.

Many economic principles can be brought to bear in a study of local problems. What caused the poverty in the first place? To answer this, the teacher might draw upon principles relating to functional and personal distribution of income. The business cycle might even be relevant. A study of the local economy in general might be necessary, especially if the area's rate of unemployment is greater than that for the nation as a whole. In examining possible solutions, consideration could be given to various economic development schemes, the tax base, problems of local industries, ideas for income redistribution, and a host of other things that call for an understanding of important economic facts and principles. One question that would have to be foremost is: "What is the *real cost* of each proposed solution?" If we decide to try to create jobs by building an industrial park, for example, what will this cost us in terms of resources we must shift from some other endeavor?

A labor dispute not only can be studied from the perspective of the immediate issues but can be used as a springboard to a broader study of the role of labor in general, of government and labor, of sharing income among the factors of production, of the importance of worker productivity, and of many other factors. Other common local problems often include the need for tax reform, air or water pollution, conservation, transportation inadequacies, slums, lagging economic growth, loss of industry, and haphazard urban development. All of these have important economic dimensions. The students can become directly involved, they can see at first hand that the problem is important to them personally, and they have access to many primary source materials.

D. *Studying the Region's Economy.* In studying the regional economy, one can start with the area as a whole and then examine the various components, or one can begin by examining a small segment and use this part as an entry point to a broader study. Let us begin with an example of the latter approach.

For many years teachers have been having their classes purchase stock in a corporation as a way to arouse the students' interest in the securities market. While this activity may be interesting to the students, it usually falls short as a means of teaching analytical economics. This is unfortunate, for it could lead to a great deal of economic thought and analysis. Let the students buy a share (or a few shares) in a local corporation. (The teacher or some other adult will be the actual stockholder of record, but each student who contributed toward the purchase can be given a certificate indicating that he or she will get a fair share, including a portion of any dividends, when the stock is sold.) As part owners of the local firm, the students would likely be interested in knowing more about it. Officials of the firm will probably be cooperative, as it is good public relations.

The purchase of the stock should lead to a study of the way in which capital is raised in the economy, the mechanics and role of the securities markets, the importance of capital as a factor of production, government regulation of the securities industries, and the like. The class should study "their" firm, asking such questions as these.

1. Why is the firm organized as a corporation instead of as some other form of business?
2. How are the factors of production organized in the firm?
3. What is the market for the firm's output?
4. How are prices established for its products?
5. How are unit costs of production determined?
6. What role does competition play in this industry?
7. How does the firm relate to other companies in the same industry?

8. With what other industries does the firm deal? Why?
9. Are there any government regulations affecting the firm?
10. How does the firm affect the local economy in general?
    a. How many jobs does it provide directly? Indirectly?
    b. What other businesses exist locally because of the firm's existence?
    c. What public resources does it utilize? (Roads, bridges, etc.)
    d. How much does it contribute locally in taxes?
    e. In what way does the firm utilize local banking facilities?
11. How is the firm affected by national economic trends?
    a. Is it vulnerable during recessions?
    b. How will it share in a growing economy?
    c. What does it contribute to the Gross National Product?
12. Does international trade affect the firm? How?

Some teachers arrange with relatively small local firms to have their students (singly or in small groups) make firsthand studies of those firms. A fairly small firm is best for this activity, as it is easier for the student to have direct personal contact with the top policy-making personnel. The data gathered by the students can become part of a study of the region. If the region under study is a town, county, city, or metropolitan area, the students should learn about the history of the area (stressing the economic reasons for its development), find out how well the area is doing economically in comparison with other regions or with the nation as a whole (and why), analyze its economic problems, and attempt to develop suggested solutions.

Whether one's locality has a diversified economy or is dominated by one industry, opportunities for learning economics by studying it are almost limitless. For example, chicken production is important in southwest Arkansas. A teacher in the town of Horatio found that many of her pupils' parents were employed in the chicken industry, and that the pupils were thus aware of their personal stake in this business. Using this as motivation, she launched a study that involved not only the chicken industry, but the economy of the region and the state, national economic problems, and even international economics.[5] Relations between the United States and the Common Market had become strained over the latter's policy on importing frozen chickens. Anything affecting the chicken industry would affect the economy of Horatio, and probably the well-being of the pupils. Before the unit was over, the students had learned about the Common Market, the principles of international trade, tariffs, the farm problem in America, the importance of the industry to Arkansas and the locality, the role of banking in serving the industry, the importance of specialization in making chicken production more efficient, economic interdependence, and many other economic facts and concepts.

In large cities or metropolitan areas, students might study such problems as the movement of manufacturing out of the central city, the erosion of the tax base as upper-income and middle-income people move out while the poor move in, urban development, and so on. A teacher in Duluth, Minnesota, recently had his pupils study the problem of teen-age unemployment. This could be the focal point for the study of a local economy and could result in something of practical value to the students. In this case, the students produced a directory of several hundred jobs available for teen-agers in the Duluth area.[6]

3. Case Studies

Case studies of an important problem can be interesting. Conflict analysis can also be employed, in such things as labor-management disputes, government clashes with business (as in the case of President Kennedy's famous confrontation with the steel industry in 1962 over price increases), and tariff squabbles between nations. A depression—in particular the Great Depression of the 1930s—should be one of the most fruitful cases for learning a great deal about economic theory. An intensive study of the Great Depression could take the class into the causes of business cycles; economic growth; national income analysis; classical theories of consumption, saving, and investment as compared with the Keynesian theory; the automatic stabilizers; monetary policy; and modern fiscal policy.

Cases from history have the advantage of being removed from today's controversies and passions, and there is usually a large amount of documentary material available for study. On the other hand, a current issue is more "alive" for the students, and they can see the immediate value in studying it. If time permits, one can do both—study the current issue (such as an impending recession) and compare it with a similar problem of the past. Either way, the study demands objective analysis and inquiry.[7]

4. Role-Playing, Games, and Simulation

The use of games, skits, role-playing situations, and similar techniques has long been popular at the elementary level. Games and simulations are now being used at the college level, however, and even college officials are receiving in-service training in university administration through these devices. Some games, such as the stock-market games "Buy or Sell" and "Transaction," are commercially produced and are carried by major booksellers. Others are being developed by classroom teachers and are often reported in professional journals.[8] The latter have the advantage of costing little or no money and of being adaptable to a given classroom situation.

Games and simulations make it possible to convey difficult concepts in an interesting and effective manner. For example, a high school teacher in Midland, Pennsylvania, has developed a simulation for teaching about international trade and the balance of payments.[9] Pupils assume the roles of different countries, engaging in transactions which involve transfers of claims on American dollars. For instance, an American coal company has its coal shipped in a Japanese vessel, at a cost of $50,000. This transaction is noted on two cards—a white card, representing "dollars in" and a red card representing "dollars out." In each transaction one country gains dollars while another loses. The transactions are recorded on mimeographed forms. Under the name of each country there are two columns, "Dollars In" and "Dollars Out." The U.S. balance of payments is summarized as follows:

Country	Dollar Claims Against U.S.	Dollars Owed to the U.S.
France		
England		
West Germany		
Japan		

The transaction cards are read aloud, discussed, and recorded; thus it becomes clear why American loans to foreigners (in the form of bond purchases, for example) are pluses for the foreigners and minuses in the United States' balance of payments. The difference between the balance of trade and the balance of payments becomes evident, and the pupils can see why more goods can be sold than are bought and still result in a deficit in the balance of payments. The simulation can also be used to deal with the mechanics of foreign exchange, relative prices, rates of exchange, the use of gold, the dollar as an international currency, the effect of devaluations, and so on.

As described here, this activity is highly structured. The teacher knows in advance exactly how it will come out, for he has carefully planned the transactions to illustrate certain points. This need not always be the case; for instance, in teaching the law of supply and demand, a market situation might be simulated in the classroom. The teacher can manipulate the situation so that at times there is a scarcity of goods, thus bringing a rise in prices, as the buyers bid against one another, but he need not "stack the cards" completely. The students can keep records of the transactions and the price changes (even developing supply and demand curves) and learn the law of demand, the law of supply, and other relevant principles by deduction.

In an open-ended role-playing situation, students are assigned certain roles and presented with a problem or a situation. They are not otherwise briefed or rehearsed in advance, although they may have some knowledge of relevant economic facts and concepts. A junior high school teacher in Tulsa, Oklahoma, illustrates the controversies surrounding the use of tax revenues in this way.[10] The pupils represent various income and occupational groups, each of which receives a designated income. The source of the income (wages, profits, interest, welfare payments, etc.) is indicated. Play money is used, and some of this must be given to the government in taxes. Those with higher incomes, of course, pay higher taxes. The fun begins when the students discuss the spending of these tax revenues. Children playing the role of wealthy people may object to higher welfare payments, even though they might in reality be from poor families receiving public assistance. The ensuing discussions can deal with schemes for reducing poverty, ways of increasing the productivity of the poor (usually through education), the degree of fairness of the tax system, and many other relevant problems.

Children can learn a great deal about economics in planning skits, plays, and assembly programs. When studying the economic background of the Civil War, for example, the effects of the tariff can be dramatized with a skit showing its impact on a typical Southern family. Labor-management negotiations lend themselves to both planned dramatizations and spontaneous role-playing. Either way, the participants should do enough preliminary research so that those playing the roles of labor leaders can talk intelligently about such things as the consumer-price index and increases in worker productivity, while the management representatives can counter with arguments involving production costs and market conditions. The dramatization can include government's role, necessitating some previous study of such things as the Taft-Hartley and Landrum-Griffin Acts.

A technique becoming popular at the junior high school level is the *model nation.* This is not confined entirely to economics, but includes other social sciences as well. The class becomes a miniature nation, writing a constitution, establishing a government, adopting a system of money and banking, setting up various businesses, and so on. If several classes in the school are doing the same thing, "international trade" can develop among them. Obviously, to do this sort of thing effectively, the pupils must study the real-life situations. Teachers using this device report that many basic economic concepts are learned almost by accident. Inflation occurs if too much money is issued and put into circulation, making it possible to develop a simpler consumer price index for the class, to have it analyze the possible causes and controls of inflation, and the like. Some of the classroom business firms make a profit and pay dividends, while others break even or go bankrupt. Again, the reasons can be analyzed in class discussions. Sometimes monopolies are formed and the "government" must take action to deal with them. "Tax laws" must be passed, so that the students are required to look into the various types of taxes and tax rates. An activity of this sort can be as simple or as complex as the teacher chooses to make it. It should not be approached in haphazard fashion, however: it requires careful preparation and control.[11] In a variation of this idea, some teachers break their classes up into small groups, each of which represents a separate nation. This device can be used to teach about international trade, the common market, and related subjects.

5. Debates and Discussions

Debates have been criticized on the ground that the students engaged in a debate tend to learn only one side of an issue. This can be avoided by having each team prepare *both* sides of the question, and by not assigning sides until the debate is about to begin. The issue should be specific, current, and controversial. For example: "Resolved: The federal minimum wage should be increased." Each side should support its argument with facts and with economic principles. Thus, the team opposing the increase should be prepared to explain the notion that a higher minimum wage can create unemployment, since it may put the wage above the productivity of certain workers. Each side should have equal time to present opening arguments, make rebuttals, and to summarize. The class can decide which team wins, but judgments should be based upon sound economic reasoning rather than upon emotion.[12]

In panel discussions and oral reports students have an opportunity to share their learnings with the class. This makes it possible for each student to become a "specialist" in some economic topic. The audience should be held responsible for learning the information presented by the speakers, and might be given a voice in evaluating the presentation. There should be time for the class to raise questions and engage in discussion with the speakers. Speakers can be encouraged to illustrate their talks with visual materials, such as maps, charts, posters, and bulletin board displays. One interesting variation of the traditional oral report is to have the pupils actually prepare and teach a lesson based upon their research.

6. Exercises in Critical Thinking

All of the activities suggested in this chapter should involve critical thinking and scholarly analysis. Too often, assignments given to secondary school pupils lack this important dimension. A term paper in which the student simply copies information from publications or describes situations has minimal value. Students should be expected to seek out causes, examine the bases of controversies, weigh varying opinions, and set forth possible solutions to problems: Why does poverty exist in a nation as rich as the United States? What are the various views on dealing with the problem? In the light of generally accepted societal goals, what can be done about it? Questions such as these call for objective and sophisticated analysis.

Students can examine the economic portions of political platforms, asking such questions as: What economic promises are being made? Are these promises consistent with our national goals? Are they feasible, in terms of existing productive resources? Will the Republican answer to inflation (for example) lead to a higher rate of unemployment? Studies can be made of various newspapers and news magazines. What stand do they take on economic issues? Are they presenting all of the relevant facts? Which side, if any, do they favor? Are their editorial proposals in accord with modern economic theory? Students often enjoy analyzing political cartoons to determine what the cartoonist is trying to say about an important issue, which side he is espousing, what propaganda devices he is using, and so on. They also enjoy drawing cartoons of their own. Any medium which is used to convey economic ideas can be the subject of fruitful analysis. Biographies, novels, plays, television and radio broadcasts, motion pictures, and even folk songs with economic content can be found.[13]

7. Behavioral Objectives and Student Learning Contracts

Implicitly or explicitly, every teacher states some sort of goal, aim, or objective for every course, unit, and lesson taught. The overall (and somewhat vague objective of an economics course might be to "give the students a better understanding of the American economy." The goal of a unit within that course might be to "have the students understand the role of money and banking in the American economy." The aim of a single lesson might be "to develop an understanding of the causes of inflation." In recent years, the traditional way of stating goals has been challenged by the proponents of behavioral (or performance) objectives. The following objectives are stated in the traditional manner:

1. To know the meaning of the words "inflation" and "deflation."
2. To understand the causes of inflation and deflation.
3. To appreciate the efforts being made by the Federal Reserve System to control inflation and deflation.

Frequently, college teachers of educational methods taught their students that ideal lesson plans included these three types of objectives—to know, to understand, and to appreciate. Some often added a fourth type, involving skills, as in "acquiring skill in drawing maps."

Critics of the traditional means of stating objectives charge that they are too vague because they usually fail to indicate how we know that the objective has been achieved. Clearly, in example no. 1 above we want the student to know the meaning of inflation and deflation, but how is he to demonstrate this knowledge? In example no. 2 we want more than mere rote knowledge; we want understanding of causes. Again, however, we are not told how the student will be expected to demonstrate that he understands the causes. Example no. 3 is tougher still, for here we are actually dealing with the student's attitude toward the Federal Reserve System, and attitudes are indeed difficult to measure.

Behavioral objectives attempt to get at these problems by *specifying student goals in terms of the measurable or readily observable performance (behavior) expected of the learner.* They also frequently specify the criteria for acceptable performance. Let us compare some objectives stated in traditional and in behavioral terms.

1. *Traditional:* The student will understand elasticity of demand.
2. *Behavioral:* Given data on the percentage increase in New York

City subway fares and the subsequent percentage decline in the number of riders, the student will compute the coefficient of elasticity correct within 1/10 of 1 percent.

All we know from the first objective is that the student is to understand elasticity. We do not know how this is to be achieved or how understanding is to be measured. The student does not know exactly what is expected of him, the teacher may have only the vaguest idea (or no idea at all) of how he will eventually determine student understanding, and another educator (say a supervisor or a substitute teacher) does not have a clear and precise idea of what the teacher had in mind.

The second objective tells exactly what the student is expected to do and establishes a criterion of acceptable performance. It does not necessarily follow that a student able to compute a coefficient of elasticity really understands what elasticity is all about—that is not the point being made here. The point is that in the second example both student and teacher have a much clearer idea of what is expected and what standards will apply. (Research that has been done thus far suggests that a significant improvement in learning occurs when students are aware of precisely what is expected of them.)

Before going on to another example, it should be understood that the behavioral objective stated above is not necessarily the best in all situations. As given here, it seems to assume that the student already knows a formula for determining the coefficient of elasticity, or knows where to find one. If this were not the case, some teachers might revise the objective to read: "Given data on the percentage increase in New York City subway fares and the subsequent percentage decline in the number of riders, and a formula for computing the coefficient of elasticity, the student will compute . . . ," and so forth. Teachers with bright students might elect not to give the students the formula, but expect them to locate one on their own. They might also ask the students to write a one-page explanation of their findings. There are still other revisions that can be made in the objective. Some might want to specify other conditions, such as:

"Working independently, the student will . . ."

"On a final examination, the student will . . ."
". . . will compute the coefficient of elasticity correct within 1/10 of 1 percent *within 15 minutes in a classroom situation."*
"Without the aid of the textbook, the student will . . ."
"With the aid of the assigned economics textbook, the student will . . ."

In short, the behavioral objective can be tailored to meet varying conditions and teacher aims. Average students might be given more time (say half an hour) than bright students, or might be permitted to meet a lower standard of performance (say, correct within 2/10 of 1 percent).

While not all educators agree that behavioral objectives are the answer to our pedagogical prayers, and while there are variations in format and usage, a commonly accepted formula for writing behavioral objectives is as follows. (Note that these elements do not have to appear in the order in which they are given below.)

Behavioral objectives indicate:

1. The person or persons who are to perform the desired behavior. (It may be an individual student, a small group, the whole class, or others.)
2. The specific behavior expected. (To list, to draw, to compute, etc.)
3. The final product or learning outcome which will be used to determine whether the objective was achieved (such as a graph of GNP from 1950 to 1971).
4. The conditions under which the learner will perform the behavior (such as with the aid of *The Statistical Abstract of the U.S. 1971).*
5. The criteria which will be used to evaluate the performance (such as with 80 percent accuracy).

Again, let us examine objectives stated in the traditional manner and in behavioral terms. In reading the second objective below, note that it includes the five elements listed above. (The figures in parentheses refer to the above elements as they occur in the statement.)

1. *Traditional:* To understand the Phillips Curve.
2. *Behavioral:* Given data on unemployment rates and the GNP deflator for the period 1954 to 1964 (#4) the student (#1) will draw a Phillips Curve on graph paper for the period 1954-1964 (#2; #3) with 90% accuracy (#5).

Clearly, objective no. 2 tells us much more than no. 1. Some parts are still vague, however. We are not told where the data will be obtained, but simply that someone (presumably the instructor) is to give it to the student. We are not quite sure what 90 percent accuracy means. Does it mean that the points on the graph for nine of the ten years must be in exactly the right place? Does it mean that there is a 10 percent margin of error allowed in the location of each point on the graph? Or does it mean both? Thus, the statement could be made even more precise; on the other hand, some teachers go overboard in specifying details ("using red ink on green graph paper . . . ," etc.).

The teacher does not surrender his time-honored prerogatives in using behavioral objectives. Thus, one often finds such statements as: "The student will write a five-page essay on the causes of inflation which, to the teacher's satisfaction, specifies . . . ," and so on. The criterion here is vague, but at least the student knows that he will be expected to demonstrate his knowledge of the causes of inflation by writing an essay and not by answering questions on an objective test or by some other means.

In summary, a well-written behavioral objective will not merely summarize content but will describe the intended outcome in terms of what the learner will be doing when he shows that he has achieved the objective. It will clearly communicate to the learner the teacher's aims, showing him the conditions under which he will be working, the assistance that he can expect to receive (if any), what will be accepted as evidence that the desired goal has been reached, and the minimum standards of performance expected of him.

The *student learning contract* is an agreement between an individual student (or perhaps a small group working together) and the teacher. The contract sets forth the purpose of the lesson and specifies the task that must be done to achieve that purpose. It states or implies the means by which the student will be tested to ascertain whether or not the goal was achieved. The student knows what is expected of him and how he will be evaluated. There may also be agreements on the time that the student will have to complete each contract and the materials and resources that can be used. The student then goes to work on his own, or with the help of the teacher and/or other students. In some cases he is told precisely what materials to use, and in other cases he relies upon a list of sources of various kinds (books, pamphlets, government reports, films, filmstrips, overhead transparencies, recordings, etc.). He may be expected to locate the necessary material himself. The activities specified in the contracts may include the writing of reports, drawing graphs, solving problems, making field studies, or any other worthwhile endeavor.

A recent study undertaken by Columbia University's Institute of Administrative Research shows that performance scores can be "greatly improved" by individualized instruction and small group work.[14] Some of the arguments in favor of individualized instruction are that it permits students greater flexibility in pursuing their own interests, allows the learner to advance at a rate that he finds suitable for himself, and takes account of differences in student ability. The bright student is no longer held back by the "lock-step" curriculum in which everyone is expected to be doing the same thing, in the same way, at the same time. The slower student need not experience the feeling of frustration and hopelessness that comes when he is unable to keep up with the rest of the class. Critics, on the other hand, charge that individualized instruction is suitable only for the better student, that many students (especially the slow learner) will do nothing, and that a lack of control in the classroom will lead to anarchy. As with all educational tools, this one can be good or bad, effective or ineffective, depending upon the skill with which it is used. Teachers who have used it successfully assert that the criticisms are wrong—that slower students improve because they can progress at a more comfortable rate and can experience success, and that young people learn to plan and to accept responsibility.[15]

It would be a serious mistake to assume that the teacher abdicates responsibility, that he will have less work to do, or that individualized instruction is a panacea. The job of planning and writing the learning contracts is a monumental one, for the teacher must try to cover everything of importance in the curriculum and prepare contracts for different levels of ability and interest. On the topic of the causes of inflation, for example, there would have to be contracts for the average, the above-average, and the slow student. Then, the class must be carefully trained in the use of the contracts. The teacher must know each student well, for he has to help them select contracts that will provide a challenge without overtaxing the student's abilities. As the students are working on their individual projects, the teacher must circulate among them, offering advice, assistance, and encouragement where needed.

The use of the student learning contract is but one of many approaches to teaching, and it is probably unwise to try to use it exclusively. Any technique can become tiresome, and from time to time there will probably be a need for all-class activities.

If an economics course is to be taught largely through the use of student learning contracts, the teacher will have to decide upon the scope and sequence of the course. It may be divided into segments, such as units on labor, on money and banking, on international economics, and the like. Each unit will then be divided into topics, such as the nature of money, inflation, banks, monetary policy, and so on. Several contracts will then be prepared for each topic. For the inflation topic, for example, there might be contracts on the meaning of inflation; the causes, the problems created by inflation; various proposals for solving the problem; and so forth. The contracts will vary in terms of difficulty, the activities specified, and the resources listed. Note the example on page 107*.

---

* In preparing this sample contract, we have borrowed freely from the format developed by a team of teachers from the public and parochial schools of Duluth, Minnesota. We have departed from their format in some respects, however.

STUDENT LEARNING CONTRACT NO. 83

Content Classification: Money and Banking

Purpose: This lesson will help you understand the major components of the U.S. money supply.

Performance Criterion:

Using the *Federal Reserve Bulletin* or other statistical sources, obtain figures on the nation's money supply for a recent ten-year period. Draw a graph showing changes in the money supply as a whole and in the portion made up of currency and in the portion made up of demand deposits. The figures for each of the ten years should be correct within 10 percent. For each of the ten years, compute the percentage of total money supply accounted for by currency and the percentage accounted for by demand deposits. The figures should be correct within 10 percent. In two or three pages, explain the relationship between currency and demand deposits in our money supply.

Key Terms and Concepts:

Money	Bank credit expansion
Currency	Monetary growth
Demand deposits	Federal Reserve System
Money supply	

Sample Test Situation:

Define the terms "currency" and "demand deposits"; explain each; and explain how they make up our money supply. Describe the relationship between them and tell how the money supply can expand or contract.

Sources:

Books:

U.S. Department of Commerce, *Statistical Abstract of the United States* (annual).
Bernstein, *A Primer on Money, Banking, and Gold.*
Weiner, *The Federal Reserve System and Its Effect on Money and Banking.*
Board of Governors, *The Federal Reserve System.*

Pamphlets:

Federal Reserve Bank of Chicago, *Modern Money Mechanics.*
Federal Reserve Bank of Richmond, *Readings on Money.*
Industrial Relations Center, *Understanding Money and Banking.*
Federal Reserve Bank of St. Louis, *Your Money Supply.*

Films:

Banks and Credit (American Institute of Banking).
Banks for Bankers: The Federal Reserve System (American Economy Series).
How Money Expands and Contracts (American Economy Series).
Money and the Fed (American Economy Series).
What Is Money? (Coronet Films).

Filmstrips:

Money (Eye Gate House).
Money and Banking (McGraw-Hill).
The Role of the Commercial Banking System (Joint Council on Economic
    Education).

The contract above might be used in a unit on money and banking
with a bright high school student. The "Performance Criterion" tells
the student exactly what he is to do and sets the standards by which he
will be judged ("correct within 10 percent"), although it is not perfectly clear how the written portion of his assignment will be evaluated.
Here it is implied that the two- or three-page paper will be completed
"to the satisfaction of the teacher." The "Performance Criterion"
meets the specifications for a behavioral objective, discussed earlier.
The "Key Terms and Concepts" section indicates terms that the
student should know and understand when he has completed this
lesson. The "Sample Test Situation" gives the student a sample of the
type of question that he might be expected to answer on a future
examination. It should be pointed out here that some teachers do not
approve of this, on the ground that many students will assume this to
be the very question that will appear on the test, prepare solely for that
question, and object if any other item should be used. Others might say

that successful performance of the task is sufficient and that no further examination is needed. The "Sources" section should be made up of books and other materials readily available. Many teachers favor a multimedia approach, and thus it is necessary that students be instructed in the use of audiovisual equipment and that facilities be available where they can view the films and filmstrips without annoying others. (In the sample contract above, we have listed authors of books and pamphlets, and publishers or distributors of some of the films and filmstrips. This may not be necessary in a classroom situation where the titles alone will suffice and where the students have been instructed in how to obtain the listed materials.) The list of sources could be longer or shorter, depending upon the intended level of difficulty, the availability of the materials, and other local conditions. It does not necessarily follow that the student must use all of the sources listed or that he must confine himself to those on the list. They can be seen as suggestions of the type of material he might employ.

Note that the number on the sample contract is primarily for purposes of identification and to enable the teacher to keep his set of contracts in order. It must not be assumed that a student has to complete contract no. 82 before he can do no. 83, or that no. 84 must follow no. 83. Opinions differ on the extent to which students should be required to follow a prescribed sequence. Some teachers would prevent a student from selecting a contract on monetary policy, for instance, before he has completed those on inflation. Others would let the student make his choice, even though it may appear to be unwise. If the student finds that he cannot complete the task prescribed in the monetary policy contract, he then goes back to the inflation contracts or to any others that are necessary for an understanding of the content of the monetary-policy item. It is argued that this, in itself, is a good experience for the learner. Also, it sometimes happens that what the teacher thought was the best sequence turns out not to be best after all. In any event, a great deal of variety and flexibility will be possible.

In summary, the student learning contract is another useful item in the teacher's tool box. Its use involves a great deal of preparation and much hard work throughout. It will not solve all teaching problems, nor will it necessarily be suitable for all classroom situations. It has been used (reportedly with great success) in the Duluth public and parochial schools at both the elementary and secondary levels.

INTEGRATING ECONOMICS WITH OTHER SOCIAL STUDIES SUBJECTS

Although most social studies teachers claim that they include economics in other courses, recent research suggests that students learn very few of the analytical principles in this way. Such events as Hamilton's financial program, Jackson's "war" on the U.S. Bank, and Bryan's silver campaign are included in most American history courses, but few teachers seize the opportunity to make these meaningful by explaining the underlying principles of money, banking, and economic development. The antitrust acts and labor legislation will be noted in government courses, but rarely does the student acquire an understanding of price/output decisions in imperfect markets or the wage theories that explain the existence of those laws. In this section, we shall briefly suggest ways of including some of the basic principles of economics in other courses.

1. Economics in History

One need not be a Marxist to appreciate the importance of economics in history. For example, economic recovery was a major problem during the reign of Alexander Severus, who became emperor of Rome in A.D. 218. The government's policies of building public works, making grants to the poor to buy farm land, extending credit to farmers, stimulating industrial development in the towns, providing state subsidies for education, and reducing interest rates and taxes on merchants in order to check the commercial decline resemble many actions taken by the United States government during the past four decades or so. Likewise, there are many economic aspects in the history of the Middle Ages and the Renaissance. The commercial revolution, the industrial revolution, the development of money and banking, and mercantilism offer opportunities to include economic analysis in European or world history.[16]

Economic concepts can be included throughout an American history course and can greatly strengthen that course.[17] The following table suggests some of the economic facts, concepts, principles, and problems that can be integrated with U.S. history.

Historical Period	*Economic Facts, Concepts, Principles, Problems*
Discovery and early exploration of America. The early colonies.	Economic background and motivation of voyages. Profit motive. Importance of labor. Definition of economics. Problem of scarcity.
American Revolution.	Free enterprise and free trade vs. economic controls and mercantilism. Effects of tariffs, taxes, and monopolies.
Confederation period and new Constitution.	Benefits of specialization and exchange. Economic aspects of U.S. Constitution.
Establishing the new U.S. government.	Need for economic unity, sound money, system of government finance. What money is and what forms it takes.
Growth of American nationalism.	Economic growth: what it is and how it is measured. GNP. Per capita GNP. Private and social capital.
The Age of Jackson.	The Second U.S. Bank. Functions of banks and need for central banks.
Sectionalism and the coming of the Civil War.	Economic differences between sections. Effects of tariffs. Tariff controversy. Inflation.
America becomes an industrial power.	Growth of big business and the corporate form. Various forms of business enterprise.
The protest movements begin.	The four factors of production and the distribution of income among them. Labor unions.

Historical Period	*Economic Facts, Concepts, Principles, Problems*
Populism	Business concentration. Economies of scale. Abuses of big business. Sherman Act.
Theodore Roosevelt	Antitrust enforcement. Conservation.
Woodrow Wilson	Income tax. Clayton Act. FTC. Federal Reserve.
World War I	U.S. becomes world supplier. Debtor-creditor positions of nations. Economic mobilization.
The 1920s	The business cycle. The Great Crash.
The New Deal and the depression	Controlling the cycle. Monetary and fiscal policies. The automatic stabilizers. Keynes.
New Deal reforms	Social Security. Wage-Hour Law. Child labor. Wagner Act. NRA. Farm programs.
World War II	Government and the economy in wartime. The production possibilities curve. Inflation. National debt. Rationing. Price Controls.
Postwar emergency	Marshall Plan and OEEC. Economic recovery.
World economic cooperation	World Bank. IMF. GATT. Trade and exchange. Laws of absolute and comparative advantage. Common Market. EFTA. OECD.
The rise of new nations	Economic problems of underdeveloped areas. Economic development. Foreign aid programs.
The cold war	Competing economic ideas: capitalism, socialism, communism. Mixed economies.
Recent times	Urban economic problems. Poverty. Automation. Youth unemployment. Depressed areas. Consumer protection. Taxation, debt, budget. Balance of payments.

2. Economics and Government

In view of the increasingly important role being played by government in our economy, there are many opportunities to teach basic economic principles when dealing with the public sector. Unfortunately, this has often been confined to mere description of such things as monopoly practices, the antitrust laws, the farm program, and government involvement in labor disputes.

In teaching about government and big business, for example, one can include the benefits (economies of scale) of big business and the problems often caused by business concentrations. The reasons why prices are higher and output lower in imperfectly competitive markets can be analyzed. This goes far beyond the fact that collusion sometimes occurs, and it requires a study of such things as marginal revenues and marginal costs in such markets as compared with the ideal situation in perfect competition. The extent to which business concentration is harmful can be ascertained in a given industry by studying facts about the elasticity of demand for the product. If demand is elastic (meaning that a rise in price would result in a more than proportional drop in sales), the monopoly is not very dangerous. It is obviously selling a product, such as a luxury item, which people can do without. If demand is inelastic (meaning that a rise in price would result in a *less* than proportional drop in sales), the product is probably a necessity. To give an extreme illustration, a 100 percent rise in food prices would certainly not result in a 100 percent drop in sales of food. Monopoly power in an industry selling necessities is dangerous. Another factor to be considered is *cross-elasticity* (a factor taken into account by the courts when determining whether or not a monopoly situation exists). This refers to the relationship between changes in the price of one product and changes in the sales of a substitute. Thus, if someone got a monopoly on butter and drastically raised its price, the sales of margarine would probably rise. These and many other economic phenomena have an effect upon government policy and action.

The concept of elasticity also applies to farm problems. The demand for farm output tends to be relatively inelastic. Thus, if farmers increase their food crop output they may not find a ready market for the surplus. Indeed, they often have to reduce their prices drastically in order to sell their crops, with the result that their total income may actually fall because of the increase in output. A knowledge of this fact helps to explain government agricultural policy. It also shows why the farm market situation is not always comparable to market conditions in manufacturing industries.

The functions of the Securities Exchange Commission, the Federal Reserve, the Treasury Department, the TVA, the National Labor Relations Board, wartime regulatory agencies, congressional committees dealing with economic issues and many other groups can be better understood if the basic economic principles and problems with which they deal are understood. Questions of taxation, proposals for a uniform federal system of welfare, revenue sharing schemes, and public budget-making require an understanding of economic concepts as well as an understanding of our constitution, separation of powers, the federal system of government, and so on.[18]

3. Economics and Geography

Geography and economics are perfect mates at the pre-college level. The student may quickly forget the locations of the Hudson River, the Mohawk Valley, and the Champlain depression unless he or she sees that they form a great Y wherein New York City's trade with the Great Lakes region to the west and with Canada to the north was enhanced by these natural highways. Indeed, the great Y helps to explain the fascinating story of New York's economic growth. Climate, topography, soil conditions, and other geographic factors acquire meaning when we see their effects upon agriculture, industry, urban development, foreign trade, and the like.

The student can be taught how the United States utilized geographic differences to bring about regional specialization, and how this economic concept of specialization and exchange helps to account for its amazing economic growth. The geographic pieces of America can be seen as parts of a great whole. In learning how to overcome geographic problems (such as mountain barriers and inadequate rainfall in certain areas), the pupil may be able to make prescriptions for the newly emerging nations of today, which are often faced with similar problems.[19]

A role-playing approach can be used effectively. For example, the classroom might be divided to represent various geographic regions of some country, continent, or general area. The youngsters in each region then obtain relevant economic and geographic facts about their region. Taking into consideration possible cultural and political differences between regions, they may meet to decide how they can work together to solve development problems for the area. Should the regions unite economically? Should they pool their resources? If so, how? What geographic factors are impeding their economic development? What factors can they turn to their mutual advantage? What sort of trade and exchange arrangements are feasible? If they establish an area-wide economic system, what system should prevail? How should they relate to other areas of the world?

In studying world geography, the motivation might be based upon the importance of every area to the United States economy. For example: Why is Africa important to us? What products do we get from Africa? What do we sell to Africa? How can trade between the United States and Africa benefit both?

4. Economics and Sociology

Economic difficulties may not be the most important causes of sociological problems, but certainly they often help to aggravate those problems. The unrest in certain ghetto areas probably exists primarily because the residents have been the victims of bigotry and discrimination. As long as the black man is condemned to second-class citizenship, he will have good reason to be dissatisfied with his place in American society, however affluent he might become in the material sense. Nevertheless, when economic deprivation is added to social injustice, the flames of discontent burn hotter. The unemployment rate among blacks tends to be about twice that of white. Blacks have greater difficulty getting jobs and getting the necessary education to obtain good positions.[20]

Frictions within families are often based upon personal incompatibility, but economic factors can provide further irritation. There seems to be a high correlation between household financial problems and family disputes. Some studies have shown that mental and emotional illnesses are more prevalent among the poor than among the middle class and the rich. Many of the symptoms of social pathology appear with greater seriousness in economically deprived areas. In New York's Central Harlem, for example, the juvenile delinquency rate is over twice that for the City as a whole, the venereal disease rate among youths is over six times as high, and the homicide rate is about six times higher.[21]

Schemes for improving the education of the poor (and thus enhancing their job opportunities), for revising the welfare system, for eliminating slum conditions, and for dealing with many other social problems must take into consideration the economic aspects. Economists are as concerned as anyone about our social problems, and have even gone so far as to estimate the loss in Gross National Product caused by racial discrimination. But they are also well aware of the fact that solutions to the problems involve economic costs. For instance, in a full-employment economy we can eliminate slum houses only by diverting productive resources away from something else. What sacrifice is the public willing to make? An understanding of the economics underlying social problems, and the re-allocation of productive resources that might have to occur in the proposed solutions, will give students a better perspective and probably encourage more realistic goals and more feasible ideas for achieving those goals.

SOURCES FOR TEACHING ECONOMICS

The economic education movement has grown rapidly in recent years. It is probable that within the next few years every school will be within reach of a center or council for economic education. The Joint Council on Economic Education at 1212 Avenue of the Americas, New York, N.Y. 10036, is a national coordinating agency. Teachers may write to the Joint Council to find out if there is a center or council in their area offering advice, assistance, materials, workshops, or courses for teachers. Councils on economic education are usually community based organizations supported by business, labor, farm organizations, and educators. They often sponsor workshops, courses, or institutes for teachers; produce materials; provide speakers; and offer advice and consultation. They attempt to be nonpartisan and objective. Centers for economic education are parts of some colleges and universities. Their services may overlap, complement, or supplement the services of councils. When they differ from councils in their activities, they tend to place greater emphasis upon research in economic education and to stress pre-service rather than in-service training in economics for teachers.

Teachers should ask to have their names placed on the mailing lists of these organizations. Centers and councils will try to provide unbiased material and will avoid taking sides in economic controversies. That is, they will attempt to help the teacher get an objective view of all sides. However, the teacher must be cautious in using free materials. There are organizations with high-sounding names which give the impression of being nonpartisan agencies for the promotion of economic literacy, when in reality their purpose is to promote one point of view, and their material is thinly disguised propaganda. Of course, material presenting one side can be useful if it is balanced by material produced by the opposition. Thus, there may be a place for both the publications of the AFL-CIO and the National Association of Manufacturers in the classroom.

Government agencies, congressional committees, and the Federal Reserve banks often provide excellent reports on current economic issues. Local and state agencies can be useful sources of information. Such annual publications as the *Statistical Abstract of the United States* (U.S. Department of Commerce), the *Information Please Almanac* (New York: Simon and Schuster), and the *World Almanac* (New York: Doubleday) are valuable reference works. The "Road Maps of Industry" charts of the Conference Board (845 Third Avenue, New York, N.Y. 10022) are available free to teachers, and provide up-to-date statistics in graphic form. Many of the larger banks publish monthly newsletters which contain a wealth of information. The newsletter of the Joint Council on Economic Education, which can be obtained by school libraries, usually includes practical material for teaching economic topics. Teachers should request a copy of the Joint Council's *Checklist* of publications.

Many state and city school systems produce teaching guides for economics. The DEEP (Developmental Economic Education Program) projects have produced practical materials to aid teachers and students. Again, the Joint Council can inform teachers of such projects in their areas. The annual booklets *Economic Education Experiences of Enterprising Teachers* are published by the Joint Council and sold at nominal prices. They are based upon entries in the Annual Awards Program for the Teaching of Economics. Edward Prehn's *Teaching High School Economics* (New York: Pitman Publishing Corp., 1968) should prove helpful.

Audiovisual aids in economics are becoming more numerous, but should be selected with great care. Films should be previewed before being used in the classroom so that the teacher can be sure they are suitable for pupils, and that they are objective. The Joint Council, or a local council or center, might be consulted on the availability of suitable materials. Many teachers make their own transparencies, but some may be able to have their schools purchase professionally produced items. One of the better commercially produced sets of transparencies is Sanford Gordon's *A Visual Analysis of the American Economy* (Boston: Raytheon, 1968).

Many resources are available in the community. Before starting a high school economics course (or economics unit within another course) the teacher might consult the local telephone directory to ascertain what business firms, labor unions, banks, or other economic institutions can be found nearby. Representatives of these institutions will often be glad to serve as resource persons or as speakers and to accommodate or arrange field trips.

An economics materials library can be developed in the classroom in a short time. All that is needed is file folders and a file cabinet (cardboard boxes will do instead). The folders should be labeled agriculture, business, consumer, labor, money and banking, international economics, taxation, and the like. Articles found in newspapers, news magazines, professional journals, and so on, can be cut out and filed in the appropriate folders, along with small pamphlets and brochures. This file provides a source of up-to-date material for the class, and will be particularly helpful to students doing term papers or reports. In short, because economics is a part of the everyday life of all people, the alert teacher should be able to find an abundance of source materials to aid in teaching it.

NOTES

1. Any of the standard texts in principles of economics can give the diligent student a fairly good background in economics. Among the better known two-semester basic texts are Paul Samuelson's *Economics: An Introductory Analysis* (New York: McGraw-Hill, 1974) and G. L. Bach's *Economics: An Introduction to Analysis and Policy* (Englewood Cliffs, N.J.: Prentice-Hall, 1968). There are shorter texts designed for one-semester courses or the general reader. Examples are Sanford Gordon and George Dawson's *Introductory Economics* (Lexington, Mass.: D.C. Heath, 1972) and Robert L. Heilbroner's *The Economic Problem* (Englewood Cliffs, N.J.: Prentice-Hall, 1968). Today there are many different varieties of economics texts, using many approaches. For example, some are problems oriented, while others adhere to a rather abstract analytical approach, and a few stress historical or institutional economics. For an excellent list and description of current texts, see Laurence E. Leamer, *A Guide to the Selection of College Introductory Economics Textbooks* (Binghamton: State University of New York) 1972 which is available free. For a list and description of relatively simple economics books, including specialized works (such as books on labor) as well as comprehensive texts, see *Suggestions for a Basic Economics Library* (New York: Joint Council on Economic Education), priced at $4 per copy. John E. Maher's *What Is Economics?* (New York: John Wiley) 1969 is designed to clear up some of the misconceptions teachers often have about economics, to set forth a means of understanding and approaching economic issues, and to suggest ways of teaching some basic concepts. Finally, the least that the teacher can do is read some of the more recent high school texts, stressing those which are analytical rather than simply descriptive. Examples are Albert Alexander, Edward Prehn, and Arnold Sametz, *The Modern Economy in Action* (New York: Pitman), 1968 and James Calderwood and George Fersh, *Economics in Action* (New York: Macmillan) 1968.
2. For a more detailed exploration of the way in which basic economic principles can be applied to personal consumer problems, see the Per-

sonal Economics Series published by the Joint Council on Economic Education. Four of the booklets show how economics can be integrated in various courses in the secondary schools, and the fifth is a standardized test of understanding in personal economics.

3. Edward C. Prehn, *Teaching High School Economics: The Analytical Approach* (New York: Pitman) 1968.

4. Over forty ideas for relating economics to the community can be found in the resource unit *Economics and Our Community* (New York: Joint Council on Economic Education) 1973. This was designed for grades four, five, and six, but many of the activities could be used with secondary students as well.

5. The teacher is Mrs. O. L. Burney, Horatio School, Horatio, Arkansas. See *Economic Education Experiences of Enterprising Teachers,* Vol. V (New York: Joint Council on Economic Education) 1968, pp. 30-32.

6. The teacher is Raymond R. Muskat of Duluth. See ibid., p. 65.

7. See Rendigs Fels and Robert Uhler, eds., *Casebook of Economic Problems and Policies* (St. Paul: West Publishing Company) 1974, and Ralph W. Hidy and Paul W. Cawein, eds., *Casebook in Business History and Economic Concepts for Use in Secondary Schools* (Newton, Mass.: Newton Public Schools) 1964.

8. See Darrell R. Lewis *et al., Educational Games and Simulations in Economics* (New York: Joint Council on Economic Education) 1974. Many issues of the annual booklet *Economic Education Experiences of Enterprising Teachers* (New York: Joint Council on Economic Education) contain articles on games, simulations, and role-playing.

9. The teacher is Dennis Cambier of Lincoln High School. See *Economic Education Experiences of Enterprising Teachers,* Vol. IV (New York: Joint Council on Economic Education) 1964, pp. 38-40.

10. The teacher is Camellia McKenzie of Cleveland Junior High School. Ibid., pp. 37-38.

11. See articles by C. B. Twiddy, in Volumes I, II, and V of *Economic Education Experiences of Enterprising Teachers,* op. cit.

12. See Marilyn Kourilsky, *The Use of an Adversary Approach in Teaching Economics* (Cincinnati: South-Western) 1970.

13. Over 150 novels published in the United States have taken labor as their basic theme. See Virginia Prestridge, *The Worker in American Fiction* (Champaign: Institute of Labor and Industrial Relations, University of Illinois), 1954 an annotated bibliography, and George G. Dawson, "The American Labor Novel," *Social Education* (May 1961). Among the recordings dealing with economic issues are *Songs from the Depression* and *American Industrial Ballads,* both issued by Folkways Records.

14. *Education U.S.A.,* May 10, 1971, p. 199.

15. *Education Summary,* June 11, 1971, p. 7.

16. Materials to aid the teacher in this respect are scarce. See Gloria Nichols, "Economics of the Feudal System: A Junior High Approach to the Beginnings of the Market Economy," in *Economic Education Experiences of Enterprising Teachers,* op. cit., Vol. III, pp. 76-83, and Nancy Fortney, "World History and Economics in Ninth Grade," Vol. IV, p. 54.

17. See George G. Dawson and Edward C. Prehn, *Teaching Economics in American History: A Teacher's Manual for Secondary Schools* (New York: Joint Council on Economic Education) 1973. A set of 120 color slides can also be obtained to be used with this manual. See the Joint Council's *Checklist* for other materials on teaching economics in U.S. history.

18. *Government and the Economy: A Resource Unit for Grades 7, 8, and 9* (New York: Joint Council on Economic Education) 1974.

19. Lloyd Kinsey of Alameda School, Portland, Oregon, selected at random a small primitive Peruvian village, had his pupils make an intensive study of its economic and geographic situation, and then draw up a feasible plan whereby the village could better utilize existing resources to improve its economy. See *Economic Education Experiences of Enterprising Teachers,* Vol. IV (New York: Joint Council on Economic Education), pp. 79-81.

20. A pamphlet on this subject, with a section on how to teach about it, is: Lester Thurow, *The Economics of Poverty and Racial Discrimination.* (New York: Joint Council on Economic Education) 1972. A filmstrip is also available.

21. See the pamphlet *The Economics of Crime* (New York: Joint Council on Economic Education) 1971 with accompanying section on how to teach the subject. A filmstrip is also available.

CHAPTER VII

Teaching Government

by George G. Dawson

WHY TEACH GOVERNMENT?

In our previous chapter on teaching economics we discussed at considerable length the reasons why economics should be taught in the secondary school. We felt that it was necessary to do this because many social studies teachers have had such poor preparation in economics that they not only lack the competence to teach the subject but they also fail to understand why it should be taught. Happily, this situation does not apply to the teaching of government. Most social studies teachers have had better (or at least more) training in government and political science than in economics, and few will deny that an understanding of government is essential for all Americans. Nevertheless, some recent research raises serious questions about the effectiveness of the high school civics curriculum as it currently exists in the United States.

In an unpublished study entitled "Political Socialization and the High School Civics Curriculum in the United States" (Survey Research Center, University of Michigan), Kent M. Jennings rejects the view that high school civics courses enhance political socialization of older adolescents and hypothesizes that such courses result in little change in many political variables which are commonly thought to be the results of civic education. Jennings's study was based upon a national sample, and his findings suggest that government courses in their current form are making little impact on students.

The shocking results of Jennings's research do not, of course, imply that we should discontinue our attempts to teach government, political science, or citizenship education; they suggest that great improvement is needed. *Citizenship education* is defined as "The study of those portions of the social sciences/social studies, and cocurricular activities, which contribute to the development of understanding and attitudes conducive to effective participation in civic affairs." [1] *Political science* is "The study of government(s) and political behavior. The subject matter provides pupils with insight into a variety of factors important to the study of governments and culture, and systems processes, policies, theories, goals, and the relationships between governments." [2] *Government* may be variously defined as "the authoritative direction of the affairs of men in a community," "the governing body of a community," "the form by which a community is managed," or simply "management" or "control." [3] In this chapter we shall be concerned primarily with the teaching of government as it applies to the United States, and with the task of preparing young people for intelligent and informed participation in our political processes.

Our laws, our political system, our governmental institutions (informal as well as formal), and the problems of government and politics in the United States have profound effects upon all who reside in this country. The Constitution affects everyone, from the highest to the lowest, and thus it should be understood by all. In some way or other, everyone can participate in our political system. One does not have to be of voting age, nor does one have to be a citizen, to take some part in the fascinating drama—with its many complex plots and subplots—being played in our political arena. The often-used term "Future citizen" is a misnomer, in most cases. It is usually applied to young Americans who have not yet reached voting age and implies that they are not citizens until they are legally entitled to vote in elections. We tend to forget that anyone born in the United States is a citizen from the very beginning of his or her life. The young American can actively engage in many aspects of government and politics long before reaching legal voting age. In a very real sense, citizenship begins (or *can* begin) as soon as the individual is capable of some sort of rational decision-making and is willing to assume certain responsibilities.

If we look upon government in its broadest sense, and strip ourselves of the unfortunate habit of thinking of government as something remote ("the bureaucracy in Washington" or the state capitol), then we can apply the principles and problems of "management" or "control" to an infinite number of situations in which individuals daily find themselves. Even the preschool child has some sort of experience with government (in this broad sense) in the family setting. Whenever people live together in groups, however small, some sort of behavioral code must be agreed upon. One parent may dominate the household, establishing arbitrary rules and punishing deviant behavior. Both parents may discuss the governance of the family, reach agreement on rules of conduct, and share in the responsibility for enforcing the rules and dealing with violations. In many modern families, however, the children participate in the formulation of family rules and policies. In the best of situations, they are led to understand why rules are necessary, what factors must be considered in setting up codes of conduct, and why infractions can have serious consequences for the group.

In many classrooms, too, children even at the primary level are being given the opportunity to decide upon proper classroom conduct and make decisions about rule enforcement. Thus, in a very real sense, children today can and do participate in government. Many of the principles that apply to government in the larger sense also apply in these "micropolitical" situations. Simple parliamentary procedures can be learned by children at an early age and, in addition to mastering the mechanics of parliamentary techniques, they can be helped to understand why such procedures are important. They can also acquire attitudes of respect for the rights of others to be heard, toleration of opposing views, and willingness to accept the will of the majority. In short, children can learn democracy at an early age if we give them the opportunity to *practice* it in daily situations. Attitudes, understandings, and knowledge of governmental principles which are acquired at an early age may well carry over to such things as the youth's social or curriculum clubs, the administration of the school, and—later—to his participation in local, state, or federal government.

To be prepared for the teaching of government in the secondary school, social studies teachers must do much more than rely upon the courses taken in college. They must keep his knowledge up to date by reading at least one good daily newspaper and perhaps a weekly news magazine. At least one basic college-level textbook in government should be in the teacher's professional library, along with a selection of readings and basic documents. Fortunately, the United States Constitution is brief enough to enable the teacher to carry a copy with him at all times. Annually published almanacs, such as the *World Almanac* or the *Information Please Almanac,* contain summaries of recent political events and an abundance of facts which the teacher of government will find useful. The *United States Government Organization Manual,* published periodically by the Government Printing Office in Washington, D.C., is a valuable source of information on the federal government. All of the aforementioned publications are available in paperbound editions at relatively low prices. Although rather expensive, *Congress and the Nation 1945-1964* (Washington: Congressional Quarterly Service, 1965) is a superb source book. (More recent supplements are also available.) The teacher might also find that membership in such professional organizations as the American Academy of Political and Social Science will constitute a good investment. There are many television discussion programs, such as "Face the Nation," which can help both teacher and student keep abreast of current issues. Many inexpensive paperbound books on political issues are available at low prices.[4] In keeping informed on governmental matters, the teacher should constantly be alert for issues (such as the question of lowering the voting age) which can be of immediate interest to students. Many facts and principles relating to American government and politics can be related to issues which concern students.

The assertion made earlier about the techniques for teaching economics can apply to government as well. Many methods can be used, and many content organizations are possible. The use of problem-solving, case studies, inquiry, conflict analysis, simulations, and developmental lessons can be effective in teaching government. Some examples will follow later in this chapter.

THE CONTENT OF SECONDARY SCHOOL
GOVERNMENT COURSES

There is less controversy over what topics, principles, problems, and issues to include in government courses than there is in economics courses. Nevertheless, the new teacher should not expect to find complete agreement on this matter. Some feel, for example, that one can teach American government in isolation, paying little or no attention to political systems existing elsewhere. Indeed, there have been times in our recent history when it was downright dangerous to teach anything about the government of the Soviet Union or other Communist or Socialist nations in an objective manner. Some are of the opinion that if one is to understand the American system he must compare and contrast it with others. Because some leading political scientists have proposed drastic changes in our governmental structure (such as adoption of the British parliamentary system), and because our government is, in fact, always undergoing subtle changes, the author of this chapter supports the view that at least some attention must be paid to systems other than our own. He favors an objective, unbiased approach in favor of the all-too-common notion that our system is automatically superior to all others, regardless of local conditions. This writer strongly favors democracy and sees little need to bring about radical changes in the structure of the American government or political system, but this does not preclude an objective and thorough examination of the whole subject. Nor does it follow that the system that works well for us will, of necessity, work well for all others. Whether or not the average high school student is capable of attacking a question so sweeping as that of changing our system of government is a matter of debate. In any event, the least that the high school course can do is to give the student a good grounding in our system as it exists and in the problems that confront it so that he or she will be prepared to tackle the more sophisticated and philosophical issues at a higher level later on.

There is almost no end to the topics that might be included in a high school government course if time permitted. Should we attempt to cover many subjects in brief fashion, or should we cover a few basic topics in depth? The writer does not pretend to have the answer to that question. The following list of topics is suggested as a possible content outline for a course in government. Some of the topics are expendable, and should be looked upon as those to be included if time permits. (For example, one should not feel compelled to deal with the topic of "Government and Agriculture" at the expense of a thorough study of the Bill of Rights.) The order in which these items are presented is not necessarily the best, but is probably a workable sequence.

1. The Principles of Democracy
2. Competing Systems—Monarchy and Dictatorship; Oligarchy
3. Historical Background of American Democracy
4. The United States Constitution
5. The Bill of Rights
6. Subsequent Amendments to the Constitution
7. Federalism
8. Division of Powers in the United States Government
9. The Legislative Branch
10. The Executive Branch
11. The Judiciary
12. The Independent Commissions and Federal Agencies
13. State and Local Governments
14. The Territories and Puerto Rico
15. Political Parties
16. Public Opinion
17. The Role of the Lobbies
18. The Rights and Responsibilities of Citizenship
19. Government and Business
20. Government and Labor
21. Government and Agriculture
22. Government and the Consumer
23. Government and Education
24. Government and Welfare
25. The Making of Foreign Policy

In giving this list of topics, we are not implying that a strictly topical approach is the best way of teaching government. Some of these items can be sub-divided into many topics of smaller scope, and some could be combined into broader units of study. Most of the topics can be taught through the problem-solving method, the technique favored by this author. A well-structured problem of interest to the students might focus upon one of these topics, or might pull several of them together. Suppose, for example, that the students show interest in the question: "Should marijuana be legalized throughout the United States?" A thorough study of this issue might involve several of the listed topics. For example: Is it consistent with the principles of democracy (Topic 1) to ban marijuana while liquor is permitted? In banning "pot," is government acting in accordance with powers granted by the Constitution (Topics 4 and 5)? Should this question be left up to state and local governments (Topics 7 and 13)? What do most Americans think about the issue (Topic 16)? In using drugs or liquor which may cause irrational behavior, are people abusing their rights (Topic 18)?

If the teacher chooses to employ the problem-solving approach to the teaching of government, there are many current issues which can be drawn upon as vehicles for conveying many important principles and facts. As this is being written, some of the problems that should serve to provide good student motivation as well as being related to our governmental and political system are as follows:

- Should the electoral college system be abolished?
- Should the federal government take action to control demonstrations on campuses?
- What can be done to eliminate corruption in government?
- To what extent should the government own and operate industries?
- Should the federal regulatory agencies, such as the SEC, ICC, and FTC, be strengthened?
- Should we have uniform nationwide divorce laws?
- Should there be some form of censorship to prevent subversion, biased news reporting, and obscenity?
- What can be done to control air and water pollution?

- To what extent should the federal government aid the cities?
- Should there be a guaranteed minimum income for all Americans?
- To what extent should the federal government use its power to enforce racial integration?
- Should strikes by government employees be permitted? [5]
- Should local governments be replaced by regional governments in metropolitan areas? [6]
- Should local and state welfare systems be replaced by a uniform national system?
- Should government attempt to guarantee a college education to all who want it?
- To what extent should government interfere in labor disputes?
- How can the war on crime be stepped up without destroying privileges guaranteed by the Bill of Rights?
- What actions should government take to guarantee equal rights for women?
- To what extent should foreign policy making reflect the public opinion polls?
- Should government take further action to control big business?
- Should the jury system be abolished?
- Should government subsidies to agriculture and others be continued?

It should be fairly obvious that any of these problems, and many more which are current, would require intensive study of our existing laws, policies, and practices, call for an analytical examination of the situation, and force the student to think and to inquire.

SOME PRACTICAL IDEAS FOR TEACHING GOVERNMENT

There are many possible approaches to the teaching of government. Future research may reveal that one method is superior to all others, but at present it is our view that no single teaching technique or content organization can claim primacy. It is important that the social studies teacher be aware of the fact that any given topic or problem in government can be approached in a variety of ways. In this chapter we shall describe some of these "teaching strategies" and leave it to the reader to decide which is best for his or her class at any particular moment.

1. The Developmental Lesson

As we stated earlier in the chapter "Teaching Economics," the developmental lesson is one in which a problem, concept, important idea, generalization, topic, or principle is introduced to the class and developed under the teacher's guidance through well-planned questions, discussion between the teacher and the class, or discussion between pupils. The reader is urged to review the section on the developmental lesson in the earlier chapter, for the same principles will apply here. The sample developmental lesson plan presented in this chapter must not be regarded as the only acceptable way of teaching the same topic, nor is the plan itself to be seen as a model of perfection. It should be studied with a critical eye, and the reader should attempt to improve upon it.

SAMPLE LESSON PLAN ON THE SYSTEM OF CHECKS AND BALANCES—HIGH SCHOOL LEVEL

Unit topic:	Our system of government.
Lesson topic:	The system of checks and balances.
Key idea:	Dictatorship can be prevented by imposing checks on the various agencies of government.
Specific aims:	1. Acquiring knowledge of what the system of checks and balances is.
	2. Understanding why the system of checks and balances is important.
	3. Understanding the arguments for and against the system.
	4. Acquiring an attitude of respect for democratic practices—specifically, the system of checks and balances.
	5. Acquiring an appreciation for the foresight of the Founding Fathers.

Motivation: Ask the students to indicate what clubs or organizations they belong to. Ask such questions as these: "How is the organization run?" "How do you prevent the president of the club from becoming a dictator?" List some of the replies on the chalkboard. For a *transition* into the lesson, ask: "What other organizations that you know about provide some sort of check on the leaders?" (Possible answers will include labor unions, corporations, governments.) Establish that a system of *checks and balances* has been built into our governmental structure. The Watergate affair should provide a good illustration.

Lesson Content	*Questions*

Powers of the president, the Congress, and the Supreme Court. List these on the chalkboard as follows:

Pivotal question no. 1: How does our system of checks and balances work?

President	*Congress*	*Supreme Court*
Veto laws	Override veto by ⅔ vote	Nullify laws
Appoint judges	Approve appts.	Serve for life
Etc. . . .	Etc. . . .	Etc. . . .

Subquestions: How can the president check the power of Congress? The Court? How does Congress check the power of the president and the Court? How does the Court check the power of the president and the Congress? Etc. . . .

Franklin Roosevelt's attempt to "pack" the Supreme Court was stopped by Congress, for example. A simple diagram such as the one below can help to clarify the concept.

Medial summary no. 1: Give examples of the powers we have listed, using actual historical events.

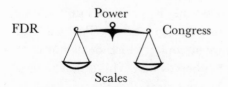

FDR — Power — Congress
Scales

Subquestions: To what extent did this incident strengthen (or weaken) the checks-and-balances system?

Lesson Content	*Questions*
List reasons for the system, such as: "Fear that president might become a dictator." "Fear that Congress would take radical actions." Etc.	*Pivotal question no. 2:* Why did the founders of the United States set up this system?
Arbitrary rule by colonial governors; abuses of British royal power; etc.	*Subquestions:* What had happened in the past to convince the founders that this system was needed?
Need for a strong central government with a powerful executive, etc.	What arguments were given against the system?
There is some justification for both sides. The system preserves democracy, but is often slow and cumbersome, for example.	*Medial summary no. 2:* How would you evaluate the arguments pro and con?
The system has worked well in many cases to keep us free from arbitrary rule. Possible examples for discussion and evaluation might include the impeachment of Andrew Johnson, passage of the Taft-Hartley Act over Truman's veto, Truman's refusal to appear before a congressional committee, and others.	*Final summary:* How well has the system worked for us? Give examples. Can the system be improved? If so, how? What principles associated with this system can be applied to our own clubs and organizations?

This sample lesson is short, and can probably be covered comfortably in the period of average length. The lesson is assumed to be part of a unit in which related material has preceded this topic. It is assumed that the students have had reading assignments based upon the content of the lesson. A brief analysis of this lesson now follows.

The lesson plan as written here shows that it is part of a unit on our system of government. This might be part of a "Problems of Democracy" course, or of a government course which deals not only with American government but with others as well. This lesson focuses upon checks and balances, but this does not mean that the topic will be exhausted in one class period. Indeed, the concepts included in this lesson should come up again and again in other contexts. The facts and principles conveyed by this lesson might well establish a framework for many lessons to follow. For example, a subsequent lesson on the executive branch of our federal government would certainly refer back to this lesson. There is reciprocity in this: the future lesson provides review and reinforcement; the current lesson lays the groundwork for lessons to come.

The *key idea* tells us that the teacher, in this case, wants the students to know that it is possible to prevent dictatorship by building a system of checks and balances into a governmental structure. This notion has universal application. It can apply not only to our federal government but to many situations (large and small) in which political power is a factor. Thus, when we start this lesson we relate that key idea to something very familiar to the students—their own clubs and organizations. We then show them that the principle applies to larger organizations, such as unions and corporations. This provides a smooth transition from the example of student clubs to the national government.

The first *pivotal question* clearly relates to aim no. 1—"Acquiring knowledge of what the system of checks and balances is." As stated in the sample lesson plan, the question appears to be fact oriented. Indeed, it does ask the students to repeat what they have learned about the system, and these facts are listed in columns on the chalkboard. It is a poor teacher, however, who will be satisfied with this, even if the responses are accurate. The teacher should demand an explanation of each key point and should challenge answers, even if they are essentially correct. He or she might ask the class to evaluate the answers given by each student. ("Do you agree with what James said about veto power?" "Was John's explanation accurate?" "Could Mary's statement be made more clearly?" "What should be added to Jane's discussion of the power of appointment?") The subquestions are designed to fill in the details of the topic to which the pivotal question was addressed.

The *medial summary* goes far beyond a simple repetition of the facts or principles elicited through the first pivotal question and its related subquestions. The students must go back and rethink the previous material and draw upon their knowledge of history to find examples. Furthermore, they must begin to evaluate the system when they attempt to answer the question, "To what extent did this incident strengthen (or weaken) the checks and balances system?"

Pivotal question no. 2, with the related subquestions, attempts to achieve specific aims no. 2 and no. 3. It might also help to achieve aims no. 4 and no. 5 as well, but since these deal with such vague elements as "attitude" and "appreciation" it will be difficult to assert with confidence that those aims can be accomplished in one lesson.[7] Pivotal question no. 2 asks for an explanation of why the system was established in the first place. Obviously, this relates the topic to historical events and provides a rationale for it. One of the subquestions is extremely important in this case, for it requires the student to note the arguments given against the system as well as those given for it. That question leads logically into the second *medial summary.* The second medial summary question—"How would you evaluate the arguments pro and con?"—again demands not only that the student review the previous material but that he or she give it some serious thought. This should be considered part of the student's training as an independent thinker, encouraging him or her to examine all sides of an issue and to make up his or her own mind in light of accepted goals and values.

To answer the *final summary* question ("How well has the system worked for us?"), the student must review all major points developed in the lesson, think about the system in relation to our past and current problems, and evaluate it in a broad but very meaningful context. In the discussion that brings the lesson to a close, the student is led back to the very beginning (the motivation) when he is asked to associate the principles of the system with the problems of his or her own organizations. This should help to emphasize the point that the concepts are not abstract and remote theories, but important ideas that can be applied to the immediate world of the student's own experience.

2. Using Community Resources

Even the smallest community will contain governmental units or political organizations which can become valuable resources for instruction. There are problems of government and politics in every village and town, and these can be studied at first hand. Of course, there are inherent dangers in drawing information from local groups. Many pressure groups will want the students to get only their side of the story and will resent attempts to study a situation completely and objectively. The individual who is lacking in courage and is afraid of stirring up controversy probably does not belong in the teaching profession however, and certainly should avoid the social studies. Even if a teapot tempest does result from a classroom study of a local problem, this in itself should be a valuable educational experience for the students.

A. *Guest Speakers.* The leaders of the local political parties and organizations can be invited to speak to the class to explain how their groups are operated, what issues concern them, why they take particular stands on those issues, and so on. Of course, it is imperative that there be balance here. It would be reprehensible to invite the local Democratic party leader and not extend a similar privilege to the Republican. Representatives of minor parties might also be called upon. Although the Democratic and Republican parties dominate our national scene, minor parties have sometimes had profound influence. In some state and local situations, the minor parties play very important roles. (The Liberal party in New York, for example, has only a fraction of the membership recorded for the Democratic and Republican parties. In close elections, however, it has sometimes been in a position to affect the choices made by a major party through its power to give its support to the major opponent.)

Representatives of such nonpartisan groups as the League of Women Voters can be valuable resource persons. Spokesmen for the various pressure groups interested in vital issues can be called in, provided that all sides are heard. Government officials, such as mayors, city councilmen, law-enforcement officers, or heads of state and federal offices in the area can discuss their roles in political and governmental processes.

The students should make careful preparation for these visitors so that intelligent questions can be raised. They should have a fair knowledge of the group represented by the guest and of the issues in which that group is involved. One class period might be devoted to a discussion of the questions that should be put to the speaker before he arrives. Each visitor should be treated with respect and courtesy, even if he or she represents an unpopular cause. The guest should be told, well in advance, what is expected of him. He should be apprised of the type of preparation the students have had for his visit.

B. *Field Trips*. Timing and preparation are vitally important if a field trip is to have educational value. Trips can be used to initiate a unit or to culminate it, or they can be part of the development of the unit. The trip should be planned to follow logically from the previous lesson and should lead into the subsequent lessons. The students and the hosts should know what the teacher expects to accomplish from the trip. Questions and activities should be planned in advance. During a trip to a city hall, for instance, the students might raise questions of the following kind:

1. Why is our city government organized as the mayor-council type? (Or whatever other type might be the case.)
2. What are the city's major sources of revenue?
3. What are the city's major expenditures?
4. What are the major problems confronting the city government today?
5. How does the city government relate to the state government? To the federal government?

3. Studying Political and Governmental Problems

Earlier, we listed a number of problems which might be studied in a high school government course. The same problem-solving approach outlined in the chapter "Teaching Economics" can be employed in the government course. Let us apply that technique to one of the sample problems to see how it might work. One of the problems listed was: "To what extent should the federal government aid the cities?" The teacher might want to change that to read "To what extent should the federal government aid *our* city?" in order to make it more practical for the students.

We have already taken the first step, by clearly identifying the problem and stating it in concise terms. Next, the current situation should be described as completely and as objectively as possible. What aid, if any, does our city now get from the federal government? How is this being used? What problems are not being mitigated by aid? What laws apply to federal aid to cities? What aid comes from the state government? Which local problems are of greatest importance? Some of the answers can be obtained from the guest speakers or from field trips; others, from documents, newspapers, official reports, and the like.

A brief history of the problem can help to shed light on its possible causes and can place it in long-term perspective. At this point, the United States Constitution and the particular state constitution can be studied to determine the legal relationships existing among the various levels of government.

The students should gather existing views on the solution of the problem, taking care to see that all sides are completely and objectively represented. How do the various political parties stand on the issue? What are the views of local civic and pressure groups? How do authorities (such as political scientists and economists) propose to solve the problem? A study can be made, also, of other cities in similar situations to see how they have handled the problem.

Then, each of the proposed solutions should be subjected to a searching and critical analysis. How does the Republican proposal differ from the Democratic? Why do they differ? Which of the proposed solutions seems most desirable in terms of the community's accepted goals and aspirations? Which solution seems to be most feasible in terms of the political and economic realities of today?

4. Case Studies

In a sense, studies of important current problems *are* case studies. Some studies might be made of past situations, however, wherein the solutions have already been obtained. This has both advantages and disadvantages. By studying a case which has already been solved, there is perhaps more opportunity for dispassionate and objective analysis. For example, it is easy to look back to *Gibbons* v. *Ogden* (1824) and examine the issue unemotionally, whereas a current case involving federal control of interstate commerce would certainly involve someone's vested interest.[8] On the other hand, current cases might be more meaningful to the student, for these involve issues now plaguing the country. One can also select cases from the past which have some bearing on current problems. Thus, a current issue involving government regulation of interstate commerce could be related to *Gibbons* v. *Ogden* and other similar cases. It should not be inferred that case studies are confined to court proceedings, however. For example, the Truman Doctrine could be studied in connection with a unit on the president's power to determine United States foreign policy.

5. Role-Playing, Games, and Simulation

Many of the concepts of government and politics can be taught through role-playing, games, and simulations. Even in the organization of the home-room class, the teacher can provide valuable experience in self-government if he or she permits the class to elect a president and other "officers," to make and enforce rules of conduct, and to practice good parliamentary procedures. Some teachers go so far as to set up a "model nation" in their classrooms, having the students write a "constitution," establish a "government," pass "laws," and so on.[9]

Games are becoming increasingly popular, and many are commercially available. A game entitled "Napoli" simulates the legislative process and its interrelationship with parties. In the game called "Plans," various interest groups try to use their influence to produce change in American society.[10] The game "Reconstruction" deals with the difficulty in achieving social and political reform in the South after the Civil War and shows the relationship between political and economic power.[11] "Section" simulates conflict of interests in a political section.[12] The simulation game "Mission" deals with the presidency and Vietnam.[13] In "Democracy" the players become members of a legislature and learn how laws are made and what factors shape the legislator's votes.[14]

Of course, teachers and students can develop their own simulations. These can be highly structured, as in a play written by the class to reenact something like the impeachment of Andrew Johnson. The students should be required to do thorough research to get the facts and should also deal with the implications of the event. In a less structured situation, the students might assume the roles of members of a legislature discussing the problem of student demonstrations. This does *not* mean that no preparation is necessary. Indeed, the students should make careful studies of existing laws relating to the issue and should know how to conduct themselves properly in the legislative setting. Armed with a knowledge of how to proceed and with good information on the current problem and the relevant laws, the students can then be given free reign to discuss the issue and try to arrive at a reasonable solution.

6. Debates and Discussions

The debate is made to order as a device for teaching government. There is never a shortage of controversial issues, and there should be little difficulty in finding many topics of interest to the junior or senior high school student. As this chapter is being written, the following topics would certainly appeal to most adolescents as exciting subjects for discussion.

- Resolved: The smoking of marijuana should be the legal right of anyone over the age of sixteen.
- Resolved: There should be harsh punishment for those who resisted the draft.

Resolved: The Congress should pass laws providing for harsh punishment of student rioters on college and secondary school campuses.

As we suggested in an earlier chapter, each team might be required to prepare *both* sides of the issue and not be told which side it will speak for until the debate begins. This will prevent students from becoming knowledgeable about only one position. The debate should be based, not upon prejudice and passion, but upon facts and principles. Much student research and preparation should precede the actual debate. The audience might be asked to decide which team has presented its case most forcefully and reasonably.

Oral reports and panel discussions make it possible for each student to specialize in one or a few topics, and then to share the learnings with the class. No single student can become an expert on everything that there is to know about government; thus, a division of labor is necessary. Suppose, for example, that a class is studying the problem of guaranteeing equal rights for black Americans. One student or group might concentrate on the current situation of the blacks—problems of unemployment and income, job opportunities, educational deficiencies, and the like. Another could examine existing federal laws that relate to the problem. A third might examine the various proposals for raising the social, political, and economic status of blacks, and so on. Each individual or group can then be responsible for making a presentation to the class. This can be done through panels, round-table discussions, all-class discussions, individual oral reports, or various other means. Various audiovisual aids can be employed in these reports. Well-prepared students can often temporarily assume the teacher's function in leading an all-class discussion.

7. Exercises in Critical Thinking

Inquiry, scholarly analysis, and critical thinking apply to all of the activities suggested thus far in this chapter. An exercise in critical thinking, then, is not always something to be treated separately. Students should be trained to detect propaganda, to distinguish between fact and opinion, and to tell the difference between proof and conjecture. They should be aware of such propaganda devices as "card-stacking" (in which only one side of an issue is presented) and the "testimonial" (in which we are told we should support a cause on the ground that it has the blessing of some noted person, even though that person may not be an authority on the subject). The class can be assigned to study newspaper editorials, political speeches, pamphlets produced by pressure groups, and other similar materials, to identify evidences of the propaganda devices. The pupils can also attempt to isolate provable facts from mere opinion.

Many of the communications media can be studied for signs of slanted reporting. Many television shows, although ostensibly designed solely to amuse the public, actually support or oppose political candidates or various causes. Some current motion pictures are also clearly on one side or the other of controversial issues. The "comic" strips which appear in most daily newspapers sometimes express political and social opinions, as in the case of the once famous senator who was depicted in a comic strip as a wildcat. (The same cartoonist depicted Nikita Khrushchev, former Soviet leader, as a pig.) George Bernard Shaw often ridiculed capitalism in his comedies and suggested that a moderate form of democratic socialism might be preferable. Some of Shakespeare's plays are said to have been propaganda for the ruling Tudor family. Modern playwrights, too, frequently use their art to express political views.

Such well-known novels as *Uncle Tom's Cabin, The Jungle, The Ugly American, Fail-Safe,* and *Advise and Consent* can be analyzed for their political content. Poetry has also been used to try to influence public opinion. In *The Deserted Village,* Oliver Goldsmith told of unhappiness caused by the Enclosure Acts; Thomas Hood's *The Song of the Shirt* described miserable working conditions; and John Greenleaf Whittier's *The Christian Slave* attempted to arouse the American conscience to end slavery. In modern times, many poets of the 1950s and 1960s have composed verses designed to influence their readers on vital public issues.

Music has always been a popular means of expressing human feelings. Songs both supporting and opposing the Vietnam war achieved popularity in the 1960s. Students might well enjoy a session which analyzes such songs, attempting to identify the position taken by the songwriter and the propaganda devices to which he resorts. (In earlier times, some of Verdi's operas were intended to rally the people to oppose Austrian rule over Italy; Beethoven's *Fidelio* glorified human freedom and condemned tyranny; Mozart's opera *The Marriage of Figaro* slyly criticized European aristocrats by making them appear stupid and ridiculous while their servants were depicted as being shrewd and crafty.) A few recordings of political songs have been produced, including *Songs of the Suffragettes* (Folkways FH 5281) and *Election Songs of the United States* (Folkways FH 5280). The famous *Sacco and Vanzetti* case resulted in a number of songs *(Ballads of Sacco & Vanzetti,* Folkways Record FH 5485) and provided the theme for Maxwell Anderson's award-winning play, *Winterset.* Much has been written about the Sacco and Vanzetti trial, and a study of this case could teach students a great deal about American concepts of justice.

If students are to think clearly about political issues, they should be aware of the various logical fallacies. Logic is a highly specialized discipline, in some ways like mathematics. We refer here to the informal or "common sense" fallacies rather than to those of formal logic, which would include syllogisms, symbolic logic, and the like.[15] Some of the informal fallacies which students should be aware of are as follows:

(a) *Argumentum ad hominem*—attacking the man. Instead of challenging an opponent's reasoning, one commits the fallacy of attacking him personally. For example, "My opponent was once convicted of a crime." Even if the statement is true, a *fallacy of relevance* has been committed if the man's background has nothing to do with the truth of his argument.

(b) *Argumentum ad populum*—appeal to the people. This is similar to the "bandwagon" propaganda device, in that one claims that his argument is valid simply because it has popular support. It must be remembered that the people favored the hanging of "witches" in the seventeenth century in Massachusetts and that many dictators have ridden to power on waves of popular support. Popular support per se does not validate (nor in-validate) an argument.

(c) *Post hoc, ergo propter hoc*—confusing time sequence with causation. For example, "The Great Depression occurred *after* Hoover's election; therefore Hoover *caused* the depression." Similarly, because World War II, the Korean conflict, and other wars occurred during Democratic administrations, we still hear it said that the election of Democrats to the presidency will cause wars.

(d) *The hasty generalization.* Too often, we form general or sweeping conclusions on the basis of too little evidence. A few students resort to violence to gain their ends; therefore we conclude that *all* students today are prone to violence. A few labor leaders have been found guilty of illegal activities; thus, it is said that all or most labor leaders are dishonest. We are cheated by one unscrupulous businessman, and we thereupon decide that no businessman can be trusted.

(e) *The fallacy of composition.* This is the false assumption that something *as a whole* must have the same qualities that each part has. No one would be so foolish as to assert that because each part of a machine weighs two pounds the whole machine must weigh two pounds. The same basic error is made in social, economic, and political situations, however. A legislative committee may be made up of highly intelligent people, but it does not necessarily follow that their collective decisions will be intelligent. Adam Smith asserted that all people in their economic activities are seeking to promote their own best interests, and it therefore follows that the result will be the promotion of the best interest of society as a whole. This is a classic example of the fallacy of composition, for these individual actions could be disastrous for the total economy.

(f) *The fallacy of division.* This is the reverse of the fallacy of composition. Here one makes the mistake of assuming that the qualities of something as a whole will correctly describe the qualities of each individual part. "This machine is heavy; therefore each part of it must be heavy." "The Congress has made a wise decision; therefore each member of the Congress must be wise." "Our society is prosperous; therefore every American is prosperous." The error inherent in these statements is painfully obvious; yet the fallacy of division is all too common. Organizations have been branded as "subversive" or "un-American" with the result that every member of them has been treated as a traitor. During World War II, Japan was the hated enemy of the United States. It was assumed by many that no Japanese could be trusted, with the result that Japanese-Americans were rounded up and herded into detention camps, although many of them had done nothing whatever to merit such treatment.

These are but a few of the informal fallacies that can be studied in a government course as profitable exercises in critical thinking.

8. Studying Other Governments

Students should realize that there are many possible ways of governing a nation. They will have a better understanding of American government if they have some knowledge of the governments of other countries. In addition to learning about monarchies, dictatorships, oligarchies, and pseudo-democracies (that is, nations in which there is totalitarian or authoritarian rule with a democratic veneer), the secondary school pupil ought to know that democracy can take many different forms. For example, our system of government can be compared with the British system and others which are in reality democratic, despite monarchical vestiges. Similarities and differences can be listed on charts or posters, somewhat like the following:

British System	*American System*
Chief executive is a member of the legislative branch.	Chief executive may not be a member of the legislature.

British System	*American System*
Chief executive is the chief minister of the king or queen. The monarch is technically the head of state, while the chief executive (prime minister) is head of government.	Chief executive is both head of state and head of government.
One house (Lords) has little real power.	Both houses have real power.
Government is more highly central-ized—unitary government.	Government is less centralized —federal system of government.
Etc.	Etc.

Of course, a simple listing of these facts is insufficient. The class should analyze each difference and discuss it in terms of which is "best" in each situation. Advantages and disadvantages of each should be noted. The failures as well as the successes of democratic structures should be understood. What brought about the governmental problems in France after World War II? Why has democratic government failed in some of the newly emerging states?

PERSONALIZED INSTRUCTION

More than ever before, educators today are accepting the idea that students are individuals and that the "lock-step" curriculum should be supplemented (if not replaced altogether) by personalized systems of instruction in which methods and materials are tailored to the needs, abilities, and interests of the individual. Thanks to programmed text-books, multimedia kits, learning modules, and the enormous variety of printed material available, it is possible to structure a program in which pupils advance at their own pace, using materials geared to individual reading abilities and interests. Students can also work in small groups, helping one another to reach common goals.

The use of behavioral (or performance) objectives and student learning contracts discussed in the chapter "Teaching Economics" can also apply to government. Suppose, for example, that a fairly bright girl has a strong interest in the women's rights movement. She might want to make a study of the U.S. Constitution in terms of the extent to which it "guarantees" equal rights for women. The objective could be stated as follows:

> Given a copy of the U.S. Constitution, the student will read the entire document and list those portions which appear to guarantee equal rights for women, such as the "equal protection of the laws" in Article XIV. For each item listed she will identify examples of apparent violations of women's rights, such as the denial of credit solely on the basis of sex.

Using articles from such publications as *Ms* magazine, books such as Marjorie Galenson's *Women and Work* (Ithaca: New York State School of Industrial & Labor Relations, 1973), government reports such as *Background Facts on Women Workers in the United States* (Washington, D.C.: U.S. Department of Labor), and other sources, the student could compile evidence of discrimination against women. She could prepare an oral report, paper, or scrapbook on her findings, and perhaps even use her data as the basis for letters to members of Congress, state legislators, and the like.

Others might examine government's role in protecting the consumer. (An experienced teacher advised the writer that such a project should be entitled: "How Can I Keep from Being 'Ripped Off'?") Many teachers report success in reaching students whose reading ability is low by capitalizing on their roles as consumers. Practically all students have experienced problems with misleading advertising, shoddy goods, and so on. Starting with a good or service the student intends to buy, he or she can make a study of the local, state, and federal agencies which have some responsibility for seeing to it that consumer interests are protected.[17] One New York City teacher, whose students had seen government as an oppressor, taught through such projects that "good government is a necessity for the preservation of individual freedom." [18]

In conclusion, there is no excuse for a dull, pedantic, or abstract course in government. The fact that the eighteen-year-old has the right to vote, the dramatic incidents of the Watergate affair, the controversy over the treatment of draft evaders and deserters, the shooting of students at Kent State University, teen-agers being elected to public offices normally held only by the middle-aged man or woman, gunfights between federal officers and Indians in South Dakota, riots over enforced busing in various cities, violence in West Virginia because of the content of school textbooks—these and a host of other current or recent events can be related to the facts and principles of government in the United States. Government can—and ought to be—one of the most fascinating subjects in the curriculum.

NOTES

1. See "Terminology for Social Science/Social Studies Curricula," extracted from W. Dale Chismore and John F. Putnam, eds., *Standard Terminology for Curriculum and Instruction in Local and State School Systems, Tentative Draft Number Five,* Washington, D.C.: National Center for Education Statistics/USOE, 1969 (Washington: National Council for the Social Studies, 1969), pp. 620-637.
2. Loc. cit.
3. *Funk & Wagnalls Standard Dictionary of the English Language,* International Edition, Vol. I (New York: Funk & Wagnalls, 1960).
4. For example, see *Paperbound Book Guide for High Schools,* published annually by R. R. Bowker Co., 1180 Avenue of the Americas, New York, N.Y. 10036. The *Guide* contains a section on "Government, Political Science & Law."
5. For a brief but very perceptive discussion of the question of strikes by government employees, see Kurt L. Hanslowe, *The Emerging Law of Labor Relations in Public Employment* (Ithaca, New York: Cornell University, 1967). Paperbound.
6. For a scholarly account of the problem of government in one metropolitan region, see Robert C. Wood, *1400 Governments* (New York: Doubleday Anchor Books, 1961). Paperbound.
7. Much more research is needed to determine the extent to which student attitudes are changed through formal education. At least two studies exist which suggest that the teacher is the important variable in affecting student attitudes. See Suzanne Wiggins, *Developmental Economics Education Program Final Report, Part II* (Pleasant Hill, California: Contra Costa County Department of Education, 1967), and George G. Dawson, "Changing Student Attitudes," *Improving College and University Teaching*

(Summer 1966), pp. 200-203. Those interested in measuring attitude changes are referred to Marvin E. Shaw and Jack M. Wright, *Scales for the Measurement of Attitudes* (New York: McGraw-Hill, 1967).

8. It would be desirable for every social studies classroom to contain several collections of source materials, such as Henry Steele Commager, ed., *Documents of American History* (New York: Appleton-Century-Crofts, 1949) and Marvin Meyers et al., *Sources of the American Republic* (Chicago: Scott, Foresman and Company, 1960). Many books of readings and collections of documents on American government have been published. *American Heritage* magazine has often published fascinating accounts of famous cases involving American government. (Consult their cumulative index.)

9. See the earlier chapter, "Teaching Economics," for a more detailed discussion of this technique.

10. "Napoli" and "Plans" are available from Western Behavioral Sciences Institute, 1121 Torrey Pines Road, La Jolla, California 92037, or Charles E. Merrill, Inc., 1300 Alum Creek Drive, Columbus, Ohio 43216.

11. Abt Associates, Inc., 55 Wheeler Street, Cambridge, Massachusetts 02138.

12. High School Geography Project, P.O. Box 1095, Boulder, Colorado 80302.

13. Interact, P.O. Box 262, Lakeside, California 92040.

14. Western Publishing Company, Inc., 850 Third Avenue, New York, N.Y. 10022.

15. An introductory college textbook in logic would be helpful here, such as Irving M. Copi, *Introduction to Logic* (New York: The Macmillan Company, 1961). There are also several good books dealing solely with fallacies, such as W. Ward Fearnside and William B. Holther, *Fallacy: The Counterfeit of Argument* (Englewood Cliffs, New Jersey: Prentice-Hall, 1959).

16. For a good reference work on contemporary governments, see Walter H. Mallory, ed., *Political Handbook and Atlas of the World* (New York: Simon and Schuster, published periodically). Lyman T. Sargent's *Contemporary Political Ideologies: A Comparative Analysis* (Homewood, Illinois: Dorsey Press, 1969) is a college text that could be useful as a reference work or for teacher preparation. Many interesting views on democracy are contained in Kurt L. Shell, ed., *The Democratic Political Process: A Cross-National Reader* (Waltham, Massachusetts: Blaisdell Publishing Company, 1969).

17. See Office of Consumer Affairs, *Guide to Federal Consumer Services* (Washington, D.C.: U.S. Government Printing Office).

18. Beatrice Liebesman, "The Teaching of Economics through Consumer Education," *Economic Education Experiences of Enterprising Teachers,* Vol. X

(New York: Joint Council on Economic Education, 1973), pp. 23-26. For an excellent scheme for teaching students with language problems, see David Fuchs, "Teaching Economics to Students for Whom English Is a Second Language," *Economic Education Experiences of Enterprising Teachers,* Vol. XII (1975).

CHAPTER VIII

Teaching Geography

by George G. Dawson

WHY TEACH GEOGRAPHY?

Geography may be defined as the subject which describes the surface of the earth. It involves a study of the earth's physical features, climates, soils, vegetation, products, and peoples. The data used by the geographer are drawn from many sciences, such as geology, astronomy, meteorology, biology, and anthropology. Although geography is closely related to such physical sciences as biology and geology, most consider it to be within the realm of the social sciences. Because geography focuses upon the character of *place,* the relationships between places, and—most importantly—the relationship of people with their habitat, it is indeed a subject that must concern the social studies teacher.

Geography, like most sciences, can be subdivided into a number of specialized fields. Mathematical geography deals with the shape, size, and movements of the earth. Physical geography involves a study of such things as natural vegetation, climate, and the oceans. (The subdivisions can be further divided into such areas as climatology and oceanography.) Human geography (sometimes called anthropogeography) studies the distribution of human communities on the earth, relative to their geographical environments. Zoogeography does the same for animals. This is a subdivision of biogeography, which is the study of the distribution of plants and animals. Political geography is concerned with the differentiation of political phenomena over the earth. The geography of the past is the subject of historical geography. Economic or commercial geography relates the earth to man's attempts to utilize scarce resources in meeting human wants and needs. Cartography is the art of drawing charts and maps.

Now, the social studies teacher who cannot find *something* from the above listing that relates to the problems of the day and to the needs and interests of students is pursuing the wrong career! Too often, of course, geography has been taught in a stale and lifeless manner. Students have been forced to memorize the names of the Great Lakes, to list the states touched by the Mississippi River, and to identify certain regions. These bits of isolated knowledge are quickly forgotten (after the final examination, if not before) unless the teacher has made an effort to make them meaningful by relating them to something which the student finds important. Someone once said that those who are ignorant of history are doomed to repeat it. The implications of that statement, of course, are that we can learn from the mistakes of the past and that we can better understand the problems of today if we place them in a historical context. Similarly, an ignorance of geography can be very costly. Human and physical resources have been wasted in ventures that had no chance of success because the entrepreneurs failed to realize the geographic limitations. For example, canal promoters (spurred on by the success of the Erie Canal in the 1820s) invested in projects without knowing the exact altitudes of the summit levels, the length of portages between rivers, or even if the available feeders could provide water of sufficient depth. Farmers foolishly settled in areas which could not support agriculture because of unsuitable soil and climate conditions. Conversely, settlement in what is now western Nebraska and Kansas was retarded by the belief that the area was a desert. (It was called, in fact, the "Great American Desert" in the textbooks and maps of the early nineteenth century.) Even today, geographic ignorance is costing an untold amount of wealth. Houses and other buildings have been built on ground not solid enough to hold them, with the result that walls have cracked and in some cases houses have been sinking into the ground. Public projects have cost far more than originally intended because of inadequate knowledge of geographic conditions that would affect construction. (One road-building project in a barren area in Africa, for instance, was slowed down by the fact that wind storms kept covering the road with sand. The builders had not accounted for this contingency, and eventually had to import snow plows to deal with the problem!)

Today, many people are deeply concerned with the problems of pollution and with conservation in general. Geography and its related sciences are essentials for an intelligent approach to these problems. (More will be said about the teaching of these problems later in this chapter.) Today, nearly everyone is excited about space exploration, and the interest that this has aroused should provide many fruitful lessons in geography. Photographs taken from space are readily available in popular magazines (such as *Life*) and can be used to good advantage in any social studies classroom.

The teacher who has a fair knowledge of geography and who is alert to the many problems—political, social, and economic—confronting the world today will have little difficulty in relating geographic facts and concepts to those problems.

PREPARING TO TEACH GEOGRAPHY

There is no firm agreement on how much formal preparation a teacher needs to teach geography competently. Many geographers suggest that the minimum preparation should be 15 college credits in geography. It is doubtful that most social studies teachers in the United States have had this much, and it is quite probable that many teacher-trainees manage to avoid the subject altogether. At least one two-semester course should be taken by every social studies major. In addition, one can learn a great deal through self-study or even through casual everyday reading. Good maps are found almost daily in such newspapers as the *New York Times*. The Sunday edition of that paper always carries many maps, charts, and graphs, as does the *Student Weekly,* which summarizes the important articles of the week. Newscasts on television are invariably illustrated with colorful maps. *The World Almanac,* published annually by the Newspaper Enterprise Association; *The Information Please Almanac,* a similar book produced each year by Dan Golenpaul Associates; and the *New York Times Encyclopedic Almanac,* a newer annual, contain a tremendous amount of information that can increase the geographic knowledge of both student and teacher. The social studies teacher who has not taken formal courses in geography can easily compensate by finding out what texts are used in such courses as economic geography, political geography, American historical geography, and the like, and obtaining copies of those books for his own use. The books can then be used as part of the reference library in the teacher's own classroom. A good world atlas is an excellent investment. Historical atlases are also available at modest prices.

The *American Heritage New Pictorial Encyclopedic Guide to the United States* is a two-volume work published by Dell which contains a wealth of detailed information on every state. It contains many beautiful illustrations in color, and it is simple enough to be used by students of average ability. The Life World Library Series is an exceptionally good set of over thirty volumes. In addition to an *Atlas of the World,* there are volumes on many individual nations (such as the Soviet Union) and on major areas (such as Tropical Africa). The cost of the full set might be excessive for the individual teacher, but the school library should consider obtaining it. A dictionary, such as W. G. Moore's *A Dictionary of Geography* (Penguin Books paperback), will prove helpful. And the annual *Statistical Abstract of the United States,* published by the U.S. Department of Commerce, is another invaluable teacher's guide.

Many good materials are available from commercial publishers at reasonable prices. *Physical Geography* by M. V. Phillips and *Map Skills for Today's Geography,* edited by John W. Maynard and David T. Peck, are inexpensive paperbound booklets published by American Education Publications. Also available from the same publisher are short booklets on special topics, such as *Our Polluted World* by Thomas G. Aylesworth and *The Conservation Story* by George F. Pollock. The publications of Scholastic invariably contain material useful in geography lessons. The Denoyer-Geppert Company, C. S. Hammond & Company, and Rand-McNally are noted for their excellent publications in geography. The teacher should consult their catalogues for details.

Many good journals are available. The well-known *National Geo-*

graphic not only contains many informative articles written in a simple and popular style, but abounds with beautiful pictures in color and excellent map inserts which can be removed without damaging the book and used for bulletin-board displays. *The Geographical Review* is a quarterly publication of the American Geographical Society of New York. The society also publishes *Focus,* a monthly newsletter presenting maps, facts, and interpretations of current problems. *The Journal of Geography* is a monthly publication of The National Council for Geographic Education. The teacher should examine these and other journals (such as *Economic Geography,* the *Annals of the Association of American Geographers,* and *The Professional Geographer)* in a library before deciding which ones would be suitable for his class.

Everyone teaching geography should be familiar with the work of the High School Geography Project of the Association of American Geographers, P.O. Box 1095, Boulder, Colorado 80302. (Information can also be obtained from the Association of American Geographers, 1146 Sixteenth Street, N.W., Washington, D.C. 20036.) The project publishes a *Newsletter* and has produced courses (such as *Geography in an Urban Age),* teacher education kits (such as *Using Simulation to Involve Students),* evaluations of materials, and handbooks (such as *The Local Community: A Handbook for Teachers).* Teachers may wish to attend summer institutes in geography (there were five NSF [National Science Foundation] institutes during the summer of 1970), and information on these can be obtained from the High School Geography Project.

Teachers should not overlook the free material that is readily available. Travel agencies, airlines, chambers of commerce, and the tourist offices of foreign countries often provide free maps and pamphlets that can be used in the classroom. However, though these materials are often colorful, they are often lacking in substance. They should be used with caution and employed as supplementary rather than primary teaching material. Designed to promote tourism, these materials emphasize the positive aspects of a country or area and rarely reveal the problem. Private industry and nonprofit interest groups can also be the sources of useful materials as long as the teacher bears in mind that they may have axes to grind or vested interests to promote. *Petroleum Today,* a colorful magazine published by the American Petroleum Institute, contains many interesting articles and maps relating to geography. Large banks, such as New York's Chase Manhattan, sometimes turn out excellent (and relatively objective) items. Chase Manhattan's *World Business* is a case in point. (Its First Quarter 1970 edition on Japan is a masterpiece.) The Conservation Foundation of 1717 Massachusetts Avenue, N.W., Washington, D.C. 20036, is but one of many such organizations today which is disseminating interesting and useful material.

Ideas for the teaching of geography can be obtained from several of the publications of the National Council for the Social Studies. Among these are:

Bacon, Phillip, ed. *Focus on Geography: Key Concepts and Teaching Strategies.* 40th Yearbook, 1970.

James, Preston E., ed. *New Viewpoints in Geography.* 29th Yearbook, 1959.

Kohn, Clyde F., ed. *Geographic Approaches to Social Education.* 19th Yearbook, 1948.

Many state and city school systems produce guides for teachers, such as New York's *Teaching Map and Globe Skills* (New York City Board of Education, Curriculum Bulletin No. 6). Some other books are as follows:

Broek, Jan O. M. *Geography: Its Scope and Spirit.* Columbus, Ohio: Charles E. Merrill, 1965. (Includes a section on teaching geography.)

Gabler, R. E., ed. *A Handbook for Geography Teachers.* Chicago: National Council for Geographic Education, 1966.

Hanna, Paul R. *Geography in the Teaching of Social Studies: Concepts and Skills.* Boston: Houghton Mifflin, 1966.

High School Geography Project. *Sources of Information and Materials: Maps and Aerial Photographs.* Washington, D.C.: Association of American Geographers, 1970.

Harris, Ruby M. *Handbook of Map and Globe Usage.* Chicago: Rand McNally, 1960.

Hill, Wilhelmina, ed. *Curriculum Guide for Geographic Education.* Norman, Oklahoma: National Council for Geographic Education, 1963.

Kolevzon, Edward, and Maloff, Rubin. *Vitalizing Geography in the Classroom.* Englewood Cliffs, New Jersey: Prentice-Hall, 1965.

Morris, John W., ed. *Methods of Geographical Instruction.* Waltham, Massachusetts: Blaisdell, 1968.

Roderick, Peattie. *The Teaching of Geography.* New York: Appleton-Century-Crofts, 1950.

Scarfe, N. V. *Geography in School.* Chicago: National Council for Geographic Education, 1965.

Thralls, Zoe A. *The Teaching of Geography.* New York: Appleton-Century-Crofts, 1958.

UNESCO, *Source Book for Geography Teaching.* New York: UNESCO, 1966. Finally, the teacher should consider joining the National Council for Geographic Education. If interested, he can write to the Council, Room 1532, 111 W. Washington Street, Chicago, Illinois 60602, for information on membership and for a list of their materials on teaching geography.

THE CONTENT AND ORGANIZATION
OF GEOGRAPHY COURSES

Many schools present the geography teacher with a course outline to follow. But in some cases, the teacher is expected to develop his own organization. If that should happen, the extraordinary number of sources and the many organizing themes should not discourage the teacher from confronting the problem: "What shall we do today?" Thus, it is foolhardy to generalize about geography courses. Nonetheless, the teacher who must develop a course should take several steps.

First, he must realize that geography is not new to secondary school students. They have been exposed to geography all through their elementary grades. In the primary grades the students will probably learn something about landforms, weather, climate, soil, water, minerals, and native animal and plant life. They may learn to associate cooler weather with northerly winds and to see the relationship between the natural environment of a people and the way they live. In fact, some of the most imaginative and creative techniques for teaching the social studies are being developed at the elementary level. Note the following examples:

- When her pupils became interested in a new housing project being built near the school, the teacher had them build model houses in the classroom. They studied the dwellings of various people throughout the world and made models of them. In each case, the children had to learn about the geography of the area. What geographic factors make it possible to build wooden houses in X but not in Y? How do climate, topography, and other geographic features affect the way in which the houses are built and where they are located?
- A teacher in a New York ghetto stressed urban geography in her classroom, took the pupils on tours of the neighborhood, and had them redesign the area so as to create a more functional and beautiful environment. They had to consider such things as the relationship of the neighborhood to the harbor, to other areas, to transportation facilities, to industrial and marketing regions of the city, and the like.
- Some teachers are making tape recordings of the sounds of an area, playing the tapes in the classroom, and having the children associate the sounds with maps. Upon hearing the sound of traffic, the child indicates on a map the point most likely to be associated with that sound. The sound of children at play would be associated with a park or residential area.
- In some areas children are actually being called upon to help plan parks, playgrounds, and schools. Some years ago, a noted geographer making a land-use survey in Great Britain had thousands of schoolchildren (under the guidance of their teachers) do the actual mapping of the country.
- Recently a teacher in the upper elementary grades developed a map test that has great possibilities. She drew maps of two imaginary countries, indicating such things as rivers, mountains, natural resources, and climate. The children were then asked to

show where towns and cities would most likely spring up, what industries the country would probably develop, what transportation problems might be expected, and what sort of trade relations might develop between the two countries.

These are but a few of the techniques being used at the primary and intermediate levels. Some of them could be refined and developed for use in the secondary grades.

To find out what has been covered in the elementary grades, the secondary school teacher can obtain and read the textbooks used in the elementary schools of his city or state. Curriculum guides can be examined, if they are available. It should not be assumed that the pupils have mastered everything found in the texts or the curriculum guides, but it is reasonable to believe that they have at least had some exposure to them. The use of maps is a necessary element in the study of geography, and the teacher should attempt to find out how much the students already know about them. For example, do they know what a *Mercator projection* is, how this sort of map can be used, and what its disadvantages are? The accompanying chart indicates the map skills that are frequently taught at various grade levels from the second through the sixth.*

It is difficult to find a course outline that can be considered "typical" because of the great number of ways in which a course can be organized. The following is derived from several outlines for high school world geography courses. It is not suggested that this is either the only way or the best way to organize a course:

Part I—Introductory Survey

    1. The nature and scope of geography
    2. Geographic contributions to man's knowledge

---

* To get an idea of what students might already know, the teacher can administer N. V. Scarfe's *Geography Achievement Test for Beginning High School Students,* available from the National Council for Geographic Education, Room 1532, 111 W. Washington Street, Chicago, Illinois 60602. A specimen set of test booklet and manual costs only 50 cents. A packet of twenty test booklets, key, and manual costs $5.

Chart of skills and concepts in *Map Skills for Today*

Skills and concepts developed	Readiness for Map Skills Grade 2	Map Skills for Today Grade 3	Map Skills for Today Grade 4	Map Skills for Today Grade 5	Map Skills for Today Grade 6
Understanding the globe	X	X	X	X	X
Understanding maps					
Relating photos to maps	X				
Special purpose maps		X	X	X	X
Map projections				X	X
Determining position on maps and globes					
Using equator; relative location	X	X	X	X	X
Using cardinal direcjions	X	X	X	X	X
Using intermediate directions			X	X	X
Using hemispheres; latitude; longitude			X	X	X
Using special grids			X	X	X
Determining directions					
Using north and south poles	X	X	X	X	X
Using the equator	X	X	X	X	X
Using cardinal directions	X	X	X	X	X
Using intermediate directions; river directions		X	X	X	X
Determining distances	X	X	X	X	X
Using a map scale '			X	X	X
Using relative distance			X	X	X
Determining relative sizes	X	X	X	X	X
Recognizing map symbols					
1. **Land forms**					
Continents	X	X	X	X	X
Hills, mountains, ranges	X	X	X	X	X
Islands	X	X	X	X	X
Trees, forests	X				
Coast, coastline		X	X	X	X
Plains		X	X	X	X
Peaks, valleys			X	X	X
Deltas			X	X	X
Peninsulas			X	X	X
Capes				X	X
Archipelagoes					X
2. **Water forms**					
Oceans	X	X	X	X	X
Rivers and creeks	X	X	X	X	X
Lakes and ponds	X	X	X	X	X
Bays and inlets		X	X	X	X
Gulfs and harbors		X	X	X	X
Ports			X	X	X
Channels, sounds, straits, and seas			X	X	X
Isthmuses				X	X
River systems				X	X
3. **Man-made features**					
Streets and roads	X	X	X		
Bridges	X	X	X		
Buildings	X	X			
Boundary lines	X	X	X	X	X
Cities	X	X	X	X	X
Railroads	X	X	X	X	X
Highways and route markers		X	X	X	X
Capitals and county seats		X	X	X	X
Airports		X	X		
Canals		X	X	X	X
Following directions to trace a route on a map	X				
Using map keys and legends			X	X	X
Comparing maps and making inferences	X	X	X	X	X

3. The origins and physical makeup of the earth
4. Problems of time, space, and location on the earth

Part II—Cultural Geography

1. The earth's cultural realms (Occidental, Islamic, Indic, etc.)
2. Social organization
3. How man and his organizations fit into the physical scene
4. How man has been conditioned by his physical environment

Part III—Economic Geography

1. How and why man works and produces
2. How the physical environment limits man's economic activities
3. How man uses his physical environment to solve economic problems
4. Economic regions and their interrelationships

Part IV—Political Geography

1. The development of political organizations
2. The state in relation to its geographic setting
3. Effects of geographic factors on international affairs

Contrast the above with the following suggested course outline:

Part I—The Human Habitat

1. Man and the earth
2. Man and climate
3. Man and soils
4. Climate and vegetation in the cold lands
5. Climate and vegetation in the hot lands
6. Climate and vegetation in the mid-latitude lands
7. An introduction to maps and their uses

Part II—Natural Resources, Food, and Industries

1. The world's forest and grass resources
2. The world's fuel and power

7. The Western Slavs
8. Italy, Portugal, and Spain
9. Greece and Turkey

Part VI—The Rest of the World

1. The Mediterranean and North Africa
2. The Middle East
3. India and Pakistan
4. China
5. Southeast Asia
6. Japan and Korea
7. The USSR
8. Australia and New Zealand
9. Africa

Which of the two outlines is better? Which is more functional? That is entirely up to the teacher. Each would have many supporters and critics. Note, for example, that in the second outline the entire continent of Africa receives no more attention than a single region in the United States. The latter outline would be much easier to follow than the former, but it contains so many topics that only superficial coverage of any given area appears to be possible. The former outline seems to allow more flexibility, but it suffers from being rather vague. Obviously, this author could easily fill the remainder of this book with outlines found in geography courses and in geography texts. However, there is no value in belaboring the point. In the final analysis, the teacher must decide what he is going to include, how he will arrange or order the content, and what teaching strategies he will employ.

SOME PRACTICAL IDEAS FOR TEACHING GEOGRAPHY

In this writer's previous chapters on "Teaching Economics" and "Teaching Government," it was asserted that many methods or strategies can be used with equal effect. The same applies to the teaching of geography.

1. The Developmental Lesson

Since sample developmental lessons were included in the chapters on economics and government, it should not be necessary to repeat all the definitions and explanations here. The same basic format will be used in the following sample lesson plan on geography, and again the reader should note that it is *not* presented as being the only good format for a lesson, nor is it being touted as an ideal plan.

SAMPLE LESSON PLAN ON THE GEOGRAPHY OF SOUTHEAST ASIA—HIGH SCHOOL LEVEL

Unit topic: Asia.

Lesson topic: The geography of Southeast Asia.

Key idea: Geographic factors affect the wealth and power of an area.

Behavioral objectives: As a result of today's lesson, the students will be able to:
1. Explain the importance of Southeast Asia to the United States and to the world.
2. Locate on maps the geographic features of Southeast Asia.
3. List the nations that make up Southeast Asia.
4. Explain how geographic factors affect the economy of an area.
5. Use maps to locate nations and identify geographic factors.

Motivation: Display pictures from magazines showing the effects of the war in Vietnam. Place on the chalkboard some figures indicating the cost of the war in terms of human lives and money. Read some statements made by noted supporters and opponents of American involvement in Vietnam. Ask such questions as these: "Why did the United States become involved in such a costly war?" One obvious answer is "To stop the spread of communism." Ask: "Why would the United States fear that control of Vietnam would be advantageous to the Communists?" A certain amount of discussion on the arguments for and against U.S. involvement can be permitted at this point, but after a few minutes the teacher should get into the body of the lesson by posing the first pivotal question.

Lesson Content	*Questions*
Rich in resources; strategic location; countries have votes in United Nations.	*Pivotal question no. 1:* Why is Southeast Asia considered so important?
Students locate them on wall map. Students identify Communist, anti-Communist, and neutral nations.	*Subquestions:* Which nations make up Southeast Asia? Which are Communist or pro-Communist? Which are anti-Communist? Which are neutral?
Western world might lose access to natural resources if area goes Communist. Area might serve as stepping-stone for further spread of communism.	*Medial summary no. 1:* If the entire area came under Communist control, how serious would this be?
List on chalkboard the student responses under the heading "Geographic Factors of Southeast Asia." Put a plus sign before those which students identify as being good for the economy; a minus sign before those which retard it.	*Pivotal question no. 2:* How do geographic factors affect the life of the people there?
Discuss the effect of the rains on troop movements and air strikes. Note how geographic factors enhance guerrilla warfare.	*Subquestions:* Which of these factors are retarding the area? Which factors are good for the economy? How is the war affected by geographic factors?
Discuss possibilities for better conservation, flood control, modern agricultural processes, etc.	*Medial summary no. 2:* How can the people use their geographic factors to better advantage?
Use of resources for domestic consumption. Importance of selling resources in world markets to earn capital for development.	*Pivotal question no. 3:* Why are natural resources so important to the area's development?

Lesson Content	*Questions*
List the major resources. List the things which are lacking.	*Subquestions:* What are the main resources? How is each used? What does the area lack?
	Final summary: (Also serves as medial summary no. 3.) How can Southeast Asia draw upon its resources and geography to grow economically? How can the nations of the area cooperate with one another in this? How can other nations help? What should the role of the United Nations be?

An actual lesson plan might be much more detailed (although many veteran teachers work with plans which are even sketchier than this). In the interests of saving space, we have not bothered to fill in many facts (such as a list of Southeast Asia's resources) that a classroom teacher might want to include in his plan. Similarly, additional questions might be prepared in the event that time remains after the above material has been covered. Among these might be test questions that will be used in unit examinations or weekly quizzes, homework assignments, lists of books and materials, and alternative ways of teaching this topic. Indeed, lesson plans run all the way from short notes on an index card to many pages of 8½ x 11 paper. In the chapters on economics and government, lesson plans were analyzed for the reader, explaining the use of pivotal questions, subquestions, medial summaries, and the final summary. Since the relationship of all of these to the aims is a matter of critical importance, the reader might want to review earlier sections where this was discussed before reading further.

A NOTE ON USING BEHAVIORAL OBJECTIVES

The perceptive reader will note that the objectives in this lesson are presented somewhat differently from those in earlier chapters. An alternative method of stating objectives is included to denote the way in which "behavioral" as opposed to "descriptive" objectives can be employed. Behavioral objectives require the teacher to:

1. Identify the *person or persons* who must perform the behavior.
2. Indicate the *specific behavior* which is intended (such as: "to locate," "to explain," or "to draw").
3. Name the *product or learning outcome* by which the achievement of the objective will be evaluated.
4. Specify the *conditions* under which the desired behavior will be performed (such as: "with the use of an outline map").
5. Establish the *standards or criteria* to be employed in evaluating student performance (such as: "must identify correctly five of the six original Common Market nations").

What follows is one possible formula for a behavioral objective.

Using information from the 1970 census, all students will be able to draw a map showing population density in their state. Rural and urban areas must be clearly distinguished, and four of the five largest urbanized centers (cities over 50,000) must be identified.

By writing the aim in this way, the learning process is explicitly set forth, and the factors needed for evaluating the results are specified. In a single statement, the content of that portion of the lesson, the learning procedures to be employed, the expected outcomes, the materials (census data and maps, in this case) to be used, and the means of evaluation are defined. The reader is urged to reexamine the objectives listed for the geography lesson and evaluate them in the light of the five criteria given above. It should be clear that they meet some, but not all, of the criteria. Try to rewrite the objectives so that they *do* conform to the formula. Study the following example. (The figures in parentheses identify the portion of the formula represented by various parts of the statement.)

Given an outline map of Southeast Asia on a 45-minute unit test (4), the student (1) will draw (2) the borders of North Vietnam, South Vietnam, Laos, and Cambodia (3), correct in relation to one another (5).

There is some disagreement among educators about the use of behavioral objectives.* This writer is neither for nor against them. The important thing is to *have* clearly recognized aims and to develop strategies for achieving them.

---

* For detailed discussions of behavioral objectives, see the following: Robert J. Armstrong et al., *Developing and Writing Behavioral Objectives* (Tucson, Arizona: Educational Innovators Press, 1968); Robert Kibler, Larry Barker, and David Miles, *Behavioral Objectives and Instruction* (Boston: Allyn and Bacon, 1970); Robert F. Mager, *Preparing Instructional Objectives* (Palo Alto, California: Fearon Publishers, 1962).

2. Using Community Resources

The teacher who fails to utilize the resources of his own community in teaching geography ought to turn in his pencil, retire from the educational profession, and get a job pumping gas. Every community, large and small, abounds with good source material. If, for example, a new highway is being built nearby, the class might examine such questions as, Why is the highway being built here? What geographic and economic factors led to its construction? How will our community be affected by it? In what way will it bring us closer to other communities? Will it help to create more jobs in the long run? What effect will it have on real estate values? On tax rates? The same approach could be used with a dam, a housing project, a park, or any other new facility.

GEOGRAPHY IN AN URBAN AGE—THE COURSE DEVELOPED BY THE HIGH SCHOOL GEOGRAPHY PROJECT

In 1970 the High School Geography project announced that its new course *Geography in an Urban Age* was available from the Macmillan Company. A sample kit, with a Teacher's Guide for each unit and representative student materials, is available from Macmillan. The teacher materials include media for a class of 30. There are transparencies, maps, activity sets, data sheets, and student manuals. A brief outline of the course follows.

Unit 1, Geography of Cities. Involves students in building a city. Students learn about factors influencing location, structure, and growth of cities. Land-use patterns are analyzed with topographic maps and aerial photographs.

Unit 2, Manufacturing and Agriculture. Students assume roles of manufacturers and farmers. They deal with manufacturing and agriculture around the world, and examine the problem of hunger around the world.

Unit 3, Cultural Geography. Slides, maps, and filmstrips are used in a study of cultural relativity. In one activity, students try to locate cities in the light of cultural clues which are provided. Trends toward cultural uniformity are examined.

Unit 4, Political Geography. Role-playing is used to get students involved in problems of distributing limited funds among sections of an imaginary state with different needs and interests, and in an international boundary dispute.

Unit 5, Habitat and Resources. Man and his natural environment are stressed. Areas similar in physical characteristics but different in the way man has modified the natural habitat are compared. The influence of geological characteristics on transportation, farming, and settlements is studied. Flood hazards, pollution, and conflicting interests in resource use are also analyzed.

Unit 6, Japan. Japan is compared with North America. Students study Japan's growth during the past 100 years and attempt to explain it. The possibility of applying the Japanese experience to underdeveloped areas should be examined.

(For information on availability and prices, see the September 1970 issue of the High School Geography Project's *Newsletter* or contact the Macmillan Company, School Division, 866 Third Avenue, New York, N.Y. 10022.)

Even without taking the entire class on field trips, the teacher can have his students study the landforms, waterways, climate, and other features of the immediate area. This can even be accomplished by having individuals make note of geographic features while traveling to and from school. Likewise, questions can be raised about why a community developed in one particular spot. Is it because of the confluence of two rivers? Because there is a good harbor nearby? What natural resources and features help to account for the economic activity of a region? (Why did agriculture fail and manufacturing succeed in New England, for example?) How does geography affect the way in which people in this region live? How does it affect values? For instance, to most people swimming, fishing, and boating are leisure-time activities. Yet for the children on the small, sparsely inhabited islands off our sea coasts, swimming, boating, and fishing were necessary for sheer survival.

Making maps of one's area can be an enjoyable activity, especially if it involves field work. It is not necessary that every student make the same kind of map. Some may concentrate on maps showing population, some on maps depicting economic activity, others on topography, others on climate and rainfall. Depending upon the aims of the teacher and the maturity and interests of the students, map-making can range from the use of simple symbols, colors, or shadings to rather sophisticated isometric lines.[1] Let the students have free reign to express their own creativity in map-making. In making product maps, for example, an artistic student may want to indicate dairying areas with a small drawing of a milk bottle or a cow, timber lands with drawings of trees, oil fields with pictures of oil wells, and the like.

The study of geography can be brought to bear on many local issues and problems. A controversial zoning ordinance, a proposal to set aside a tract of land as a wildlife preserve, or public opposition to a new power plant can each be examined for its possible effect on the existing environment and on the prevailing relationships between people and the land.

Most people now live in urban areas (an *urban place* is officially defined as any place with a population of 2,500 or more). Urban geography is a fascinating and vitally important science dealing with the spatial aspects of urban development.[2] Today, many cities are losing industries, the major reason being the obvious *lack of adequate space*. Another factor is that available space is often used inefficiently. Buildings that might be suitable for a manufacturer are too far from transportation facilities, markets, or sources of supply. Traffic congestion slows down deliveries and increases production costs. Poor planning and haphazard growth have characterized many of our cities, and they are now paying dearly for it. Here again, ignorance of geography helped to create these problems. With these problems becoming more severe, the urban geographer, who is concerned with location, interaction between manufacturers and suppliers, accessibility, distribution, circulation, and population movements, will undoubtedly be called upon (along with architects, economists, engineers, sociologists, and others) to help mitigate the ills of the cities.

Only a few of the activities that can be used in the geography class in the urban school have been mentioned here, but for a better understanding of the city, students might be asked to make a study of its structure. Does the *Concentric Zone Theory* (developed by Ernest W. Burgess with respect to Chicago) apply to other towns? According to this theory, cities have five generalized zones. See the accompanying diagram.

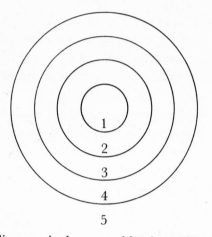

Zone 1 in the diagram is the central business district, the focal point of commerce, transportation, and social and civic life. It contains department stores, office buildings, hotels, major banks, and theaters. *Zone 2* is a transitional zone, typified by deteriorating houses, slums, poverty, crime, cheap roominghouses, and some light manufacturing. *Zone 3* contains workingmen's homes—the dwellings of laborers and factory workers who have moved out of Zone 2 but wish to be close to their jobs. *Zone 4* is a middle-class area inhabited by professional people, white-collar workers, and the owners of small businesses. *Zone 5* is the commuter's area. Often beyond the city's limits, it contains high-quality houses inhabited by many who have jobs or businesses in the central business district. To answer the questions, students would have to become intimately acquainted with their city and the way in which its space is utilized.

Studies might also be made of transportation in and around the city. Students in New York, for example, have learned that commuter railroads are much more efficient than automobiles in getting people to the city. (It was found that cars using one highway lane can transport 2,200 persons per hour over a given distance, while commuter trains can carry 50,000 people per hour.) Because of traffic congestion, it costs five times as much (in terms of man-hours of labor) to unload a truck in New York City's garment district than it does to unload the same truck in a suburban area. Even the problems of the poor are related to the city's geography and transportation factors. Residents in one of New

York's poorest ghettos find that it takes longer to get to an industrial area three miles away by public transportation than it does to get to a wealthy neighborhood seventeen miles away. Since there are more jobs for unskilled workers in the industrial area than in the wealthy neighborhood, the public transportation system is often cited as a factor inhibiting the initiative of the poor. Similarly, anyone who has flown to or from New York knows that it may take longer to get from midtown Manhattan to the airport than to get to one's destination in another part of the country. Those who suggest that New York's traffic problems can be alleviated by building underground parking garages may be failing to realize that Manhattan sits upon solid rock and that the costs of building underground facilities are greatly increased by this geological phenomenon.[3]

To learn what *can* be accomplished by the intelligent use of space and by careful planning, the students could study the *new towns,* such as Reston, Virginia, and Columbia, Maryland.[4] They might attempt to learn about the excellent zoning practices of such places as Manheim Township in Lancaster County, Pennsylvania,[5] where certain areas are reserved for farming and related services. Such questions as the following might be examined: "Can we apply these principles to our own area? If so, how? If not, what *can* we do? How can we best utilize our existing resources to promote our economic development?" To suggest that high school students can tackle these problems is *not* unrealistic. There are many cases in which elementary teachers have had their pupils study the geography of their area and develop feasible plans for development.

3. Studying Current Problems

The study of problems was implied in the previous section, for certainly poor transportation, the loss of industry, poverty neighborhoods, and other urban ills are crying for a solution. Other problems, such as pollution, conservation, the farm situation, and the balance of payments, all have aspects which require a knowledge of geographic situations. Perhaps the following two illustrations will make this point.

Since pollution is one such issue obviously related to geography, any unit dealing with this subject would of necessity have to include the issues mentioned below:

- Geographic features can contribute to air-pollution problems. (In one major city, mountains on the landward side prevent ocean breezes from blowing polluted air away. Thermal inversions are more common in hollows and valleys.)
- During a thermal inversion, a layer of warm air forms over an area and traps the cooler air beneath it. Pollutants which would normally move up and disperse over a wide area are trapped below, forming haze or smog. (Thermal inversions in such places as New York and London have caused hundreds of deaths.)
- The concentration of automobiles, industrial plants, and buildings into relatively small spaces is a major factor in air pollution.
- Mercury pollution has been found in the waterways of thirty-three of the fifty states.
- In the past waste could safely be discarded in streams when they had enough oxygen to sustain underwater life. Bacteria in the stream attacked the wastes, the bacteria were consumed by higher organisms, and the water was pure when it reached the next town. But as cities and towns grew, urban areas developed so close to one another that downstream towns were forced to use water polluted by upstream towns. The water no longer flowed far enough for oxygen, the sun's rays, green plants, dilution, and bacteria to purify it. (What is the water supply situation in *your* town or city?)
- Nearly half of the people in the United States are drinking water that is below federal standards of quality or of unknown quality.
- Pollution is costing the American people billions of dollars a year. In one way or another, everyone is paying the price.
- Some industries have been virtually destroyed by pollution. Commercial fishing has been terminated in some areas because of pollution. Pollution killed at least fifteen million fish in 1968.
- Great damage has been done to many forests and farm crops by air pollution. Who really pays for this?
- A geographic factor can have both positive and negative effects. For example, Baltimore's harbor is a major source of income to

that area, but the discharge of human waste from the 6,000 ships that enter that harbor each year is equal to the sewage of a city of 25,000 people.

- Good watershed management can help control pollution. A watershed acts as a giant blotter, sopping up and holding water in an area. Destruction of the timber in the area can cause water to run off too quickly, eroding the soil and polluting the streams. Are the rivers of *your* area protected by good watersheds?
- Recognizing that geographic factors often cross state lines, regional cooperation is often necessary to cope with pollution. Note, for example, the Ohio River Valley Water Sanitation Compact (ORSANCO), in which eight states joined together to clean up and protect this important waterway.[6]

There are, of course, many other geographic facts and concepts that can be used in a study of pollution.[7] The topic of pollution can be a separate study or part of a unit on conservation in general. A few ideas for teaching about conservation follow:

- *Soil conservation.* All food, directly or indirectly, comes from the soil. Cotton, linen, fur, wool, leather, and wood products depend upon the soil. Millions of acres of precious topsoil have been lost because of poor conservation practices. Students could study this problem for the nation as a whole and for their region in particular. What economic activities in your region depend upon the soil? Where are they located? Are there problems of erosion, leaching, and soil exhaustion? If so, what is causing them? What can be done to correct the situation?
- *Water conservation.* Study the water supply situation for the world, the United States, and for your region. How do we rely upon our waterways for transportation, recreation, industrial uses, drinking, and so on? What threats exist to our water supplies? What are the causes of flooding, pollution, and other such problems? Study the water cycle (or hydrologic cycle). What is a water table, and what is its importance? What is the level of the water table in our area? How much water is used by industry? By individuals? How

can we purify polluted water? How can we prevent further pollution in the future?

- *Forest and grass conservation.* Forests and grass help protect the soil from wind and water erosion and help prevent rivers and streams from flooding. They are also valuable resources, but much of our grassland has been depleted by such things as overgrazing. There are at least 4,000 uses for timber, but in one forty-year period the nation reduced its timber supply by 43 percent. Overexploitation of our timber, forest fires, diseases, and failure to reseed timber areas are some of the causes of the problem. What are the major timber areas of the United States? What industries rely on timber? How do we as individuals rely on timber? What has been the history of woodlands in your area? How can good forest management to ensure adequate supplies of timber in the future be established? How does the problem of forest and grass conservation relate to the other conservation problems (water, soil, wildlife)?

- *Mineral conservation.* Minerals are nonrenewable resources, and much of this nation's supply is being exhausted. Where are our major mineral deposits located? What is their importance to our economy? We burn more petroleum and natural gas in one year in the United States than nature can create in one *million* years. How long can we continue at this rate before exhausting our supplies? Can we rely upon foreign sources? If so, for which minerals? What steps can be taken to economize on our use of minerals?

- *Wildlife conservation.* Many wild creatures are very beneficial to man. (Note the value of the beaver in preventing floods and erosion, the value of birds in destroying insects, and the value of fish as a source of food.) Because of uncontrolled hunting, the destruction of natural habitats, and pollution, many valuable species are becoming extinct. What are the wild creatures of greatest importance to man? Where are they located? What is the wildlife situation in your area? (Even heavily populated urban areas have birds and other wildlife which somehow aid man.) What is the *balance of nature?* How is man helping to upset that balance? What problems is this causing? How can we help to preserve our valuable wildlife?

Teachers today are making good use of student interest in conservation and the problem of pollution.[8] Indeed, it would be possible to build an entire geography course around these two issues. Students could tackle real problems of their area and become active in some of the conservation organizations. They might study some of the controversies and conflicts, such as the fight among several states for the use of the waters of the Colorado River, issues involving the building of power plants, and damaging oil spills. (Note how students rallied in early 1971 when oil from a damaged tanker spilled into San Francisco Bay and threatened sea birds and other wildlife.) The study need not be confined to the United States, for the whole world is suffering from the same ills. (World consumption of raw materials in recent years has been outstripping the increase in population, leading to predictions of widespread poverty and hunger by the end of this century.) Since many young people have an admirable concern for the welfare of others, and many teachers are finding that their students want to know why millions of people are malnourished, why hundreds die every day from starvation, and why some nations get poorer while others become more affluent, geography may provide many of the answers, especially when linked to economics and the rest of the social sciences.

4. Case Studies

The problems discussed above are, indeed, case studies. But studies can also be made of situations which are not so directly and dramatically problem oriented. A study of the famous Seabrook Farms in New Jersey could show how farming can become an efficient and modern operation. Studies might be made of the Saint Lawrence Seaway, of the New York Port Authority, of the Delaware River Compact, and of the TVA. The work of such government agencies as the Bureau of Mines, the Geological Survey, the Bureau of Reclamation, the Forest Service, the Atomic Energy Commission, the Environmental Science Services Administration, the Soil Conservation Service, the Council on Environmental Quality, the Department of the Interior, the National Council on Marine Resources, the Extension Service, the Federal Advisory Council on Regional Economic Development, the Federal Power Commission, the Federal Water Quality Administration, the Fish and Wildlife Service, the Bureau of Land Management, the National Park Service, the Committee on Oceanography, the Bureau of Outdoor Recreation, and the Upper Great Lakes Regional Commission can be examined.[9] State and local agencies might be studied, along with relevant federal, state, and local legislation.[10]

5. Role-Playing, Games, and Simulation

Students could play the roles of city planners or of members of regional planning agencies, charged with the responsibility for developing feasible schemes for the development of their areas. They would have to study the many geographic, economic, social, and political features of the area (and the interrelationships among them) to develop intelligent and workable plans. Ideas could be obtained from the plans for Columbia, Maryland, or Reston, Virginia, and from the New York Regional Plan Association's materials.[11] The students might act as advisers to one of the underdeveloped nations. In recommending development plans they would have to learn about that nation's resources, state of its technology, the educational level of the population, economic relationships with other nations, and so on. In one of the activities contained in The High School Geography Project's *Demonstration Kit* (published in 1968), students examine the causes of floods, the adjustments people make to flood damage, how two similar habitats are used differently by man, and what factors affect the water supply. They must make decisions about the management of gaseous, liquid, and solid wastes. In one of the Project's simulation units ("Manufacturing and Agriculture" from *Using Simulation to Involve Students),* students become involved in an issue involving factory location. Given the specifications of a factory, its needs, and its production, teams, composed of five or six members, try to choose among several cities the best site for the firm. Among the roles assumed by the students are: (1) the firm's president; (2) the personnel manager; (3) the treasurer; (4) the sales manager. The students meet and discuss their needs and their individual responsibilities, do research on similar companies, study the cities available, and select a site. Each team makes a presentation to the rest of the class explaining why it made the choice it did. In the *Game of Farming,* students must make and justify decisions in a manner that dramatizes the risks farmers take. The *Game of Section* helps students understand conflicts of interest among sections in an imaginary state. They must consider political decisions involving resource use, public investment, and development. The Project's games can be integral parts of units on "The Growth of Cities," "The Geography of Culture Change," "Manufacturing," "Agriculture," and "the Political Process." In "Operation Bigger Beef" the students become members of research teams from the U.S. Department of State specializing in different regions of the world, selecting underdeveloped countries, and trying to aid them in cattle production.

INTEGRATING ECONOMICS WITH OTHER SOCIAL STUDIES SUBJECTS

Some ideas for combining economics and geography were set forth in the chapter on the teaching of economics. (Refer to the sections entitled "Studying the Region's Economy" and "Economics and Geography.") In this section the teaching of geography in history, political science, and sociology will be discussed.

1. Geography and History

It is the opinion of this writer that the social sciences are inseparable. One cannot ignore geography, economics, political science, sociology, and geography in a history course and still do a competent job of explaining historical trends and patterns. Indeed, many social scientists today are beginning to accept the idea that they can no longer exist in neat little compartments. Of course one may major in history, political science, or what have you; but some knowledge of all the other social sciences and of their relationship with one's own field is imperative. More colleges and schools are adopting interdisciplinary social science courses in which all of the disciplines are brought to bear upon the problems of the day. This is a healthy development even when separate courses continue to exist in each of the social sciences.

Herodotus (484-525 B.C.) is sometimes credited with being the father of history. He seldom failed to place historical events in a geographic setting, however, so some geographers also see him as the father of geography. Thus, there is nothing new about relating these two subjects. In studying American history, geography is a "must" when one deals with the voyages of discovery and the early explorations of the New World. Real or imagined similarities in climate and vegetation led early settlers to believe that America was much like their European homelands. But the geographic advantages and disadvantages of various regions were soon discovered. Natural harbors and rivers became the early sites of settlements, for obvious reasons. Settlers who failed to take geographic features into account often met with disaster. Students might study the settlement patterns in the North as compared with the South and ask which scheme was more functional—the compact towns of New England or the sometimes haphazard expansion in the South. In what ways did the early settlers use the natural environment wisely? Unwisely? What problems of government were presented by the topography and the patterns of settlement? How was early transportation and communication affected by geographic elements? What was the role of shipbuilding, fishing, and the carrying trade in the early American economy?

How did our geography affect the War of Independence? In what ways did it give us advantages over the British? Disadvantages? What geographic considerations entered into the peace settlement; into boundary questions then and later; into the writing of the Northwest Ordinance of 1787; into the writing of the Constitution? What problems did we have with the administration of public lands? How were our inland waterways important? To what extent did mountains impede settlement? What was the importance of the Lewis and Clark Expedition? How did geography enter into the problems we had with the Indians; with our neighbors, such as Canada and Mexico? What was the significance of the Louisiana Purchase? Of the Mexican War? Why did some Americans once feel that the West Coast should belong to *China?* What were the arguments for and against the purchase of Alaska? What problems were faced by people moving west? How did geography both hinder and encourage the building of transcontinental railroads? How effective was the Homestead Act, in the light of its stated purposes? What role did the discovery of gold play in America's development? How did the closing of the frontier affect us? One need do little more than scan a standard text in historical geography to come up with dozens of questions such as these.[12]

2. Geography and Political Science

Almost as obvious as the relationship between geography and American history is the relationship between geography and political problems. For example, students can compute the distance that a tanker would have to travel to carry oil from Kuwait to New York by going around Africa's Cape of Good Hope and compare this with the distance if the ship could use the Suez Canal. Such a simple analysis would make graphic the political and diplomatic costs of the Suez Canal's closure. The strategic position of the Suez Canal could be a subject for study, along with the Panama Canal, the Mediterranean, the Dardanelles, the Bosporous, and many other similar waterways. What is the relationship between the problem in the Middle East and the fact that this area is on the crossroads of continents and sea arms? In what ways has geography been used as an instrument of political control? Did many nations locate their capitals near the geographic center of the country so that armies could be sent easily to any point where a rebellion might occur? Did the Romans show an understanding of geography in the building of their roads? For example, were the roads placed in such a way that legions could be sent to rebellious provinces quickly? Have some countries been protected by geographic features (such as mountains and oceans) while others have been vulnerable? Has geography affected important treaties? Are some historians right in saying that our geography helped promote the development of local democracy, since the vastness of our land and the natural features which impeded transportation made it difficult for the central government to exercise its authority? How is the problem of government different in a land such as Somalia, where many of the people are nomads, from that in a land more conducive to stable agricultural settlements? What problems are created for the Ethiopian government when Somali nomads wander into Ethiopian territory seeking water and grass for their camels? What geographic features in Europe led to the development of the Common Market and may possibly lead to a united European government? In what ways have such problems as pollution, conservation, and low farm incomes brought about more government involvement in the economy? [13]

3. Geography and Sociology

There is disagreement among some geographers on the extent to which geography shapes patterns of living. Without doubt, however, geography can have some effect on human attitudes, values, habits, and mores. What must be avoided is the notion that geography *determines* these things in any automatic way. For example, the climate and topography of New England had some effect on the way in which the earlier settlers lived, but most of their values, habits, and attitudes were formed long before they arrived. A barren and inhospitable land might affect people in different ways. Some might be impelled to join with other people in meeting the challenge posed by the harshness of the land. Others might become fiercely competitive, thinking that the land cannot support everyone and thus that only the strong and ruthless will survive. Or elements of both may occur.

The life of the Somali nomad has clearly been affected by adverse environmental conditions. In this semidesert land, poorly endowed with water and grazing resources, most of the people attempt to eke out a meager existence by raising sheep, goats, and camels. Because water and grass are scarce, they travel in small groups and often clash in bloody tribal encounters with other such groups. Thus, the Somali people value physical strength and aggressiveness. Strangers are greeted with suspicion and hostility; yet, on the other hand, there is an unwritten code of hospitality. A lone Somali will often set off on a journey on foot, with no food or water, confident that he will receive sustenance from any other Somali he meets on the way.

The life of the pastoral nomad is idealized in Somalia. Only the members of lowly outcast groups would engage in such degrading occupations as shoemaking or metalwork. Tending camels is noble and is reserved for the men and boys. Since camels are not easy to handle, the women and girls tend the sheep and goats. This sometimes causes family separations, for the camels can wander far from the water holes while the sheep and goats must cluster near them. And as a consequence Somali men usually give no thought to being far from their families for long periods. Thus, divorce is very common, and a man may have as many as four wives at one time. (Few avail themselves of this privilege, however, for it is a costly and troublesome proposition.) Although looked upon as inferior to the man, the Somali woman is actually tough, self-reliant, and influential. (She has to be to survive.)

The camel is "the Cadillac of Somalia." The ownership of many camels helps a man to acquire more prestige. Values are often expressed in camels; damages in civil suits in the Kadi courts are assessed in numbers of camels rather than in money. The number of camels a man and his family give to the family of his bride reflects, in part, the value he places upon the woman. An educated girl (a rarity in Somalia) commands a much higher camel price, for example. Because the camel helps the Somali to survive in a land that defies survival, its value is often beyond computation. This is clearly reflected in the literature of the Somali, especially in the poetry. Note the following verses from love poems:

> Like a camel sick to the bone,
> Weakened and withering in strength,
> So I, from love of you,
> Oh Dudi, grow wasted and gaunt.
>   • • •
> All your beauty is to me
> Like a place where the new grass sways,
> After the blessing of the rain,
> When the sun unveils its light.

When the Somali poet wishes to pay the highest possible compliment to his loved one, he compares her to "a place where the new grass sways"—for such a place means life itself to him.

Finally, the teacher might go *beyond* the social studies in providing instructional experiences for his students. Quantitative techniques are important in geography, so perhaps the mathematics teacher can cooperate in such things as correlation analysis (such as an analysis of the correlation between population growth and fuel consumption). There are many ways of relating science lessons to geography. Studies of climate and the weather, earth science, and oceanography are but a few.[14] In this chapter are described only a few of the many ways in which geography can be taught in an interesting manner, but for the potentially creative teacher these descriptions can be expanded into an almost infinite number of stimulating lessons.

NOTES

1. For a brief and simple discussion of the use of maps (including the employment of isometric lines), see Jan O. M. Broek, *Compass of Geography* (Columbus, Ohio: Charles E. Merrill, 1966), pp. 64-71.
2. A good college-level text on urban geography is Raymond E. Murphy's *The American City* (New York: McGraw-Hill, 1966). The High School Geography Project's unit *Inside the City* offers many interesting suggestions for teaching urban geography.
3. See George G. Dawson, "Applying Analytical Economics to Regional Studies," *Economic Education Experiences of Enterprising Teachers*, vol. V (New York: Joint Council on Economic Education, 1968).
4. Write The Rouse Company, c/o Information Department, Village of Cross Keys, Baltimore, Maryland 21210, for information on *Columbia Today* and other publications.
5. Jean Gottman, *Megalopolis: The Urbanized Northeastern Seaboard of the United States* (Cambridge, Massachusetts: The M.I.T. Press, 1961), p. 331.
6. For an excellent history of the compact, see Edward J. Cleary, *The ORSANCO Story* (Baltimore: The Johns Hopkins Press for Resources for the Future, Inc., 1967).
7. For other ideas on teaching about pollution, see Harold Wolozin, *The Economics of Pollution* (New York: The Joint Council on Economic Education, 1970). This pamphlet contains sections on the teaching of

pollution by Patricia Reilly. Also see Patricia Reilly, "Teaching About Environmental Pollution," *Social Education* (January 1971).

8. Two of the outstanding organizations providing information on these problems are Resources for the Future, Inc., 1755 Massachusetts Avenue, N.W., Washington, D.C. 20036, and The Conservation Foundation, 1250 Connecticut Avenue, N.W., Washington, D.C. 20036. An excellent text-book for secondary level students is *Our Natural Resources*, 3d ed., by P. E. McNall and Harry B. Kircher (Danville, Illinois: The Interstate Printers and Publishers, 1970).

9. A good source that should be on hand in all social studies classrooms is *The United States Government Organization Manual* (Washington, D.C.: Government Printing Office, published annually). For ideas for case studies, see Richard M. Highsmith, ed., *Case Studies in World Geography* (Englewood Cliffs, New Jersey: Prentice-Hall, 1961).

10. An outstanding source of information on federal legislation is *Congress and the Nation, 1945-1964* (Washington, D.C.: Congressional Quarterly Service, 1965). This huge volume has nearly 2,000 pages of data.

11. For a list of its publications, write the Regional Plan Association, 230 West Forty-first Street, New York, N.Y. 10036.

12. Two good texts (for the college level) on historical geography are Ralph H. Brown, *Historical Geography of the United States* (New York: Harcourt, Brace & Company, 1948), and Ray Allen Billington, *Westward Expansion: A History of the American Frontier* (New York: The Macmillan Company, 1949).

13. See Paul Buckholts, *Political Geography* (New York: The Ronald Press, 1966). This is a good standard text showing the relationships between geography and politics.

14. The U.S. Naval Oceanographic Office has published a set of Ocean Science Study Kits for students and teachers. Teacher kits are $3.20; student kits are $1.60. Write the Naval Oceanographic Distribution Office, 5801 Tabor Avenue, Philadelphia, Pennsylvania 19120.

CHAPTER IX

Teaching American History

by Herbert I. London

WHY TEACH AMERICAN HISTORY?

For the past two decades spokesmen for the teaching of American
History have argued, somewhat as Thucydides did, that history should
be *de*romanticized and told *exactly* as events of the past occurred. While
this view has obvious appeal, even if it is not entirely practical, it has
ignored and tended to obscure the myths on which a national heritage
are based. What is singularly omitted from this "objective" approach
are the reasons why myths arise and survive despite the best efforts of
the historians to refute them.

If American history recounts the collective memory of the people,
there is every reason to assume that those recollections are inexact,
reflecting what many wished rather than what actually happened.
Still, this memory bank, with all its inaccuracies, is one of society's
compasses that guides man into the future.

The study of American history is therefore indispensable, not only to
discover where we came from, but who we are. And in so doing the
mythology takes on almost as much significance as the factual
evidence. Knowing that George Washington did not cut down the
cherry tree probably has less importance than knowing why the myth
had national acceptance. Similarly, debunking Paul Bunyan's exploits
is not as interesting as discovering why his exaggerated achievements
made the annals of classical folklore. In a very real sense legend is

184

history, for it tells about the aspirations, superstitions, and customs of a people. Folklore is also useful insofar as the historical setting is established. Horatio Alger makes sense only as a pre-World War I mythical hero, while Tom Rath is obviously understandable only as a 1950s antihero.

From the growth of mental attitudes and from the evolution of historical events, the qualities of nationhood emerged. It is around these attitudes and events that an American history course should be molded. To understand the past is not perforce to guarantee its acceptance; on the contrary, sifting the evidence may very likely produce skepticism. But this is the chance an educator takes in the hope the questioning, critical mind will also be the one best equipped to make the history of another era.

A second, somewhat hackneyed, reason for studying American history is the mental training it affords its students. As a discipline it can develop analytical skills, give events space-time coordinates, and increase one's ability to make decisions.

That the historical method can develop—sharpen, at the very least —analytical skills is obvious. In fact, once the method is sufficiently mastered, it serves to inhibit precipitous conclusions, assertions without proof, simplistic cause-and-effect relationships, post hoc fallacies, and the host of logical inconsistencies that characterize untrained minds. American history is particularly well adapted to this method, since widespread exposure to the media has undoubtedly given all students exposure to some aspects of American life. A discussion of the "causes" of recent events from urban riots to American involvement in the Vietnam war can, without elaborate preparation, elicit student responses and consequent methodological procedures.

No less important is the ability to conceive of events in a time continuum and a social context. Presumably, studying past epochs will give the present one a clearer focus, even if it does not necessarily preclude the possibility of committing the past's mistakes. Studying the compromises at the Constitutional Convention and those compromises of the 1830s, 1840s, and 1850 might have illustrated the differences inherent in the national system, but recognizing these potential conflicts probably could not have prevented them and the subsequent Civil War. Still, the study of the past may at times prevent superficial antidotes for long-standing problems. The reaction of the New Deal to the economic vicissitudes of the 1930s, notwithstanding the controversy surrounding it, was, at least in part, a studied response to the question of how to control economic depressions. By studying the climate in which events occur, the complexities of social evolution and the variety of societal responses to similar events may become apparent. The nation's reaction to Andrew Jackson's "pet banks" and William Howard Taft's concessions to private bankers was obviously different, yet the actions themselves were in the main similar. Likewise, it has been argued that the Vietnam commitment was, at least in the minds of its architects, a response not dissimilar from that in the Korean conflict. Yet even when the nuances and obvious differences are noted, they do not account for the different public responses to the two events.

Historical studies have the potential of presenting to students problems whose solution will not permit glib group discussions. A skilled teacher can present issues that depend on a thorough familiarity with the chain of historical events responsible for a particular problem. For example, the attempt of collective political action to control monopolistic economic interests is best understood by tracing the development of the Populists, Progressives, and New Dealers and their proposals for dealing with the problem. This kind of study doesn't assure greater ability to make decisions, but it is the kind of exercise that encourages more sophisticated consideration of the contingencies that account for specific events. Concurrently, the study of historical problems permits students to test actual solutions with their own hypothetical solutions. In most cases students will casually dismiss the errors they can identify with historical hindsight, but careful examination of the possible consequences of their decisions may lead to greater modesty and greater appreciation of critical decision-making. By simulating Lincoln's major decisions during the Civil War or Eisenhower's response to the U-2 crisis or Kennedy's decision during the 1962 Missile Crisis, students may be freed of the belief that solutions, without hazards, are easily achieved. With the escalation of rhetorical simplicities and societal complexities, the mind's analytical

attributes—its problem-solving capacities—assume greater importance every day.

Consistent with the aim of encouraging analytical skills is the
development of the politically conscious citizen. This much-discussed
goal still seems beyond our grasp, but it has been self-consciously
mentioned as an educational objective by every social commentator
from Dewey to Conant. In a practical sense, familiarity with the
national heritage should lead to more intelligent political decision-
making in order to maintain the viability of government institutions.
Presumably, apathy is the greatest danger to truly representative
political systems; without the vote, with blind choice, or with one
choice, the representative character of democracy is lost. The study of
American history can describe the virtues of a representative system as
well as the flaws, but it can also impress upon students their obligation
to participate intelligently in the electoral process. Those students who
maintain that the vote is a sham, "a liberal hoax," or an empty gesture
threaten the perpetuation of the representative heritage. Ignoring the
means for change can reflect a faith in the status quo, a complete lack
of faith in the electoral system of politics, or an unconcern with social
conditions. In each case, regardless of the motives, a challenge has been
presented to the political system that could in fact sound its death
knell. It is not an overstatement to suggest that a public aware of its
national antecedents could prevent the breakdown in the representative system. For some, this is little more than a conservative conclusion;
but for those grounded in the nation's history, it is an expression of the
belief that change through an enlightened electorate is endemic to the
American political process.

CONTENT

The story of American life is variously related chronologically,
topically, problematically, and systematically. Each approach has advantages; yet each is also flawed. Either the underlying concept is that
history is a total record of the past, including art, literature, politics,
law, religion, philosophy, and so on, or that history is best examined as
a microcosm, a source of intensive analysis. The two assumptions are

not necessarily incompatible, but in practice that often appears to be the case.

Since no historian can possibly examine all the records and documents of every government, not to say every generation or each individual in that generation, he relies on the collected material of archivists, a process that is inherently selective and very often unconsciously arbitrary. The chronologically oriented historian attempts to start at the beginning and, by sifting through collected records, suggests the important acts and men that have changed national events. Approaching his subject as a relatively orderly progression, this kind of historian selects from the already collected documents in order to present a coherent record of the past. In order to denote periods of dramatic change, he often demarcates eras or epochs, a shorthand way of dividing his available material. The method, while the one most often chosen by historians, raises several fundamental questions. What is the beginning? When, for example, does American history commence—with Columbus, the Indians, the Vikings, or perhaps the Asians who at various times frequented the West Coast of America? How does one determine what are important events? Are those situations having national significance to be preferred over those having local or personal importance? And if so, does one run the risk of writing a history that ignores the common man? Can one be sure that the archivist's collection of records is complete or accurate? And even if there is no reason to doubt their veracity, how does one select the data to be emphasized? Does a chronological progression exist in history? Or are events more often moving in different directions; or are they overlapping or subject to arbitrary rise and decline? Does a chronological approach very often suggest a post hoc assumption, a feeling that what came after was a consequence of what came before? Isn't the idea of denoting eras a way of imprisoning ideas? What, after all, does the Jacksonian Age mean when Jackson was no longer president? When did the Progressive Era begin or end? Or has it ended? Is the Age of Big Business anything more than a useful phrase in which to fit information relating to the modern corporation? A chronological orientation poses, at the very least, these hazards and challenges. Since most textbooks are organized in this way, teachers usually opt for this approach; but it is merely one way of discussing the content of American history and as such should not be used exclusively.

A second method of organizing American history is by topics. This method often involves a chronological approach for a specific area. For example, the rise of unions from the Knights of Labor to the AFL-CIO merger. Or it may involve a "problems" approach for a certain unit; for example, What role did geography play in developing political attitudes? But the central feature of the method is its thorough examination of separate aspects of American history—labor, industry, politics, foreign affairs, and so on. The criticism of this approach is the difficulty in applying data from one area to another. Presumably the totality is blurred or, at least, less comprehensible for the student than the chronological approach. Crosscurrents are usually not emphasized. And the whole issue of transfer is very often dependent on a student's ability to see relationships and the teacher's concern with emphasizing them.

A "problems" method has the kind of elemental simplicity and emphasis on contemporaneousness that has an irresistible appeal for students. It is an approach that demands policies, that forces students to speculate. In the analysis of a problem such as "Why has pollution become a national dilemma?" a natural corollary is "What programs should be adopted to most efficiently control pollutants?" In order to find solutions, a situation should be studied, however retroactively, in which pollution was not a problem with national repercussions. For some, the *zeitgeist* is all that counts: "our times provide our solutions." But for those not subscribing to the obvious fallacy, the past can be a useful guide, even if it suggests only what not to do. The warning that should accompany utilization of the method is that student solutions should not only be feasible; they must also be politically acceptable. Could, for example, rigid government pollution bills be passed as long as key industries have the power to suspend such legislation? Would the employees of a polluting industry accept such legislation if the consequence of its passage were their unemployment? Speculation, therefore, is only valid if seen within the constraints of reality, a lesson that usually frustrates but rarely fails to enlighten.

The last approach may be the boldest. A systems analysis infers the study of stated objectives, the methods used to implement those objectives, and the measurement of the relative ability to achieve the objectives. If New Deal legislation was partially designed to curb the effects of the depression, one can isolate the economic acts sponsored by President Roosevelt, measure their effect on the standard economic indicators—unemployment rate, interest rate, investment rate, gross national product, etc.—and evaluate the extent to which stated goals were achieved. The method depends on a careful analysis of objectives. But this is precisely the contentious point. Politicians are imprecise by design; ambiguity may be translated into political capital. Similarly, history as a system cannot always account for fortuity, the forces of chance that are not predictable and that obscure value judgments. To continue the analogue, was Roosevelt's accomplishment his spiritual force, his ability to maintain faith in the system—a factor that could not be predicted from his patrician background? And if this assertion is valid, how does a historian measure or even delineate his spiritual effect?

The real concern for the teacher of American history is not what approach to use but why it is being used. If the study of American history has some relationship to political decision-making and to the development of national identification, and of analytical skills, then data should be identified that complement the objectives of the course. In far too many cases little attention is paid to the fundamental reasons for teaching a course—leading, as one might expect, to a situation in which results cannot be predicted. An essential dimension of the teacher's role is making this kind of decision before the semester begins, before he even steps into the classroom. Content, and the approach to it, often emerges from this decision-making process.

A complementary consideration for every teacher should be the structure of American history as a discipline. Perception of history differs from one epoch to the next. At times, the differences seem illusory or trivial, but they do remain. Nonetheless, one can still refer to conceptions that are endemic to history and universally applied. What is the peculiar subject matter that only an American historian will investigate? What particular competencies must he possess to carry on his work? What modes of inquiry must he employ to seek explanations?

What is the expected outcome of the investigation? These are the questions that define a discipline and that give direction to a course. Presumably, student directed and conducted research is a course objective if the teacher expects the development of analytical skills. Yet in order to reach this goal, competencies must be defined and encouraged, various modes of inquiry explored—the historical method, systems analysis, polling, content analysis, etc.—and conclusions subjected to rigorous tests of logic and verisimilitude. Only by stressing the structure of history as a discipline can the pluralism of causes, ephemeral answers, and differential perceptions make sense to a student. American history has no guaranteed locus of truth; it is only as reliable as the inquiry that produced it.

STRATEGIES

If what makes an American distinctive is the combined past of other Americans, then teaching strategies should necessarily reflect the records of those Americans. And in examining those records one cannot be restrictive: a poem or song or personal budget can be as valuable as historical tools as personal memoirs. In fact, the basic rule guiding research for the historian applies equally to the teacher of American history: do not arbitrarily exclude evidence that could provide another insight about the past. The teacher is obliged to explore the primary materials, the artifacts, the contrasting interpretations, and the literature, for they represent his teaching strategies.

One very effective way to observe changing American social attitudes is in song lyrics. In 1931 one of the most popular tunes was "Life Is Just a Bowl of Cherries":

> Life is just a bowl of cherries
> Don't take it serious, it's too mysterious
> You work, you save, you worry so
> But you can't take it with you when you
> go, go, go.
> Oh life is just a bowl of cherries so
> live and laugh at it all.

The lyrics reflect a naïve insouciance, as well as good-humored fatalism—values that were consonant with a generation eager to forget a war, yet unsure about the future. One year later (1932) Jay Gorney's "Brother, Can You Spare a Dime" captured the heartbreaking anguish of the beginning of the Depression.

> They used to tell me I was building a dream,—
> And so I followed the mob
> When there was earth to plough or guns to bear—
> I was always there—right there on the job.
> They used to tell me I was building a dream
> With peace and glory ahead—
> Why should I be standing in line just waiting for
> bread?

The contrast between the two songs is obvious. Yet despite their differences, both songs capture the historical atmosphere of their eras in a way that sometimes eludes the professional historian.

Art is another historical reflector. By examining, as opposed to just looking at, art objects, one can obtain ideas about a period, about its problems, conflicts, beliefs, and achievements. The basic strategy is simple. From an analysis of art objects, particularly art schools, one can generate hypotheses about a certain era.

In the period immediately after national independence, artists whose styles were shaped by the colonial age could not, perhaps would not, extricate themselves from a derivative European school of painting. Self-conscious about the lack of a distinctive American tradition, these artists imported and maintained a dry and formal neoclassicism in the New World. Rather than seek new solutions for art in a newly created state, they fought to maintain the only art familiar to them. Their attitude has been described as "extreme nationalistic self-consciousness." Some historians argue that the post-Revolutionary period was filled with this kind of social ambivalence. On the one hand, independence encouraged assertiveness; on the other, independence led to insecurity. Despite proclamations of new and distinctive social forms, men tended to act in a manner that was obviously akin to the colonial customs and manners they knew best. This is one historical hypothesis readily explored through an analysis of the paintings of De Peyster Manner and his contemporaries.

With the Age of Jackson and his presumed tide of democratic assertiveness appeared a group of painters eager to satisfy an American yearning for paintings of their own lands. Thomas Cole and his followers Asher Durand, John Kensett, and John Casilear (the Hudson River school) discovered their native land and a native style. Their paintings, for example, *Oxbow of the Connecticut, Kindred Spirits, Delaware Water Gap*, reflected the spirit of a nation that had come of age. The crudeness of their style compared to that of the Europeans was unnoticed by a public that wanted to capture the vision of the New World. And this the Hudson River painters gave them. Without stretching the analogy, one can find that Andrew Jackson, despite his personal predilections, became the symbol of national assertiveness, democratization, leveling, and American distinctiveness. His style was consciously imitating the stereotypical common man. He was nationalistic, outwardly forceful, seemingly contemptuous of tradition, and was a reflection of the historical tide that produced the Hudson River school.

When national interest focused on reform, painting, and particularly its subject, changed as well. At the turn of the nineteenth century came a rise in social reform inspired by a new interest in the proletariat. One art school, mocked by the critics as the Ashcan school because of its interest in slums, soon captured the muckraking indignation of this progressive era. The Ashcan painters may not have been as outraged at social conditions as were Jacob Riis or John Spargo, but they did shift the emphasis in art from bucolic hills to urban life. Elevated trains, baby carriages in parks fringed by skyscrapers, vaudeville, and air made gray with smoke were part of the new genre. In many respects these painters marked the end of an age of innocence—the American *fin de siècle*. The style was still curiously romantic even though America's future was identified as pragmatic and realistic. Through painting, a generation observed its present while tenaciously clutching to thoughts of a past, less complex age.

These illustrations present one useful strategy for distilling the endless facts about American life. In fact, teaching strategies of any kind are designed to bridge a gap between the fragmented vision of the past and the contemporary student world. Another teaching tool that attempts to establish this reciprocal relationship is poetry. For poetry, like history, is written to suggest where we have been, are, and will be. Similarly, poetry, like history, reflects the spirit of an era as much as it does the personal feelings of its creator.

Robert Frost's "The Gift Outright" discusses, in a way Frederick Jackson Turner would have appreciated, the effect of abundant and seemingly omnipresent land on the American nation. William Cullen Bryant captured emerging nineteenth-century romanticism and nationalism when, in "Thanatopsis," he wrote, "Go forth, under the open sky, and listen to Nature's teachings"—a statement presaging Horace Greeley's advice to young men. And Edna St. Vincent Millay, a disillusioned poet of her times, portrayed the carefree character of the rebellious 1920s when she wrote:

> My candle burns at both ends;
>   It will not last the night
> But oh, my foes, and oh, my friends—
>   It gives a lovely light! *

Obviously the poet, if true to his times, presents a historical legacy for all times. That explains why poetry is a teaching source that illuminates the past and partially explains some of the universal forces motivating men at any time.

Using primary materials whether they are poems, paintings or songs automatically involves the investigator in determining their authenticity. Access to primary sources opens a range of teaching strategies. For example, determining the composer and origins of the song "We Shall Overcome" could demonstrate the basic techniques in historical investigation. Any number of answers might apply: Pete Seeger wrote the song after hearing one verse of it in the South; two black men associated with a labor movement wrote it; it's an old Scottish tune; or none of the aforementioned is valid. Studying Gilbert Stuart's portraits

* "First Fig" from *A Few Figs from Thistles* (Harper and Brothers, 1918).

of George Washington offers two similarly perplexing questions for students: How does one know Stuart was the painter? And how can one be sure Washington was his subject?

This particular strategy is a way to elicit curiosity. There are several educators who maintain that history should be taught *only* as an inquiry. On this point there is unlikely to be any consensus. Teaching American history should involve a variety of techniques, since no one method affords all the answers.

In recent years the realization that interpretations do inevitably vary has led to a strategy in which competing interpretations are juxtaposed and considered for their relative merit. Perhaps the following will serve as illustrations: Franklin Roosevelt was, was not a "conservative"? Andrew Jackson was, was not in favor of a strong federal system? The attack on Pearl Harbor was, was not a surprise invasion? Alexander Hamilton was, was not in the "conservative" tradition? The Populists were, were not reformers? Postwar American foreign policy was, was not a response to Soviet aggression? The Civil War was, was not irrepressible? The Founding Fathers did, did not want to retain the slave institution? "Rugged individualism" was, was not a frontier myth?

If, as John Dewey suggested, the student learns most effectively by doing, simulating historical situations in the classroom so that students are actors should work effectively. Most teachers assume that students cannot "make" history, and, indeed, they probably cannot. But students have the capacity to re-create it, to solve similar problems as they arise anew. This is the purpose of historical games.

While there are many games already mass produced, the teacher would do well to create one of his own. For example, decisions in American foreign policy can be argued by describing a Communist coup in the Caribbean on the island of "Domhaiba." The situation, including the number of insurgents, the previous government, relationship between the island and nearby islands, implications for security in the region, effect on regional power relationships, and the potential consequences for the island's people, should all be detailed. Decision-making roles could then be assigned with a list of primary responsibilities and concerns for each official (secretaries of defense, state; chairman of National Security Agency, Joint Chiefs of Staff, other cabinet members, chairmen of the Senate and House foreign relations committees, the ambassador to "Domhaiba," etc.) Let each assigned student write an independent scenario including his description and evaluation of the situations and recommendations for government action. Proceed to let the class act out their scenarios and then compare their conclusions with the published reports of similar situations—American intervention in the Dominican Republic, for example. In this author's opinion, learning of this kind apprises students, in a way rarely achieved through other techniques, of the relative costs, benefits, risks, and rewards of alternative decisions-making. And even if mistakes are made, which is both inevitable and desirable, they will be historical errors—wrong decisions—not student mistakes—an inability to remember the name of the British vessel sunk by a German submarine in 1915. Game theory is one strategy that incorporates the human dimension of analytic problem-solving into the American history classroom.

INTEGRATING AMERICAN HISTORY
AND OTHER DISCIPLINES

Notwithstanding the efforts of some university and public school educators to maintain discrete departments, American history remains a subject that is at once part anthropology, economics, geography, political science, sociology, psychology, and, of course, history. History by its very nature is already integrated.

Any discussion of American life ultimately suggests something about American character and organizations. For the historian, an anthropologist such as Margaret Mead has invaluable clues about the American system. In *Keep Your Powder Dry* and more recently *Culture and Commitment* Professor Mead describes some relationships between child-rearing practices, national values, and cultural antecedents that encourage historical analyses with completely different kinds of hypotheses from the conventional historian. The economist John Kenneth Galbraith is not only writing polemics about a "more efficient" economic arrangement; he has indicated how certain economic assumptions held by nineteenth-century classical economists have precipitated major crises in our history, including the Great Depression. Frederick Jackson Turner relied on geographic evidence to deduce a theory of the American frontier—a theory so pervasive that for two generations even those historians skeptical about its implicit determinism still went to the trouble of coming to grips with the argument's implications. Samuel Lubell, by relying on behavioral political techniques, provides as much insight into the factors that created the New Deal's political coalition as all of the histories of the pre-New Deal era. Max Weber's theories of Protestantism and its effect on the capitalist system are cited, almost as a cliché, by every serious student of America's past. In several respects the theory, regardless of its validity, has played so prominent a role among social scientists that many have obtained prominence and "made" history by relying on Weber's findings. One could argue that Weber's notion has not only served as a source for explaining the past, but that it has also been a catalyst for factors in the history it was designed to interpret. The recent publication of Woodrow Wilson's biography by Bullock and Freud once again points out the contribution that Sigmund Freud and psychological theory have made to understanding American history. Many findings in psychology, as is the case with other social sciences, remain inconclusive, but the theoretical models suggested by psychology have been used to test historical phenomena. One can only guess that Wilhelm Reich's *Mass Psychology of Fascism* will serve as a model for a future history of American social events in the 1980s.

For the student of America's past, ideas are not restricted by disciplines; American history becomes more intelligible when it is interlarded with the theories and formulations of the other social sciences. This is one lesson future teachers should try to remember and employ.

BIBLIOGRAPHY

Barzun, Jacques, and Graff, Henry. *The Modern Researcher*. New York: Harcourt, Brace & World, 1957.

Bassett, John Spencer. *The Middle Group of American Historians*. New York: Macmillan Co., 1917.

Brubaker, Dale, ed. *Innovation in the Social Studies.* New York: Thomas Crowell Co., 1968.

Commager, Henry. *The Nature and Study of History.* Columbus, Ohio: Charles Merrill Books, 1966.

Feldman, Martin, and Seifman, Eli, eds. *The Social Studies: Structure, Models, and Strategies.* Englewood Cliffs, New Jersey: Prentice-Hall, Inc., 1969.

Fenton, Edwin. *The New Social Studies.* New York: Holt, Rinehart & Winston, Inc., 1966. Chapters 27, 29.

Gardiner, P., ed. *Theories of History.* Glencoe, Illinois: The Free Press, 1959.

Hofstadter, Richard. *The Progressive Historians.* New York: Alfred Knopf, 1968.

Metcalf, Lawrence, in N. L. Gage, ed., "Research on Teaching the Social Studies," in *Handbook of Research on Teaching.* Chicago: Rand McNally, 1963.

Muller, Herbert. *The Uses of the Past.* New York: Oxford University Press, 1957.

New York State Department of Secondary Education. *Teaching American History.* Bureau of Secondary Curriculum Development, New York State Education Department, Albany, New York.

Niebuhr, Reinhold. *The Irony of American History.* New York: Charles Scribner's Sons, 1952.

Oliver, Donald, and Shaver, James. *Teaching Public Issues in the High School.* Boston: Houghton Mifflin, 1966.

Popper, Karl. *The Poverty of Historicism.* Boston: Beacon Press, 1957.

Shaver, James, and Berlak, Harold, eds. *Democracy, Pluralism, and The Social Studies.* New York: Houghton Mifflin, 1968.

Wish, Harvey. *The American Historian.* New York: Oxford University Press, 1960.

CHAPTER X

Teaching World Civilization

by Leon Clark and Donald Johnson

I have made a ceaseless effort not to ridicule, not to bewail,
nor to scorn human actions, but to understand them.

—Spinoza

AROUND THE WORLD IN 180 DAYS

In 1873 Jules Verne sent his hero, Phileas Fogg, around the world in
eighty days. Fogg took his servant with him to share the adventure.
The servant was appropriately named Passepartout, the French word
for picture frame, or a mat on whih a photograph or other impression is
made.

More than one hundred years later, world history teachers are doing
the same thing as Fogg, except that now the trip takes 180 days and the
impressions are made on 120 high school sophomores instead of on one
Passepartout. In point of fact, however, Fogg spent much more time on
his trip than students do today. A school year of 180 days means
approximately 100 hours of social studies instruction, considering the
length of class periods, the interruptions for other school activities, and
the time spent on logistic concerns.

Our academic Fogg, however, is an intrepid traveler; and, once he
takes off, he follows an impressive itinerary. With his reluctant passengers in their seats, he flies over 3,000 years of world history, moving

chapter by inevitable chapter from Ancient Egypt to World War II—if he is lucky enough to get that far. Fogg, it should be acknowledged, is a well-organized leader; besides the textbook guide, he provides countless ditto sheets of additional information, distilling and synthesizing for his passengers all the important facts they must know. They "must know," for example, the major Egyptian Pharaohs like Thutmose, Ramses, Hatshepsut, Ikhnaton, and of course Cleopatra and her famous nose. Nobody knows *why* he "must know" all this, except that there will be a test, and that is sufficient reason for some of the passengers who are anxious to complete Fogg's trip so they can take another one next year.

From Egypt and Mesopotamia Fogg goes to "The glory that was Greece and the grandeur that was Rome." Again there are more chapters, more lists, more notes, and as time becomes the enemy, there is more lecturing from a frantic Fogg. As winter approaches, Fogg's voice becomes a bit more strident. "You must know Solon, Draco, Cleisthenes, Pythagoras, Thales, Pindar, Socrates, Plato, Aristotle, Themistocles, Vergil, Cicero, Horace, Livy, Plontinus, Cato, Domitian, Hadrian, Constantine, Tiberius Gracchus, Octavian, Marcus Aurelius, Pepin, Charles Martel, Charlemagne, Alfred, and William. And then the battles and their causes and their results. And when these books, these works of art, these places, and these inventions."

This pattern continues until June. Fogg may occasionally wonder about the value of what he is doing, but when he recalls the duties of a tour guide, he thinks there is no other alternative. And if he actually reaches World War II and has a couple days left to cover the cold war, the Common Market, the growth of technology, and the Westernization of the underdeveloped world, he feels confident he has done his job. A few passengers will reinforce this confidence by answering correctly eighty to ninety of his most difficult multiple-choice questions.

Now, any teacher who has faced the task of teaching world history in 180 days should be able to identify with at least some of Fogg's dilemmas. To try to "cover the world" a la Sherwin-Williams, the paint company, is to ask for superficiality. Paint may cover, but it doesn't illuminate what's inside. In fact, it may hide what's underneath. This approach means a reliance on essentially one expository textbook; emphasis on content and neglect of the process that led to that content; exclusion of three-quarters of the world that lies outside the West; a narrow focus on history as a discipline, ignoring the other social sciences; and finally, and perhaps worst of all, a water-glass theory of learning that assumes (at least implicitly) that education is a pouring in rather than a drawing out.

The problems with this traditional approach to world history are numerous, but here are some of the obvious ones:

(1) *It is impossible to cover the world.* There is so much information about any *one* nation that it is impossible to cover it all in a decade of study, not to mention 180 days. Moreover, any attempt to *try* to cover unwieldy amounts of information leads to force-feeding, usually in the form of teacher-dominated lectures, which lead to rote memory on the part of students and finally to regurgitation on a test. People usually do not eat what makes them sick, and students have a tendency to behave very much like people.

(2) *Facts in themselves are worthless.* It is what we do with them that counts. And students will never know what to do with them if facts are all they learn. Moreover, facts are not durable: Students lose them and the information explosion destroys them. How many facts can we recall from our own high school history courses? If anything, we retain vague impressions. And if we were extremely lucky we developed a few good habits of clear thinking. Mark Twain hit close to the mark when he said: "I never commit to memory anything that can readily be found in a book." Instead of cluttering minds with facts, we should clutter libraries with students who are learning methods of research.

(3) *Africa, Asia, and Latin America are part of the world.* A world history course that ignores these vast areas of the earth should change its name. It is not only a lie intellectually to equate the West with the entire world; it is an act of supreme arrogance. It is also educationally deceitful, for students will never really see themselves until they see others and learn how others see them. "He who knows only England, does not England know," said the poet. Examining only the West and calling it the world is like examining an elephant by looking only at its

trunk, and then calling it a snake. This does an injustice not only to the elephant but also to the examiner, for the total elephant is infinitely more interesting than any one of its parts.

(4) *History is only one view of the world.* And the historical view so happens to be the one most difficult for young people to develop. Few people under twenty years of age (perhaps under thirty) have a genuine historical perspective. Young people tend to be rooted in the here and now. If we hope to grab their attention, we better begin where they are. Why did Americans begin reading histories of Vietnam? Not because they were interested in 1000 B.C., but because they were interested in 1965. They were interested in the present and wanted to know how it got to be the way it is. A chronological survey—the form of organization of most world history textbooks—may be an unnatural ordering of human experience. We all begin with the present and then work back. If we then persist with our study and become history professors, we write histories from the past to the present to satisfy some laws of cosmic logic, not to replicate our own process of discovery. Students should not be expected to begin at the end of the process. They should be allowed to go through the same steps of discovery that all of us go through—in spite of school. Chronology may be fine from God's point of view, but not from the perspective of a fifteen-year-old.

(5) *Expository textbooks are a finished product.* They have done all of the thinking and analyzing. They are the end result, leaving little for the student to do but memorize. The authors of such books may have learned how to uncover information, how to compare views, how to draw conclusions; but if students are to learn these things, they must be allowed to do them. Teachers must allow students to use primary sources (raw data) and write their own textbooks, so to speak.

The question is, then, How do we bring about some of these changes in the traditional world history courses? One thing is clear: Little will change by adding new elements to the existing base. Bringing Africa, Asia, and Latin America into an already-crowded course will not solve the problem of crammed content; adding sociology and anthropology to a survey of the entire world will not automatically solve the problem of chronology. That is simply to add new floors on the same building. One ends up with a content structure as high as the Empire State

Building and a methodological elevator which can take us only to the fortieth floor. What is called for is a radical reorganization and methodology.

RADICAL CHANGES

Perhaps the best way to approach this change is to escape completely from our present situation. We are too earth-bound to get a new perspective. Imagine for a minute that you are a creature from another planet and that you are approaching earth for the first time. (Students, in fact, are approaching much of the earth for the first time in world history courses.) To begin with, your chances of landing on Europe are very slim. Your chances of landing on Africa or Asia are much, much better, about twenty times better in fact.

One of the first things you would notice, of course, would be the appearance of men (biology, anthropology) and the nature of their surroundings (geography). Once you became accustomed to these immediate perceptions, you would probably notice the activities of these human creatures. You would see them working, trying to make a living (economics). You would see them interacting in groups (sociology) and establishing authority and power in these groups (political science). You then might notice the rituals they perform such as marriage, worship, entertainment (anthropology). In examining these rituals, you would begin to see underlying values and beliefs (religion, philosophy, anthropology).

As you moved about the earth, you would find this pattern time and time again: people working, forming groups, establishing authority, performing rituals, and holding values. If you sent a report home to your own planet, you would probably say, with Confucius, "The nature of man is always the same, it is their habits that separate them!" You might point out certain slight differences in skin color, clothing, tools, and so forth, but by and large the similarities would strike you as more significant than the differences. Incidentally, the *last* thing you would do, after comparing different peoples, would be to investigate the reasons they developed the way they did, that is, go back in time (history).

If you wanted to make more sense of these earth people, you might simplify your study by dividing human activities into categories. You might put all economic issues together, all political issues together, all social issues together, and so forth. In short, you might divide (and therefore hope to "conquer") the whole spectrum of human experience by creating what are known as the social sciences. Moreover, within each discipline you would discover certain major ideas that appeared time and time again as you traveled around the earth. For example, in economics you might discover that all people make *demands* for goods, thereby leading other people to *supply* these demands. In sociology, you would discover that all adults teach the young how to behave *(socialization)*, according to certain *norms*. And in political science, you would discover that some people have *power* while others do not.

Having once isolated some of these major ideas in the various disciplines, you would have a handy method for making sense of any society you visited. If you wanted to understand the political system of an area, for example, you could simply ask a few questions about *power*. Who has power? How do they get it? How do they use it? How is it regulated? The answers to these questions (and a few more) would give you a very good understanding of the basic political structure of any society.

It should be obvious by now that words like "demand," "supply," "socialization," "norms," and "power" are concepts, the building blocks of the social sciences. The questions surrounding each concept (e.g., Who has power? How do they get it? How is it regulated?) are known formally as *analytical questions*. Our space traveler, if he is armed with a few basic concepts and the ability to ask analytical questions, can quickly organize data and make sense (draw conclusions) about the various societies he visits. And with enough evidence, he can *generalize* about his conclusions, making broad statements about one society or about all societies on earth. At the same time, he can apply his method to ancient Greece as well as to contemporary China. Ideally, students of world history should approach the earth in very much the same way our visitor from space does.

Notice, however, that generalizations appear last in the process of

analysis. Traditional approaches to world history usually put generalizations first. They begin with such statements as these:

- Natural environment has a limiting but not a determining in-
  fluence on peoples' behavior.
- The more complex a society, the more it will exhibit widespread
  division of labor.
- History may repeat itself, but each repetition has unique qualities.
- Culture determines the way a person sees the world.
- The more government power is centralized, the greater the chance
  for dictatorship and the less the chance for democracy.

About fifteen years ago, Paul R. Hanna and Richard Gross of
Stanford University set out to identify the major generalizations that
could be made about human societies. Their ultimate goal was to
create a frame of reference for organizing social studies content. By the
time they had finished, they had collected a total of 3,272
generalizations.[1] Commenting on this approach, Edwin Fenton
writes:

> Lists of generalizations are inert. They become ends in themselves,
> tempting teachers to choose generalizations from a list, Smorgas-
> bord-fashion, for their students, rather than means to an end. No one
> can remember more than 3200 generalizations—one and a half every
> school day for twelve years—even though many are self-evident. Nor
> do the generalizations help students to learn the process by which
> social scientists develop a generalization. Process is important. In the
> midst of a knowledge explosion, each of us must either know how to
> build new generalizations, or be content to live in tomorrow's world
> with yesterday's knowledge.[2]

In a very real sense, generalizations are little more than sophisticated, abstract facts. As Fenton points out, they are inert ends in
themselves, subject to obsolescence and useless in helping us analyze
new situations. Concepts, on the other hand, are focal points for an-

alysis; they lead us into a study of the dynamics of society rather than into a collection of observations. "Norm," for example, does not tell us anything about a particular society; it simply presents the occasions to ask a series of analytical questions: What are norms? How do they affect behavior? (Or, inductively: How does social behavior indicate the norms of the society?) How do the social institutions embody these norms? What are the sources of these norms? The process of analysis can be applied at all times and to all societies. In short, learning to ask questions is much more important than learning answers.

For world history courses, then, the conceptual-discovery approach provides a way out of the "coverage" problem. By emphasizing process, it avoids the problem entirely. It focuses on the *how* rather than on the *what*. It asserts what scientists—from Aristotle to the present—have always known, namely, that understanding principles is the basis of all wisdom. A doctor, after all, does not have to know what every human being's circulatory system looks like to be a good doctor. He simply has to know the principles involved. With this insight, he can treat any man, anywhere, and (hypothetically) at any time in history. Likewise, students who understand the basic principles (concepts) of the social sciences can make sense of any social situation. Our job as educators is to give them these tools of analysis.

Take, for example, the sociological concept of socialization—the process by which any society conditions its young to conform to the norms of that society. Like all concepts, *socialization* is universal; all parents teach and discipline their children. *What* they teach them, however, will depend upon the values of that society. American youngsters, for example, might find it strange that African boys of sixteen can give commands to their older sisters and even to their mothers. They might also find it strange that six- and seven-year-old girls have major responsibilities in rearing their younger siblings. If we leave American students will these facts only, they will always think Africans are strange, and, even worse, they will never know why. If, on the other hand, we ask students to hypothesize why they think Africans treat their children the way they do, and then have the students collect data that will either confirm or alter their hypotheses, we are inviting them into the inner machinery or society; they are likely to see how it works.

Ideally, we would have data available for students to investigate; in this case a firsthand account of growing up in an African family would be ideal. (Materials such as these are now becoming available.) But even if we do not have such ready references, we have the life-experience of our own students. After all, they know all about socialization; they are going through it every day—in the hands of their parents, their teachers, their religious leaders, their peers and the community at large. (The very process by which these students learn about *socialization* is itself part of the American socialization process: We value rational, critical, and independent thought; hence we encourage our students to think this way in analyzing the nature of society.)

To help students discover the process of socialization and how it is related to the values of a society, ask them some obvious questions.

Why do American parents teach young children to eat with a fork and not with their hands? Why are children taught to say "thank you"? Why are twelve-year-old boys considered babies if they cry? Why are girls of the same age allowed to cry? Why are teen-agers given their own room, if it is at all possible? Why do teachers (some, at least) ask students for their opinions, instead of simply dictating to them?

When students begin to discuss the answers to these questions, they will begin to see that reasons—important social and cultural reasons —lie behind the process of socialization. They will also discover a number of other concepts in the process. They will realize that men and women often play different *roles* in various societies (women take care of children, for example, whereas men fix broken doors), which explains why girls and boys are reared differently. Girls, for example, are allowed to play with dolls, whereas boys are given a carpenter's set. They will also discover that roles approximate *ideal types,* that is, ideal notions we have of what a man and what a woman should be. American men, for example, were once seen as strong, decisive, and the breadwinners in the family; women seen as soft, nonargumentative, and custodians of the home. (For a lively discussion, ask students: What is the ideal American male, female? How do we try to create these ideal types in America? How do we mold our boys and girls?)

After the connection is made between the process of socialization and the roles and ideal types in society (i.e., the values), then an analysis of African society (or any society) can be made. Students will see immediately that young Africans are socialized so that they will approximate the ideals of their society. If African boys of sixteen are allowed to command their sisters and mothers, then men (ideal men) in that society are extremely dominant. If young African girls are expected to take care of children at a very early age, then child-rearing is extremely important for African women. Students should be able to infer from such data on socialization the values and ideals of the society. They also should be able to discover the notion of *cultural relativism.* By simply asking, "How happy would a teen-age African boy be in American society?" students will readily see that he would probably miss the dominant position he held at home. Conversely, an American girl would probably dislike the subservient position given her in African society. Both would be somewhat unhappy in each other's social system because both have been socialized for their own system. It follows, of course, that neither system is superior or inferior; they are simply different.

Arming students with basic concepts—or, more precisely, allowing them to discover the social dynamics surrounding concepts—gives students the cognitive framework for making sense of new realities, allowing them to move to any society at any point in history and make some sense of it. Instead of stopping where most students stop today—with a few exotic facts about other cultures which simply confirm their inbred sense of superiority—these students should be able to see that every culture makes sense in its own terms. They will see, for example, that socialization in Africa is designed according to African ideals; that socialization in America is designed according to American ideals; and, most important, that the American process of socialization would not meet the needs of African ideals, and vice versa. In short, every society is a self-contained whole, consisting of interrelated parts which can be understood only in the total context of that society. Conceptual analysis forces us to examine societies from the inside; hence it goes a long way in breaking down negative value judgments that invariably arise from ethnocentrism. In other words, it deals with the affective domain of learning as well as with the cognitive.

The objectives of a unit of study similar to the one just described might look something like this:

Knowledge Objectives

(a) To know some of the daily experiences of African tribe X
(b) To know how boys and girls are treated in tribe X
(c) To know that division of labor is often based on sex
(d) To know what *role* is
(e) To know what *socialization* is
(f) To know that socialization is designed to further the *values* of society
(g) To know that differences in human behavior result from conditioning (socialization) and not from race.

Critical Thinking Objectives

(a) To be able to form hypotheses based on observation
(b) To be able to test hypotheses with new evidence
(c) To be able to draw inferences from unanalyzed data
(d) To be able to form generalizations from specific data
(e) To be able to compare societies objectively in terms of social process
(f) To be able to frame analytical questions for purposes of discovering the values of a culture.

Value Objectives

(a) To develop empathy for tribe X by sharing in their daily activities
(b) To relate personal experience to the experience of people in other cultures
(c) To see that customs in one society are not superior to customs in another

(d) To judge other societies (in this case, tribes) simply as units of social organization, designed to achieve certain ends, and not as inferior or backward groupings of people.

Most curriculum builders divide the cognitive domain of learning into two sections: (1) simple knowledge objectives, such as the recalling of facts; and (2) critical-thinking objectives (sometimes called methods-of-inquiry objectives), such as the ability to form hypotheses, see relations, and make inferences. The second category is obviously much more difficult than the first, but it is also much more important to teach, for this is where process lies. And it is precisely the process of arriving at insights and conclusions that traditional world history courses never taught. The third category of objectives, or course, deals with the affective domain of learning, an area of social studies learning that has been neglected perhaps as much as, if not more than, critical thinking.

One answer to both of these past oversights is to use primary source materials in the place of expository textbooks. Not only are such materials unanalyzed, thereby forcing the student to develop his own methods of analysis, but they are usually concrete and therefore have an emotional impact that affects attitudes and feelings. It should be obvious that the numerous objectives listed above would have to be taught over several class periods, with perhaps only two or three objectives in each category designed for each class. Some objectives, of course, would be repeated.

ORGANIZING THE WORLD

It has been our contention that the struggle for answers and insights—the learning how to learn—is much more important than any conclusions that might be reached. However, in this approach, the time spent will be greater and the area covered will be less than under the more traditional approach to world history. This raises questions concerning how to organize the world for study. If much more time is to be spent on the learning process, then what content do we eliminate, and what do we include?

There are several ways to organize a world cultures course while still applying the methods of "the new social studies." An examination of four of these ways to "organize the world" is presented in the following section.

Organization by Disciplines

One method of organization that follows naturally from what we have been discussing is the *discipline approach*. Here the traditional social science disciplines of sociology, anthropology, economics, political science, and so forth, are used as the organizing principle. The educational goal, of course, is to give the student an intimate acquaintance with the basic concepts and methods used by the various disciplines. If, for example, we were using sociology, we might identify a set of basic concepts—role, norm, primary group, secondary group, socialization, ideal type—and then set about finding interesting and perhaps contrasting examples of how these concepts interact in various societies. Our study might carry us to Japan, China, Russia, Nigeria, India, Brazil, and Poland. The common denominator at all times, however, would be sociology. Introductory college courses often follow this pattern.

After spending a certain period of time on sociology, the class might then move to anthropology, developing such concepts as *kinship, culture, structure function, culture diffusion,* and *culture conflict.* An attempt could be made to use illustrations from societies not studied in the first unit on sociology. After anthropology, the other social sciences could be handled.

The advantage of the discipline approach is twofold: First, each discipline has a well-developed set of concepts that interrelate, thereby giving us a tidy framework in which to work; second, the disciplines can be applied to every area of the world, allowing us to pick and choose our data as we see fit. For example, if we were studying kinship formation, we would probably want to tap some of the rich varieties of kinships that exist in Africa and Asia. If we were stuck to an area-studies approach—let's say Latin America—we would not have this variety of data available to us.

The disadvantages of the discipline approach are also twofold: First, the disciplines tend to be weak in historical analysis, focusing most of their attention on the twentieth century; second, the disciplines tend to diminish some of the "special" qualities found in different cultures. By emphasizing only one discipline at a time, the discipline approach loses some of the more subtle aspects of the unique interrelationships found from culture to culture. After all, the relationships among religion, social class, economics, and politics in India may be quite different from these relationships in Nigeria.

Organization by Basic Institutions

If we accept our basic postulates of organizing by concepts and questions and of always rooting our subject matter in the frame of reference of the student, we might create a year's organization based on man's basic institutional formulations. Using this method, the teacher would perhaps begin by discussing with students, and helping them identify, what their basic needs are: Probably they would list sex, food, warmth; the need to create something; the need for answers to such questions as Where did we come from? and How was the earth created?; the need for physical security; the need to pass on their culture and knowledge to the next generation; the need to have physical comforts; and many, many other needs. From this list of needs the teacher can further develop with the students, through discussion, readings, pictures, and other data, that man tends to solve these needs in groups. When a group of people try to solve a basic need, they create an institution.

The next step is to synthesize the various needs into basic institutions. For example, one may begin with the need to reproduce offspring and rear them. The basic institution to achieve this we can call *family*. Students may then be asked to organize some of the possible forms this institution might take. They may come up with many women and one man, a collective of men and women, several women and one man, a kibbutz, one woman at a time, and so forth. Source readings may be used here to give tangible examples of such organizations. From here students can develop other basic questions about the *family*. What is the role of wife (wives), sons, daughters, husband(s)? What is the basis for marriage, property, family arrangement, love, status, and so on? Is divorce allowed? What is the pecking order among brothers and sisters? How is extramarital sex viewed? Is virginity before marriage advocated? Does the wife have mobility? Can she work, travel, talk to other men? Must she stay covered (purdah)? Comparisons can be made between our own family structure and that of others. Selections from *How to Be a Jewish Mother* may be contrasted with excerpts from *Coming of Age in Samoa* or *Nectar in a Sieve* (Indian) or *The Good Earth* (Chinese). The root idea in this is that all cultures will have and have had some type of family structure. Once the list of questions is developed about the institution of the family *by the students,* so that the questions are *their questions,* they may be applied to any culture at any time in history.

Another institution which can be developed from the students' questions is the institution of religion. Man has always wanted to know where the universe comes from, what meaning life has, what happens after death. As he tries to solve these questions, collectively, religion is being created. Questions students might raise to understand a specific people's beliefs might be: Is there a god? How many gods are allowed? Is it (they) inside or outside the world? Is there a class of priests and a defined ritual? Does all life manifest a spirit (we might later call this pantheism)? How is evil represented? What is the creation story? How is nature treated? A teacher might compare Genesis, where man has dominion over nature, with parts of the Indian *Ramayana,* where man is in unity with nature. Pictures of totems, rituals, cathedrals, and representations of deities may all be used for illustrations of how various peoples deal with these religious questions. The key is the questions and how people answer these questions. Answers may reveal differences between the concepts of Allah and Siva, and they may reveal similarities between such seemingly diverse phenomena as a metal Krishna in an Indian household and a plastic St. Christopher's medal on the dashboard of an American automobile.

A third institution would be man's answer to the eternal problem of the production and distribution of goods. What do most people do for a livelihood: farm, hunt, gather, engage in commerce, work in industry?

How do these people then distribute the goods—according to need (people of the Kalahari Desert), through private initiative (1850 America), by a combination (1969 Great Britain)? What is used as a means of exchange: leaves, beads, barter, rare metal, pieces of paper, credit cards? How is economics used for status? (Compare the Potlatch ceremony, the Bar Mitzvah, and the Hindu wedding.) How important is wealth in the society? Who owns the land and the machines? What skills are important? These are all basic questions which may be developed. There are many more equally valuable questions that could be asked about each culture studied.

Still another basic institution, again developed through student questioning about their own lives, is government. How does the group maintain a social order, allow for change, satisfy individuals? How are leaders chosen? How is power transferred? Are the trappings of power symbolized by a crown, a staff, an entourage, a jet plane, or charisma? Are the people allowed to participate in the decision-making process? If so, how and to what extent? What training for political life does the group offer the people? How much communication is there available? Is the basic framework of the group a clan, tribe, city-state, nation-state, regional organization? Is there any inherent value in any of these types of organization? Does one sovereign unit relate to others through power, law, compromise, or diplomacy?

Other suggested basic institutions that would be more or less universal would perhaps be: the arts (painting and sculpture, literature, music and dance), a recreation, a science of some type, most likely a military organization, and an educational system. Basic questions for each of these institutions would be developed by students and teacher, both drawing on their own experiences, reading sources from other cultures, looking at art and relics, listening to poetry and music, and using a variety of other data sources. Questions in art might be: What medium is used? What are the objects of representation? What is the concept of space, and what are the important symbols used? For literature, we might ask: What is the concept of the hero? Is there a plot? Characterization? What symbols are employed, and what is a basic model of expression—essay, epic poem, short story, novel, drama? For music, we would be interested in knowing what instruments are played, what the themes of the songs are, and what they symbolize. Is improvization or structure involved? Is music linear or cyclical? For science, we perhaps would want to know if trial and error or magic, or if what we call the scientific method, are utilized? How much is science imbedded in religion? Is it part of the educational system?

Through this institutional organization, several basic institutions may be identified, and a series of questions can be posed for each institution. These questions then become the basis for a year's organization of world civilization. The questions can fit a format of historical development where they would be asked for all the civilizations dealt with in a traditionally chronological world history course. Or they may be used as a key to contemporary cultures, which the organization of the New York State ninth-grade course in world cultures suggests. This approach draws on the social science disciplines as well as on the disciplines of art, literature, music, science, and even military tactics if desired. This organization offers ample opportunity for the "why" questions to be raised. Implicit in the scheme are such fundamental questions as: Does civilization develop in a progressive direction? For example, in government, is a nation-state inherently superior to a tribal organization? Is the novel a superior form to that of the folk tale? Is industry a more "developed" system than herding? Is a Bach cantata "better" music than a New Guinea rain song? Is astrology an inferior method of explanation to Einstein's second principle? And so forth.

Also implicit is a constant comparative approach to world civilization. How was the role of Greek women different from my mother's? How is an Arabian wedding different from/similar to my brother John's? What is Longfellow's *Song of Hiawatha* saying that is echoed in the Indian *Ramayana* and in the *Iliad?* Is Bobby Dylan using the same art form the twelfth-century English troubadors did? Why do I react negatively to the idea of arranged marriage? Is that St. Anthony's festival I saw in Greenwich Village saying the same thing as the event I read about of a northern Indian village, where villagers carried their deity around and clothed and washed him? The list of comparisons is almost infinite. Your individual list will reflect your interests and philosophy. The list of your students will reflect their experience, their sophistication, and their own needs. If one trusts the questions to guide him, much seemingly alien and undifferentiated information may take on some sense and meaning. This system will also offer a criterion for selection. A teacher can't "cover" everything. The questions one asks can determine the material with which to deal. One must tailor it to suit the time, the students, and a sense of practical possibility.

Organization by Themes

A third possible organization for a world cultures course might be thematic approach. In this system the teacher, with or without student planning, might select movements or themes that seem to be basic to man's behavior and history regardless of time or place.

One such theme might be how peoples make changes in the society in which they live. To put it succinctly: Do they make changes through reform or revolution? To begin as usual with the students, it may be worth the investment of time to have each member of the class respond to a controversial question such as "Should students evaluate teachers?" or "Should grades be abolished?" Those who offer a firm no as an answer may be seated on the far right side of the room. Those who answer yes may be seated on the extreme left side of the room. Finally, those with opinions between the parameters of right and left can be placed along a continuum based on the degree of support they offer for either no or yes. From this tangible exercise, labels such as radical, revolutionary, liberal, conservative, reactionary, may be induced.

Once the concept of "left" and "right" is established, the teacher might proceed to develop the question of how the two extremes of the spectrum can relate to one another. Here the making of some type of decision must be introduced. If those on the left side of the room should take the position that "Here we stand. God help us, we can do no other," and if they refuse to compromise with those on the right side of the room, we have a classic example of polarization. We might then ask our group on the right side what their opinions are in regard to the left. They can continue to negotiate, give in to the left, or, if they are in the majority, use their superior power to force the left to capitulate to their will. In this little classroom exercise we have the model for reform or revolution. Then case studies may be introduced, such as the America of 1850-60, Rome in 80 B.C., China from 1946 to 1950, Russia from 1905 to 1918, Columbia University in 1968, and countless other classic situations where polarization took place and where compromise failed. Examples where compromise worked might be used also. The Compromise of 1850 in the United States, Japan after the Meiji Restoration, and a general election in India would be examples of successful compromise. Of course it is helpful if the teacher is familiar with such works as Crane Brinton's *Anatomy of Revolution* and other classic works on the subject.

This is one theme that may serve as a thread either for a chronological approach to world history, for area studies, or for selection by social science disciplines. The focus would simply be on those times in a society where large groups of people polarized around a basic issue or issues. If a historical organization is used, the teacher might select Egypt under Ikhnaton; Athens under Draco, Solon, and Cleisthenes; Rome during the period of Marius and Sulla, the early Caesars, or under certain of the emperors; the reforms of Charlemagne; the Reformation in Europe; the English Civil War, the French Revolution; the American Revolution; and a host of other equally good choices. India under Asoka; China during the Ch'in, T'ang, Manchu dynasties, or the people's Republic under Mao; Latin America at almost any point, and Nigeria in the 1960s can also be included if the course is truly world civilization.

The "Golden Age" and its demise may be another central theme around which to organize the year's course. The basic question here is: Why do civilizations seem to experience periods of ebbs and flows? What causes these recurring periods of great creativity in the arts, politics, power, philosophy, and so on, in the world's civilizations? One may select Periclean Athens, Rome under Augustus, the Guptas' India, the T'angs' China, Elizabethan England, France under Louis XIV, the Muslim Middle East, Mogul India, the Ghanian Kingdom in Africa in the eleventh century, and Mayan Central America as examples of the "Golden Age." Of course, one makes his own selection. Then the teacher must ask: What were possible factors which contributed to the ending of these great ages? Why did Ghana go into eclipse to later become replaced by the great Mali civilization? Why did Rome "fall"?

What happened to the Gupta creativity after the sixth century A.D.? Why did Chinese culture after the great T'ang period tend to become conservative? In dealing with this open-ended and virtually impossible question, various hypotheses might be offered by students: military invasion, being surpassed in technology, the people losing their dynamism, some inner law of decay (Henry Adams, Oswald Spengler), changes in geographic environment, and many others.

The advantage of this theme is perhaps its open-endedness. No one really knows why civilizations fall or why or even "if" they attain a "Golden Age." Study of such a question could teach the difference between fact and interpretation. In addition, this theme will provide ample opportunity for analysis by the students of their own age and its symptoms of greatness or decline. The Roman circus and professional football, the Gracchi brothers, and the Kennedy brothers, internal disorders of the second century B.C. China, and contemporary urban America are but a few of the possible analogies that may be drawn.

Another grand theme that may serve as a context for the study of world civilization might be "When cultures meet." Here again the class itself offers much potential data for analysis. This would be especially true in an urban setting where many religious and ethnic groups are in constant proximity. The teacher might begin by asking students to trace their own cultural roots and family trees and to focus on certain unique features of their particular cultures. Ethnic foods, dress, words, religious customs, and the like, might be the place to begin. What is the source of such things as chop suey, pizza, soul food, cowboy, Mardi Gras, Los Angeles, St. Anthony's festival, the Steuben Day parade, and St. Patrick's Day? From here the class might go on to study the process of cultural diffusion as it happened in America and how the disparate strains, represented by numerous immigrant groups, came to be absorbed and practiced in America. Conversely, there is material for fruitful study of modern cultural diffusion. Coca Cola is almost a universal symbol; the spread of American popular music, baseball, beauty contests, and clothing styles may be observed in Asia, Africa, and Latin America. Kung Fu, the dashiki, the Che Guevara look, and the sitar, Zen, and the bossa nova are some examples of diffusion in the opposite direction. From the superficial level of clothing, music, customs, and the like, it may be possible to go a bit deeper into ideology, philosophy, literature, and political organizations that have been spread, adopted, and modified, in the modern world and in man's history. The British parliamentary system in an African or Asian setting, Christianity in Guatemala, Eastern mysticism in New York City and San Francisco, and Western Marxism in a Chinese setting would be a few such examples in the present-day world. In history, the meeting of cultures in the Alexandrian Empire, the Roman Empire, medieval Spain, Kievan Russia, Norman England, Mogul India, Manchu China, the Middle East during the Crusades, and the spread of Buddhism in Asia are but a few of the colorful and fascinating periods characterized by a meeting of differing cultures and the synthesis that was subsequently made. The mode of cultural contact and diffusion also offers material for organization of the course. Was the contact peaceful or violent; overtly imperialistic or subtle; carried on by commercial tradesmen, missionaries, refugees, and so forth?

Some other grand themes that might serve for a course organization might be "Religious reformation," "How the artist confronts reality," "How society chooses its hero," "Man's view of nature," and "War and peace." All of these themes could draw on all areas of the world, be studied in a historic context if required, and offer a thread of continuity which would allow for the use of facts and information as building blocks for large concepts and questions. These themes also expand the potential storehouse of knowledge to include music, art, literature, philosophy, and even popular fads and habits. The organization will teach such skills as how to use data in a variety of ways, how to use a culture's symbols as vehicles of understanding, and the important truth that world culture is a reality that, despite local differences, includes the contributions of all peoples who have gone before us.

Like all the organizational patterns suggested, the thematic approach attempts to use the students' own lives and experiences as the basic source of data and to expand those experiences to a wider context and perhaps to a higher level of abstraction and critical thinking. It uses the world in its entirety as a stage of activity and stresses the comparative approach of study. Most important, it offers questions and configurations as the goal of learning and assumes facts to be means to a greater end.

In all the organizations of the world discussed so far, the focus has been on universals. Whether we use social science disciplines, man's basic institutions, or themes as our approach, we are attempting to examine certain fundamental phenomena in man's behavior that are universal. A possible flaw in this type of organization is the tendency to teach that behavior is standard and to lose the particular genius and cultural pattern of individual civilizations. One way to correct this tendency is always to work out the particular concept being considered in a specific place with actual people in a given time. Thus, a teacher deals with the revolution in Russia in 1917, family patterns in North India in 1969, urbanization in Kenya in 1958.

Organization by Cultural Areas

A fourth possible organization for the world cultures course is to study several cultural areas which, because of their creativity, great achievement, and uniqueness would be used as case studies for intensive research. Such a selection probably should include Indian civilization, Chinese civilization, the Muslim Middle East, an African kingdom, ancient Greece and Rome, perhaps two medieval cultures (Japan and northern Europe), and the post-Renaissance West. The treatment of these great cultural areas would not be an encyclopedic listing of dynasties, names, and dates. Rather, it would stress the world view, the cultural character, and the unique institutional organization of the cultures under consideration.

The aim in this approach is to get inside the civilization and to attempt to see it according to its own standards and values. There is a strong propensity to carry with us a bias in favor of the goals of our culture: individual freedom, social mobility, materialism, and scientism. Thus, Indian caste becomes a "problem to be solved"; medieval Christianity may be viewed as the superstitious "opiate of the masses"; Chinese group consciousness becomes "premodern"; African communal economics become "primitive communism." Instead of this, the

Indian caste system, for example, should be evaluated against the goals of Indian society.

One way to achieve this is to use the metaphor of a game. The students would try to treat each civilization as a game—played for certain ends (goals, runs) and by certain rules. The object of study would be to understand the rules and ends of the civilization under study.

One way to get at the "end" of a civilization is to understand its world view—how it makes sense of the universe. A knowledge of the metaphors which set forth the cosmology of the civilization is an essential part of this task. A teacher could start with the student's world view. Ask him: "Is there a god?"; "Where is he located?"; "How does the literature talk of god?"; "How have the holy men gotten to him?"

For most people in the West, God is outside the world. He is a creator separate from man; he is reached through man's relationship to him, either personal or corporate. When the student turns to an Indian temple, to an Indian dance, to the direction of the eye in an Indian "holy man," or to a bronze "dancing Shiva," he begins to see another world view. Here God is an integral part of the universe—within it—the universe and god are one. The metaphor of the game is that westerners play life in order to reach God outside themselves while many Indians play in order to become one with God within.

Another set of questions might be concerned with whether the universe is subject to rational law or is capricious. Again, start where the student is and ask if he must sacrifice to make the universe work or if it functions by itself. Does nature or God stand at the acme of the universe? Who is responsible for carrying the truth from God—the priests, the church, each individual, the men of knowledge? Perhaps tradition is the basic source of truth in a particular civilization; if so, who in the society is responsible for maintaining it? Does man attempt to dominate nature, or is he a part of it?

These questions on cultural world views are absolutely essential for an understanding of any society or people. Without them, it is doubtful that any student "can transcend the parochialism of his own time and place." Under the impact of Marx and the great stress on economic growth and faith in technology, American students are sorely tempted, as are their teachers, to assume a monolithic world view based on progress, growth of the economic sector, and a civilization whose status is measurable materially. This propensity tends to enhance an already strong ethnocentricism and serves to downgrade the rich cultural heritages of lands like Africa, India, and China. Those areas deserve to be studied on their own terms and in the context of their own world views and value systems.

In addition, American students at this point in our history are becoming increasingly interested in philosophic and spiritual questions. In a recent workshop for high school students, a New York City student was heard to say, "We're talking a lot about God these days at Ben Franklin (High School)." It would seem to be unfair to students, and a gross distortion of historic truth, to leave out the rich and varied world views of the world's great cultures and simply to assume that all the world's people believed in a transcendent god dedicated to material progress.

In selecting the areas that constitute world views from the cultures of the world, again one must be somewhat arbitrary and perhaps oversimplify. These are just some suggested possibilities: Hebrew—a transcendent God with human qualities like justice and mercy, a deity who makes contracts with his chosen group; Greek—a notion of the universe as basically an orderly one which can be understood by reason, empiricism, and science (a universe where individuals count as the basic units of society; a social organization which assumes individual membership in a polity); Roman—much the same, with more emphasis on man's legal responsibilities; medieval Europe—God-centered universe with a society more group oriented, static, and authoritarian in nature; Africa—a basic unity of body, mind, and spirit, a collective feeling of belonging to the group (unlike the Greek notion of separation of mind, body, spirit); India—a view of divinity being within the universe, with gods subject to the same pressures and factors as man, a sense of man *in* nature rather than man having dominion over nature (a sense of truth being beyond the empirical world and the mundane level of worldly activity, which is illusion); China—a sense of the universe as one of growth, the unity of man and nature, a wholeness to life, an emphasis on ethical behavior and an elaborate system of human relationships, an honoring of the learned moral man, a vivid sense of history; post-Renaissance West—an emphasis on individual rights and behavior, a strong belief in rationalism and science, power and materialism raised to almost religious heights, a fragmentation of man into a myriad of personalities and functions with little integration of the whole, a growing secularism.

Another way to get a hold of civilization is to grasp the characteristic way of life or style, or what is now called national character. This approach attempts to extrapolate a unity in the civilization and describe its "way of life." How does one attempt this definition of a unique and enduring cultural personality? There are the geographic facts; climate, topography; wars; invasions, the rise and fall of governments; small people and great politicians; and writers, thieves, and saints. Even the highest intellect can digest and make sense of only a small fraction of these infinite data. The mind must make an abstraction from the data, and the abstractions must be greater than the sum total of all the facts. This mental picture must be the sinew that holds the impressions, the data, the facts together; otherwise, they would disintegrate into a thousand unrelated bits and have meaning for us roughly equivalent to the Manhattan phone book. The heart of this task is for the teacher to have the ability to select only those data for the student to consider that serve to *symbolize* the whole.

One might start by selecting those institutions which are basic to the social fabric of the civilization. For India, they probably would be caste, family, and village; for Ancient Athens, perhaps the legislature, theater, and lyceum; for Rome, the legion, the Senate, and law; for medieval Europe, the manor, the church, and perhaps the town or fair; for China, the family, the bureaucracy, and the court; for modern America, the corporation, the constitutional system, the public school, the ghetto. This selection, of course, is somewhat arbitrary. Others equally symbolic could be selected for analysis which would offer a symbolism for the whole.

Another method of getting to know a civilization is to get a feeling for it. This sense of feeling is perhaps rather vague but is nonetheless indispensable for the good of knowing the civilization. This feeling can best be apprehended by experiencing the manifestations of the culture, looking at the art it produced, listening to the music it wrote, reading autobiographies of its intelligentsia, studying the literature of its writers, seeing its films. All these media will help the student become enmeshed in another culture and to develop a sense of its identity. Further, it would be good to smell the odors, taste the foods, and perhaps even wear the clothes of the culture. It would be ideal if a school could set aside a special room for each culture and turn them into total environments of Africa, India, China, Latin America, ancient Greece, and so on. This could quite easily be done by arranging (even building) the furniture; draping the walls with art and scenes; creating the foods and smells; and saturating the environment with books, tapes, films, and records of the language, music, sounds, and sights of the culture. How much more meaningful this contrived reality would be compared to the mere abstract words in a textbook. This feeling about a culture necessarily implies a far greater use of the humanities than we have traditionally made. It may be that there is no more immediate avenue to another culture than the intuitive feeling one gets from its art, literature, and music. As Albert H. Marckwardt has written in this regard, "a great work of literature will put into terms of concrete experience the values, concepts, and ways of life which the social scientist is likely to treat in the abstract or at best in detail less powerful than that which serves to make concrete the *Weltanschauung* of a great poet, novelist, or dramatist." [3]

Once having created a feeling for the central character of a given civilization, it is important to place the society in a larger context, into the mainstream of world civilization. One would want to check the specific culture against the larger generalities that have been made about all civilizations. Was there a period of urbanization, of commercial revolution, an internal revolution, one or more cultural renaissance, a religious reformation? How did these great universal movements become particularized in the culture we have been dealing with? Can our generalizations about revolution, expansion, and so on, be modified? Was this civilization an exception to any of the generalities?

Implicit in the study of cultural areas is a comparative approach to civilization. The student constantly places his own culture against the one being studied; thus, the subject matter is constantly in the frame of reference of the student.

This comparative-civilization approach should furnish some answer to the question of the relevance of world history. The use of a civilization as a case study, if handled correctly, offers both teachers and students the opportunity to analyze man's attempts to work out answers to social, religious, economic, and political questions and to use them as possible options for today's problems. This comparative approach furnishes the raw materials for a personal value system and philosophy. Instead of the pragmatic basis of getting into college, getting a job, or meeting state requirements, a study of different world cultures becomes a sort of testing ground for the creation of a personal philosophy of life. This is a true liberal arts education.

CONCLUSION

Any organization of the world civilization course will leave out much that is valuable—even essential. Any method of organization will tell only part of the story. None will apprehend the total truth of man. No one method completely frees man from the curse of ethnocentricism or from the fallibility of his own understandings.

Should one opt for the inductive approach, using the social science disciplines, he must make a further selection of which disciplines to employ. No one teacher can handle all the processes of sociology in a year, let alone anthropology, economics, and political science. Furthermore, there is intense disagreement within the disciplines themselves, for there are no real laws of social science that have the reliability of the law of gravity.

Perhaps the most important caution about the discipline approach is that it employs an ordering of knowledge that has evolved largely out of Western thought. Prospective teachers should remember the example of Arnold Toynbee, who ultimately admitted his use of Greece and Rome as models for all civilizations and came to see the fallacy in holding that model to be universal.

The discipline approach may also tend to obscure the importance of man's collective knowledge. Professor Mark Krug has observed that man must stand on the shoulders of past giants to go on. Therefore it is necessary to know what these giants did in history and what they have contributed to total civilization. A student who has mastered the social science processes may still be missing a vital element in his education: the ability to identify and appreciate the collective knowledge of man.

One might also suggest that learning basic social science processes or generalizations may inhibit creative thought on the part of the students. There is a tendency for the teacher already to have arrived at the generalizations that the raw data are *supposed to reveal.* A teacher may even *stack* his raw data so that students will be led to conclusions that he or the textbook author have already decided are valid. This is more closely related to scholasticism than to an open-ended induction, which allows data in the hands of students to come out where they will. Creative thought is the breaking through of old thought patterns and yesterday's generalizations. Creative thinkers of the past—men like Galileo, Freud, Darwin, or Einstein—broke from established methods of inquiry when they made their great discoveries. By teaching known processes to our students, teachers must not inhibit their own potential spontaneous responses to knowledge.

To avoid some of these potential dangers, an area-studies approach might be used as an organizing system. Here one would try to teach the notion that, as Ruth Benedict observed, "Each culture has an organic unity which makes it unique." The area-studies emphasis may offer that opportunity to see the social, economic, political, and other phenomena in a context which is a unique cultural synthesis. This approach also allows the use of literature, art, science, philosophy, and any other data which serve to give insight into the culture.

The area-studies or single-culture organization, however, also has its limitations. Students may get the impression that cultural differences are exaggerated and that cultures have developed in isolation. If an attempt is made to study a single area in some depth, teachers may find themselves back in the habit of stringing together endless facts which will end in more student confusion. Students may become so involved in a given culture that they fail to perceive the larger abstractions about man and his behavior. The allocation of time may also be a factor against the area-studies approach. In a given year, it would be necessary to limit sharply the number of civilizations that it would be possible to study. This type of organization may make a less economic use of the hours and days available than the social science disciplines method.

An emphasis on area studies, social science processes, institutions, or themes does not imply that all or any of them are incompatible. In the organization any teacher wishes to construct, segments of all may be appropriated and synthesized. One could take the social science process organization and use it as the basic structure for a historical approach starting from the ancient civilizations of Egypt, Sumeria, the Indus Valley, and China. Or history could be left out, and selected societies could be used as subjects of analysis.

If an area studies approach is the organizing structure, the teacher can again use a historical approach or concentrate on only contemporary cultures or do a little of each. This system in no way contradicts the social science discipline approach. It is still necessary to make choices. It must be decided which disciplines are to be used as tools for analysis in the culture. One may want to use several in a sequence. For example, economic questions may be stressed for Japan, anthropological questions for Africa, political questions for Europe, and sociological questions for India. It would be decided in advance which areas and which social science processes would be used. Whichever are chosen, they should be few. It is far better to use four or five processes, such as cultural diffusion, economic growth, urbanization, transfer of political power, than to try to cover all for all cultures. Again, the key is selection.

It would be possible to use much the same organization with selected area studies using a thematic approach. Again, specific cultures or civilizations would be chosen in advance. Then the theme would be chosen from any field of knowledge. The objects that the culture chose for artistic representation, the attitude toward nature of the selected civilizations, the reform movements that were carried out, revolution, renaissance, the subjects for art, the most honored ideas, the type of music—all of these could be analyzed in any selection of cultures, historic or otherwise, that was made.

Using man's basic institutions as a format can also be synthesized with the other organizations. Working with the students to develop questions based on their own experiences about family, government, economics, religion, science, warfare, education, and the arts would necessarily include the use of anthropology, political science, economics, philosophy, art, and literary criticism. These questions, as already discussed, can then become the keys for whatever areas are selected for study. Again, a historical approach can be used to trace the development of government, economic systems, literature, while art or history can be left out. Each area or culture may be analyzed by asking the same questions about each culture. As in all these approaches, the student would be comparing other answers to those his culture and he himself has evolved. One advantage of this method is that it invites the inclusion of the humanities, philosophy, science, and other disciplines which normally are excluded in a regular historical analysis and would be left out with a purely social science process organization. The use of art, literature, and music especially offer tangible cultural expressions and therefore give the student an emotional as well as an intellectual experience with the culture.

The types of organizations are almost infinite. Whichever is chosen is bound to leave out valuable concepts and important areas, but this is the reality of selection. Certainly the teachers' strengths, the background and interests of the students, the important problems of the day, the wishes of the community, and the philosophy of the teacher and the school would all be important factors in making the selection. Whatever the choices made, they must, of course, always rest on certain guiding principles. These would seem to be: (1) choices must be made which offer a direct correlation with the student's own life and experience; (2) selections are to be made in conceptual areas, not informational areas (revolution, socialization, relation of man and nature, golden age, power are conceptual areas; the age of Louis XIV, Roman Empire, T'ang dynasty, Age of Exploration are informational areas); (3) selections are kept to a minimum of areas and processes, probably no more than five or six for any given year; (4) selections are made to insure that knowledge will be approached in question form; therefore, selections must offer examples of man's great questions about which most students are interested.

These guiding principles may suggest course organizations which on the surface bear little relationship to one another, but a deeper look should reveal that these principles are always being employed.

To end on a didactic note, nine postulates are offered as guiding principles that should be adhered to no matter what the organization of the world history course may be:

1. Never abstract from abstractions; always abstract from something that can be felt, heard, smelled, seen, tasted. It must be concrete. Start going up the abstraction ladder from the student's own life and experiences. Set his home against a Chinese home, his relationship to father, and grandfather against Indian counterparts. Deal only with basic questions he has raised or can raise with help.

2. Use facts and data as means to an end. The end is an understanding, a conceptual framework of a culture or process, not the data themselves.

3. Have a hierarchy of concepts in your mind or written down for the year (or at least periodically during the year). What are you trying to get across about China, India, ancient Greece? If you have only forty-five minutes on Athens, what is the most basic concept you want to get across—individualism, rationalism, birth of philosophy, life-style—or what?

4. Let students come to their own insights, conclusions, understandings; give data and materials which challenge students to think and draw conclusions. Beware of telling, preaching, or imposing your own values and conclusions. Let students have the thrill of going through the process of anthropology, sociology, history, political science. Stress the idea that you, too, have biases, tastes, etc., and that your view is not the only one and is subject to modification if challenged.

5. Don't make a fetish of covering curriculum. You may cover all the ground, but you won't cultivate any. Be realistic as to what you expect students to remember. What do you remember now from your tenth-grade world history course? Why do you think that is?

6. Test for processes and concepts. Perhaps even give students the facts to do something with. It is more important to know what to do with data than to remember the data. Data banks will soon make available all the data one wants at one's fingertips. The question is how to handle them.

7. Use every unit of study to enhance basic generalizations about history and the social sciences. Go deeper each time you deal with a process. Revolution, urbanization, reformation, commercial revolution, thought, renaissance, etc. Select your areas so that they offer a chance to deal with these generalizations in each culture.

8. Always teach from the point of view of what the questions are, not what the answers are. If students can learn to raise good questions, they can always find the answers easily.

9. Don't ever assume one world view or cultural criterion as a basis for studying other cultures, especially the Western world view. The basic questions our culture raises are fine to use for studying other cultures, but the answers are not.

NOTES

1. Paul R. Hanna and Richard Gross, "Generalizations from the Social Sciences," in *Social Studies in Elementary Schools,* John V. Michaelis, (ed.), Thirty-second Yearbook of the National Council for the Social Studies (Washington, D.C., 1962), pp. 62-89.

2. Edwin Fenton, *The New Social Studies,* New York: Holt, Rinehart and Winston, Inc., 1967, p. 13.

3. A. H. Marckwardt, "Humanities in Non-Western Studies," in Bigelow and Legter (eds.) *Non-Western World in Higher Education,* The American Academy of Political and Social Science, November, 1964, volume 356, p. 50.

CHAPTER XI

Teaching About Latin America

by Professor Emeritus Durward Pruden

The contemporary teacher of Latin America faces an intriguing and challenging panorama of human experience about which far too little is known in the United States. In this brief chapter of a "methods" text, it is utterly impossible to give even a condensed version of the complex history and civilization of all the nations "south of the border," so it will be assumed that the classroom social studies teacher already knows this "content," or at least has available sources for learning it by independent study. Consequently, this treatise will deal primarily with *how to teach* about the area. The discussion will be divided into four sections: I. The Conventional (though not necessarily "old-fashioned") Approach; II. Some Newer Methods and Possibilities; III. Some Suggested Dos and Don'ts; IV. Bibliographical and Other Resource Materials.

I. THE CONVENTIONAL APPROACH

Depending on the amount of time available and on the resources at hand, the teacher uses texts, magazines, newspapers, maps, films, discussions, and even a bit of entertaining and dynamic lecturing to organize the material in something like the following manner:

A. Background of the early Hispanic peninsula, which congealed into the nation-states of Spain and Portugal and produced the culture and character of the *conquistadores* and early European colonial settlers.

231

B. Background of the period of exploration and discovery that resulted in the conquest of the New World.

C. Brief survey of the so-called New World—especially the area south of present-day United States.

  1. Its essential geography
  2. Its flora, fauna, and other resources
  3. The aborigines
     a. Aztecs of Mexico
     b. Mayas of Yucatan
     c. Incas of the Andes
     d. Minor groups
        (1) Caribs and Arawaks of the Caribbean
        (2) Chibchas of Colombia
        (3) Araucanians of Chile
        (4) Guarani of Paraguay

  D. Conquest and settlement

  1. Cortes in Mexico
  2. Pizarro in Peru
  3. Almagro and Valdivia in Chile
  4. Ponce de León in Florida and the Caribbean
  5. Coronado, De Soto, Cabeza de Vaca, and others in the southern United States
  6. Captaincies in Brazil

  E. Colonial era (concept of mercantilism)

  1. Government—institution of vice-monarchies
  2. Economic exploitation—looting, mining, *encomienda* system
  3. The society—class system
  4. Role of the church

F. Wars of Independence

1. European background (Napoleon)
2. Hidalgo and Iturbide in Mexico
3. Bolívar in northern South America
4. San Martin in Argentina and other parts of southern South America
5. Bernardo O'Higgins in Chile
6. Unique situation of Dom Pedro I in Brazil

G. Common problems of independence

1. Monarchies or republics?
2. If republics, centralist or federated? [Note: The term "federal" is largely misused or reversed in the United States and has come to refer to centralist activities of the national government.]
3. Dreams of continental union versus local separatism

At this point, the teacher is faced with a very difficult task of selection, because it is simply impossible to cover in a satisfactory manner the national history (since independence) of *all* the Latin American nations in any conceivable time allotment below the university level—and it is difficult even then. A customary choice at this point is to deal rapidly with the national history of the nearest Latin neighbor of the United States—Mexico, plus that of the important A-B-C countries of Argentina, Brazil, and Chile—though some experts now feel that in recent decades Venezuela has become important enough to be included also. If only one country can be worked in, it should, of course, be neighboring Mexico. Its history since independence is customarily organized in the following manner:

H. Independent Mexico

1. Santa Anna period of semianarchy, 1821-1855
2. Benito Juárez period of reform and idealism, 1855-1876
3. Porfirio Diaz period of stability and stagnation, 1876-1911

4. Mexican Revolution, 1910-1920
5. Modern Mexico of reforms, progress, stability, and wavering between the Left and the Right

It must be remembered, of course, that the history of *all* the nations of Latin America is just as detailed interesting history as is Mexico's—Brazil's unique experiment with a continuation of monarchy for a while being a good case in point.

Not many secondary teachers with intense interest in Latin America have had the good fortune of Dr. Robert Meredith of the Mount Kisco, New York, public schools, who for some twelve years has been permitted to teach an entire senior, elective year of the subject. On the basis of his experience, he divides the year's material as follows:

1. Precolonial and colonial period (as above), about 8 to 10 weeks.
2. National period (as above, but with variations depending on the "news of the day"), about 16 to 18 weeks
3. Contemporary problems, about 8 to 10 weeks
   a. Economic underdevelopment
   b. Political instability—newness of democratic tradition
   c. Maldistribution of wealth—class structure
   d. Military intervention
   e. Population explosion, etc.

Teachers who have a much briefer period to teach the subject—such as those teaching the usual world history course—will have to do much picking and choosing and condensing, depending on time and resources available, curriculum requirements, and local considerations. Perhaps the following section may offer some help in this matter.

II. SOME NEWER METHODS AND POSSIBILITIES

Probably the most basic element in modern teaching methodology is *motivation.* Experienced teachers realize that many students—perhaps the majority of them—simply will not learn merely for that ancient and perhaps mythical reason, the sheer joy of learning and knowing.

However, it is almost universally recognized in the profession that practically all normal children can—and likely will—learn about things in which they are intensely interested. How, then, can students be so motivated toward parts of the world that seem to be so far away and even nebulous? Creative American teachers have a distinct advantage in this area:

A. A vast part of the United States—virtually the entire Southwest —was once under the Spanish flag, and was later a part of Mexico. No other non-Latin nation has entire states with such obviously Spanish-derived (sometimes Indian-derived) names as New *Mexico,* Texas *(Tejas),* California, Arizona (the dry zone), Nevada (the snowy place), Colorado (the red [clay] place), and Montana (the mountainous place)—to say nothing of cities with such Spanish names as Los Angeles (the angels), Sante Fe (Holy Faith), and hundreds of others, as well as various rivers, mountains, areas, communities, foods, popular sayings ("savvy," "vamoose"), songs, dances (rumba, conga), etc. Surely the students of these areas, as well as those of other areas, can be motivated as to the background causes of these non-Anglo terms.

B. In an earlier chapter, Professor London has written extensively about using the class itself as a resource unit. What better example of the possibility of this use can be given than the presence of hundreds of thousands of students of Mexican ancestry in hundreds of schools in the Southwest of the United States? To these may be added the many thousands of students of Puerto Rican descent in the schools of the Northeast, especially in the New York area; and more recently the children of Cuban emigrants in the Florida area—as well as smatterings of these and others throughout the United States.

Some of these children, whose families may have suffered either overt or subtle discrimination because of their ethnic background, may at first seem reticent about it; but once assured and convinced by a sincere teacher that their "mother culture" is not only understood but actually admired and respected, most such students will respond warmly and enthusiastically in class, carrying the entire class along into a sort of firsthand participation in the joys of Latin life—its music, songs, dances, foods; its customs and family life—and, hopefully, its history and its problems. Most Latin-background children in a friendly environment are quite uninhibited about singing, dancing, and the like, so that very interesting class programs can be worked out, perhaps drawing in the school's Spanish language class and various non-Latin students.

What more enjoyable class or school Christmas celebration could there be than the traditional Spanish *piñata* party, with a few chosen students blindfolded and trying to poke poles into the hanging clay vase to break it and spill its "goodies" out, to the shrieking enjoyment of the onlookers? Such "goodies" could include, among other things, such widely available Mexican tidbits as toasted *tortilla* chips, known to any American child who has been through a supermarket as *fritos*. These are just a few typical examples of enjoyable motivation techniques with which a creative and imaginative teacher can begin.

C. Miscellaneous community resources. Many American communities now have all sorts of Latin-related resources—some often unnoticed but available to a resourceful teacher. In addition to the types of people and things previously described, there are often various Latin American officials around—from ambassadors and United Nations missions personnel to local consular officials and official tourist agents. Many local museums—even small ones—have sections on Latin America, and there is currently a "rage" about pre-Columbian art and artifacts (see almost any antique store!). Various movies, television programs, magazines, and daily newspapers deal with aspects of life "south of the border." Various American citizens, usually including some students, have vacationed or toured there. Airlines have brochures and public relations people eager to speak, as do some commercial interests. Alert students can help a good teacher dig them up—all toward the goal of a more meaningful study of this important area of social studies.

D. Examples of student projects. There seems to be no end to the myriad interests of motivated students. Here are only a few from the hundreds that might arise: A student, or a committee of them, might keep a running scrapbook on current newspaper and magazine articles on all the nations of Latin America and be prepared at any time to summarize for the class yesterday's events there. A student particularly interested in clothing fashions or textile designs can make beautiful color reproductions of Indian and colonial motifs. An art student with some talent in portraiture can copy old textbook pictures of famous characters in history and put the same faces into modern settings without the beards and armor of the originals—Columbus as a modern sea captain, Cortes as a modern business executive, or Queen Isabella in evening gown and walking her little dog, make interesting conversation pieces. A student interested in calendars will be amazed at the accuracy of the double (secular and sacred) calendar of the ancient Mayas—which was more accurate than that of the Spaniards at that time! And mathematically oriented students will be equally amazed at the Maya invention of an entire mathematics system based on units of twenty (vegesimal)—from their even more ancient ancestors counting on both their toes *and* their fingers (from which the decimal system probably originated). The Inca *quipu* (a tassle of different-colored strings) is always fascinating as an ancient way of communicating by tying certain kinds of knots in certain positions on certain strings—as well as Inca efforts to transplant living teeth. Home economics students can prepare tasty native dishes—Latin American (especially Mexican) cookbooks are available in English, and most supermarkets carry such items as canned tamales, chili and beans, as well as the aforementioned fritos. Amateur musicians can really make their guitars strum on such stirring songs as "El Rancho Grande." Sombreros and serapes may strangely appear far from their native lands. Literature and films (both commercial and documentary) are filled with endearing Latin children.

Inquisitive students can not only learn some elementary research techniques but also develop a critical and analytical attitude toward so-called popular history by inquiring into such interesting questions as:

1. If Columbus had never lived, when would the New World likely have been discovered? (Answer: Certainly no later than eight years after 1492, when in 1500 the Portuguese sea captain Cabral accidently touched the eastern bulge of Brazil while trying to sail around the western bulge of Africa.)
2. Did Magellan really circumnavigate the earth? (No, he was

killed in the Philippines—his captain, Elcano, completed the voyage.)

3. How did "America" happen to get named after the wrong person? (The French map-maker Waldseemuller had seen Amerigo Vespucci's article but had not yet heard of Columbus.)

4. Was it really Marco Polo who led the famous expedition to the Far East? (No, his older brother Nickoli Polo took along the boy, Marco, who later wrote about it.)

III. SOME SUGGESTED DOS AND DON'TS

So far this chapter has dealt with some of the fairly well-established facts of history and some possible teaching techniques. What follows may possibly be deemed by some to be somewhat controversial, so the individual teacher may use, or not use, particular items, according to his own overall political predilections. They do, however, seem to some who have taught the subject many years, to be worthy of consideration.

A. Probably all groups everywhere in the world are afflicted with some degree of ethnocentrism—the idea that the way they are, and the way *they* do things, is right and best—and that others who are different are either wrong or at least peculiar. Americans have not escaped this tendency, and studying Latin America furnishes several good opportunities to point this out to students:

1. To many Latin Americans, the term "United States of America" seems to be an overly grandiose name, since all of the Western Hemisphere from the Bering Straits at the north to the Strait of Magellan (or Tierra del Fuego) at the south is America; thus, all peoples of the hemisphere are, technically, "Americans." There are officially other "United States" *in* America; for example, The United States of Mexico and the United States of Brazil. So, many informed Latin Americans insist on calling citizens of this nation *norteamericanos* or by a Spanish term meaning merely "United States-ians"; and they point out that a more proper name for this nation would be the "United States of the Central Portion of North America"! Another

example might be that if the "United Statesian" visiting in Argentina who remarked to the people there: "It seems so strange down here beneath the equator for your seasons to be reversed, and to have summer at Christmastime." To this an Argentine citizen replied: "Oh, no, *señor norteamericano,* we have had summer at Christmastime all my life, and for many centuries before—it is *your* seasons that are reversed." Another example would be that of the United States professor trying to establish rapport with Chilean university students by saying: "I have great respect for the 'father of your country,' the great Bernardo O'Higgins—in fact, he was the George Washington of Chile." Immediately the Chilean students answered most respectfully: "Oh, no, *señor professor norteamericano,* your great George Washington was the Bernardo O'Higgins of the United States!"

2. Likewise, most nations of the world are at times afflicted with a bit of chauvinism—including the United States. So it may come as a sobering thought to students to learn that some historians consider the Spanish-American War of 1898 to have been completely unnecessary —whipped up by jingoistic elements of the American press and by a contemporary spirit of "imitative imperialism"; and accomplishing little more than (as one writer puts it humorously) "enabling Teddy Roosevelt to charge up San Juan Hill in Cuba—and right into the White House." And it might be pointed out that a few years later Latins were filled with righteous indignation when the same American president gave as his excuse for intervention in their affairs that he would ". . . teach those Dagoes how to behave"—to say nothing of his manipulations to get the Panama Canal Zone away from Colombia.

Despite the wealth, beauty, and importance of the great Southwest to the United States, it is nevertheless true that some historians consider the Mexican War of 1846-48 to have been thinly disguised imperialism under the slogan of Manifest Destiny to expand "from sea to shining sea"—and fortunately just before the California gold rush of 1849! A young congressman from Illinois, skeptical of the whole idea, introduced the Spot Resolution to try to ascertain whether the first shot was actually fired on Mexican or American soil. His name was Abraham Lincoln.

3. It is also thought-provoking for American students to consider the

proposition that their nation has somewhat damaged its moral image in the eyes of some educated Latins by choosing to divide dictators into "bad guys" and "good guys," as in the 1965 landing of American marines in the Dominican Republic "to prevent communism," while blithely ignoring the other half of the same Caribbean island with its stern dictatorship of "Papa" Duvalier in Haiti.

4. It has been customary to assume that Colonial Spain's imperialists, *conquistadores*, and even its church, were entirely greedy and ruthless. Of course, some of this was true, but probably no more so than it was for other imperialist nations of the time; and the Spanish conquerors never claimed, as did the settlers to the north, "that the only good Indian is a dead Indian." There was no religious freedom, and the church did destroy the Mayan literature it considered pagan. However, the little care there was for the infirm, poor, and orphaned usually came from the church; and, even in their overzealous conversion of the Indians to Catholicism, the early missionaries insisted on respect for Indian family life—a far cry from the tearing apart of families in the nefarious slave trading in American history.

Closely related to this matter is the often overlooked fact that the Spanish and Portuguese empires in the New World endured almost twice as long as did that of England; and the final demise of the Spanish Empire was caused not so much by autocratic government as by the economic practices of mercantilism, which were, incidentally, also a major cause of the rebellion of England's thirteen colonies.

B. It is also proper to stress that, even though there are some common historical elements and problems applicable to all of Latin America, it is not one vast homogeneous unit; each nation is also unique in some respects. For example, the largely Indian, rural nations such as Bolivia, Mexico, and Paraguay are different from (but not inferior to) the more sophisticated, Europeanized (but not necessarily more democratic) Buenos Aires, Montevideo, Rio de Janeiro areas.

C. The teacher should avoid stereotyping Latin Americans as lazy *mañana* people; because, in truth, the very opposite is largely true, as is well known to anyone who has observed these energetic, ambitious people working hard at their jobs—sometimes against great handicaps. One stereotype that persists is that of the Mexican *peon* sitting on the sidewalk, leaning against a wall or fence, sombrero pulled over himself as he drowses the day away. This version is in the television cigarette commercial in which the nagging wife (or *señorita* of the moment!) yells to her Wally Beery-Pancho Villa-type man: "Paco, you don' feeneesh your revolution—you don' feeneesh de shelf—you don' feeneesh nuthin'—not even your cee-garette!" But the next day, after she has introduced him to the glories of Brand X cigarettes, and Paco is mounting his horse, the lady inquires: "Paco, you gonna feeneesh your revolution today?" But Paco childishly answers: "No—maybe *mañana* —today I gonna feenesh my Brand X cee-garettes."

The teacher can assist the students in not jumping to the previously mentioned ethnocentric conclusions that various Latin customs are extremely odd—the midday *siesta*, for instance. This custom makes considerable sense where the midday is unbearably hot but the early mornings and evenings are nice and cool (even without air-conditioning)—and where large families enjoy the togetherness of a midday lunch and rest period at home before continuing their work until, perhaps, 8 or 9 P.M. Nor is the 5 or 6 P.M. "tea," with sandwiches, cakes, and ice cream, so peculiar when the customary dinner hour is not until 9 or 10 P.M. Closely related is the idea that Latin food is so hot that eating it is like consuming unbridled fire! Students can readily understand that the mucous linings of Latin stomachs are exactly like those of other people and that many of their foods are, in fact, extremely bland—Mexican *tortillas,* for instance, are made solely of the pulp of fresh corn meal. Of course, the early Indians, lacking herds of beef cattle, did manage to make their protein-rich beans more palatable with seasonings, sometimes including hot peppers; but the really hot sauce *(picante)* is usually served on the side, to be used or not—or sparingly—just as coarse ground red peppers might be sprinkled over Italian spaghetti or a little Louisiana Tabasco sauce over vegetables in the southern United States.

D. Finally, American teachers are urged not to waste too much time in "going overboard" about Castro's Cuba. Considering the current climate of American excitement (especially in the news media), it is easy to magnify the little island nation out of all proper perspective. It is, and long has been, a very unimportant nation—not too well known to most Latins themselves, nor to Americans except for the few pre-Castro tourists to its gambling casinos or to its lovely beaches. It seems likely that the "Cuban situation"—if it has any lasting effects at all on Latin America as a whole—will probably be in: (1) spurring liberal leaders, including some of the formerly conservative clergy, to accelerate long overdue democratic reforms, especially in the economic area; and (2) furnishing the old landlord oligarchies (joined by some newly rich commercial interests) a popular polarization point in opposing needed democratic changes. Of course there is also the legitimate fear among many Latin American leaders that Castro is intent on exporting his revolution to every part of the continent, a fear that was borne out in part by Che Guevara's abortive revolutionary activities in Bolivia.

IV. BIBLIOGRAPHICAL AND OTHER RESOURCE MATERIALS

A discussion of bibliographical teaching resources may be found in other chapters of this book. Classroom teachers are also urged to watch continuously the new book lists of all publishers and the available book reviews, and to maintain contact with their school librarians, since a veritable avalanche of books on Latin America (many of them inexpensive paperbacks) is flooding the market at the moment.

As to specific text material, if the work on Latin America is merely a unit in a world history or regions course, the official school text for that course will likely contain a condensed coverage, as well as suggested related readings. If the teacher wishes to use a separate, brief paperback covering the entire history and life of Latin America, he might consider: Harold F. Peterson's *Latin America* (New York: The Macmillan Company, revised edition, 1971), 150 pages; or Samuel Steinberg's *Latin America—Past, Present, and Future* (New York: Oxford Book Company, 1952), 214 pages.

Those few teachers fortunate enough to be able to offer an entire senior, elective year on the subject might consider using at least parts of any of the several good college-level survey texts, of which one fine example is: Hubert Herring's *A History of Latin America* (New York: Alfred A. Knopf, 1961, latest of the frequent revisions).

For outside readings on special student interests the constantly expanding list is almost endless. A few fine ones chosen at random are William H. Prescott's classical *Conquest of Mexico* (New York: E. P. Dutton & Co., 1929) and *Conquest of Peru* (Philadelphia: J. B. Lippincott & Co., 1869), still interesting to advanced readers (paperbacks by Modern Library Giants); and Victor W. Von Hagen's *The Aztec: Man and Tribe* (New York: New American Library, 1959), *World of the Maya* (New York: New American Library, 1960), and *Realm of the Incas* (New York: New American Library, 1961), also available in inexpensive paperbacks from Mentor: *Ancient Civilizations,* the New American Library. Gertrude Diamants's *The Days of Ofelia* is typical of the many poignant books about appealing Latin American children.

A good overall summary of modern Latin American character and life (for high school students) may be found in Frank Tannenbaum's *Ten Keys to Latin America* (New York: A. A. Knopf, 1966).

In addition to various types of source material previously mentioned in other parts of this chapter, good materials—some of them free—may be obtained from:

- The Pan American Union, central organ of the Organization of American States (OAS), Washington, D.C.
- The Library of Congress, Washington, D.C. Its Hispanic Foundation Reference Department has excellent bibliographies, as well as many of the materials themselves.
- The University of the State of New York, New York State Education Department, Office of Foreign Area Studies, Albany, N.Y., distributes excellent bibliographies and other materials, as well as holding occasional summer workshops on various world regions. In fact, many American universities and colleges now offer courses on Latin America; and several have well-financed Latin American research institutes—the University of Texas, Austin, for example.
- The United Nations itself, as well as various related private

groups, such as the U.N. Committee of the National Council of Women, distribute material.

- The National Council for the Social Studies (a department of the National Education Association), 1201 Sixteenth Street N.W., Washington, D.C., has excellent material on *many* aspects of curriculum, methods, and materials on all world regions; and its official journal, *Social Education,* occasionally has articles on teaching about Latin America.
- The Foreign Policy Association, 345 East Forty-sixth Street, New York, N.Y. 10017, handles much material about the area.
- Various magazines—both scholarly and popular—from *Current History* to *Life*—often run individual articles and occasionally devote entire issues to Latin America. The latter also publishes excellent picture books on various nations. *National Geographic Magazine* often has articles, excellent photographs, and well-researched artists' representations of pre-Columbian life. Some of these are fine for opaque and overhead projector showing in class. The ever present school magazines such as *Scholastic* frequently have pertinent articles.
- Fine films, some in beautiful color, may be rented from such film libraries as the one at New York University, Washington Square, N.Y., N.Y. 10003. John Steinbeck's classical *Forgotten Village* and Jacques Soustelle's *Pre-Columbian Mexican Art* are just two fine examples. Or films and filmstrips may be purchased outright from a number of the flourishing documentary film companies—one being Universal Education and Visual Arts, 221 Park Avenue South, N.Y., N.Y. 10003. Some publishers, such as Mc-Cormack-Mathers, New York, N.Y., put out, not only small booklets on individual countries, but teaching kits as well. The standard map publishing companies have an abundance of both general and specialized maps of the area.

CHAPTER XII

Teaching About Africa

Professor Emeritus Durward Pruden

There has never been anything dark about the so-called Dark Continent of Africa except the shadow of ignorance that surrounds discussion of that vast area. Actually, the great continent is the very *opposite* of dark or drab: It is, rather, a giant kaleidoscope of brilliant, flashing light, of beating equatorial sunlight, vast deserts, huge rain forests, grassy plains, lofty mountains, roaring rivers, crashing waterfalls, canyons, lakes, invigorating highlands, flourishing foliage, unbelievable subsurface wealth, and an almost endless variety of the most majestic animals the earth has produced—and probably the ancient cradle of man himself.

As was said previously about Latin America, it is utterly impossible in this brief chapter on a "methods" text to give even a condensed version of the complex history and fascinating civilizations of *all* of the continent; so it will be assumed here that the classroom social studies teacher already has an objective and balanced sufficiency of this "content," or at least has available sources for learning it by independent study. Consequently, this treatise will deal primarily with *how to teach* about Africa. The discussion will be divided into sections on: I. The Difficulties and Problems of Organizing a Unit on Africa, II. Suggested Delimitations of the Unit on Africa, III. Several Possible Approaches to the Organization of the Course on Africa South of the Sahara, IV. Some Great Concepts That May Be Emphasized, V. Some Suggested Dos and Don'ts, and VI. Source Materials.

I. THE DIFFICULTIES AND PROBLEMS OF ORGANIZING
A UNIT ON AFRICA

If there is any one thing on which practically all African scholars and experts agree, it is that there simply is *no one* correct, or best, or even "most logical" way of organizing a course on this huge, complex, and diversified area. For example, Europe is often taught under such subdivisions as "Ancient," "Medieval," and "Contemporary." United States History courses often include the settlement, the colonial era, the early national era, and up to the Civil War in the first half; and from the Civil War to the present in the second half. A course on Latin America may be logically divided into a first half about the aborigines, the discovery and conquest, the colonial era, and up to the wars of independence; and a last half dealing with the national history (since independence) of the various nations up to the present. But none of these types of neat and "logical" divisions precisely fits the majestic panorama of human development and existence that is Africa. How, then, does the teacher approach this complicated problem? Perhaps a good first step is to ascertain whether some parts of the continent may logically be eliminated from the course so as to narrow the field.

II. SUGGESTED DELIMITATIONS
OF THE UNIT ON AFRICA

Shocking as it may at first seem, it is strongly urged here that the northern, Moslem, largely Arabic tier (Morocco, Algeria, Tunisia, Libya, and Egypt) be omitted. Its history is, of course, extremely important, especially that of ancient Egypt and Carthage; but many experts feel that it is more properly a part of the history of the Arabic world, or of the Middle East, or even of Europe. One authority has even gone so far as to quip that it is not true that Egypt, for example, is *separated* from Europe by the Mediterranean Sea, but, rather, is *joined* to Europe by it; and is *separated* from Africa by the Sahara Desert! Be that as it may, it is probably true that most American students approaching a course on Africa tend to assume that it will be primarily about Negro

Africa—black Africa—in effect, *Africa south of the Sahara.* This line of demarcation is not absolutely accurate, but will suffice; nor is it accurate to refer to Negro Africa as "tropical Africa," because millions of blacks live far south of the tropics in more temperate climate—as, for example, in the Union of South Africa.

Equally surprising as the above elimination of "North Africa" is the suggestion to eliminate from a study of Africa itself the history of the Negro *in America.* This is a very important part of *American* history, and perhaps should now be strongly emphasized as a sort of "compensatory" history to try partially to make up for past neglect and unfairness; still, it *is* American, *not* African history. Sadly enough, once the blacks were loaded onto the slave ships, they ceased to be a part of Africa and became, in one manner or another, a part of the United States—or of Brazil, or of the Caribbean. Only a few pathetic vestiges of their ancient heritage survived the stultifying and rigid conformity of New World slavery—notwithstanding the current effort to reidentify with the mother country.

An exception to the above delimitation can, of course, be made if Liberia and Sierra Leone are studied in the African unit, because here there is a valid relationship, Liberia having been established as a haven for freed American slaves, and Sierra Leone having been established by British abolitionists.

III. SEVERAL POSSIBLE APPROACHES TO THE ORGANIZATION OF THE COURSE ON AFRICA SOUTH OF THE SAHARA

A. The Historical Approach

Despite the previous comments about the difficulty of establishing logical guidelines about the teaching of the history of the entire continent of Africa, this historical approach has, and can be, used—sometimes with considerable success, at least concerning the last hundred years. The historical treatment may be broken down into the following sections:

1. *The Ancient Period in Africa South of the Sahara*

This will, of necessity, be the most vague and least explicit part of the unit because of the paucity of exact knowledge of Africa's ancient past once one gets below the aforementioned northern tier without the written records of ancient Egypt, Carthage, and so on. There is, or has been until recent decades, a sort of historical vacuum about the other parts of the continent because:

(a) Of the approximately 900 different dialects spoken, very few developed into a *written* language in ancient times; thus, most of whatever history survived had to be "oral" history, which is likely to become intertwined with folklore, legend, mythology, and so forth.

(b) Until the last few decades, few European or other Western historiographers, anthropologists, and other social scientists did much professional work in or about Africa—and even much of the fairly recent work has been in the French, Portuguese, or German languages.

(c) During the past hundred years under colonialism, black scholars were, if not prevented, at least not particularly encouraged in this activity. Nor were publishers (nor seemingly, the public) particularly interested.

(d) However, in recent decades, and especially in recent years, some very fine scholars, both black and white, are beginning to piece together valid evidence that there were, indeed, a number of highly developed societies in sub-Saharan Africa in ancient times, such as the Sudanic civilization, the ancient kingdoms of Cush and Ghana (far more vast than the present nation by that name), and are indicated to have existed by the artists of Benin and the activities of the wide-ranging Bantu (Swahili-speaking), the Bushmen, the Pygmies, and others.

2. *The Period of Exploration and Discovery*

(a) The futile efforts of Prince Henry the Navigator to conquer the Moors and to find the semimythical Prester John.

(b) Other fifteenth-century Portuguese expeditions down the west coast of Africa: (1) arrival of Bartholomeu Diaz at the Cape in 1488; (2) Vasco da Gama's rounding of the Cape and going on to India in 1498, thus discovering the long-sought all-sea route to Asia.

(c) Declining interest in Africa as Spain, France, England, Portugal, and the Netherlands shifted their mercantilistic exploitations to lucrative North and South America, India, and other parts of Asia.

3. *The "New Imperialism" of the Late 1800s and the Early Twentieth Century*

(a) Appearance of the new nations of Germany and Italy on the scene after about 1870, demanding "their share" of wealth-producing colonies.

(b) Renewed "Mad Scramble" of Britain, France, Germany, Portugal, Italy, and Belgium to divide the only remaining available area (besides China, perhaps)—Africa.

4. *Colonialism in Africa from Shortly After 1870 to Approximately 1960*

(a) The Portuguese in Angola on the west coast and Mozambique on the east coast.

(b) The Germans in South *West* Africa and east coast Tanganyika: (1) World War I loss of German colonies.

(c) French seizure of vast French West Africa, French Equatorial Africa, plus Morocco, Algeria, and Tunisia.

(d) Italy in Libya and Eritrea and Somaliland and (eventually and briefly) in Ethiopia: (1) World War II loss of Italian colonies (Libya a bit later).

(e) King Leopold and the Belgians in the Congo.

(f) Britain's "Cape-to-Cairo" hodgepodge, including Egypt, Sudan, part of Somalia, and parts of East, Central, South, and West Africa.

(g) The unique history of the Union of South Africa from the arrival of the first Dutch Afrikaners, through the Boer Wars, to unilateral independence and apartheid. World War I loss of German colonies.

5. *Independence and the "New Freedom"*

(a) Post-World War II rise of African nationalism and anticolonialism.

(b) Demise of French African Empire: (1) tragedy in Algeria; (2) de Gaulle's decision for individual plebiscites—French Community of Nations.

(c) Belgium's abrupt departure from the Congo.

(d) Britain's more orderly retreat—Commonwealth of Nations.

(e) Portuguese dictatorial "hanging on" in Angola and Mozambique.

(f) Present situation: (1) considerable stability throughout, but a few military junta revolutions, and civil war in Nigeria; (2) confusion in the former Southern Rhodesia—Ian Smith, etc.; (3) continuing situation in the Union of South Africa; (4) continuing "moderate" rebellion in Angola and Mozambique.

B. The Geographic Approach

1. *Africa as a Whole*

A mid-twentieth-century American writer who tried somehow to organize *all* of Africa into one easily readable book was the journalist and popular historian John Gunther in one of his famous series of "Inside" books in 1953. Faced with the problem of covering (however superficially) the entire continent for popular reading, and not bound too heavily by the rigid discipline of historiography, he simply started with Morocco and swept across the northern tier to Egypt, and then southward along the *east* coast to the Union of South Africa, and from there up the *west* coast back to where he had started—with occasional "switchbacks" to pick up central areas, such as the then "Rhodesias," and the east-west split between the two large Portuguese colonies. Granted that this was rather a "shotgun-scatter" approach, still he managed it fairly well. Using this approach, the American secondary school teacher, if omitting the northern, Moslem tier, as previously discussed above, could:

(a) Discuss with less thoroughness the Sudan and the nations of the Horn—Ethiopia and the Somalis—not that they are unimportant, for there is still some Arab influence and historical relation to the Middle East (for instance, the Shebean dynasty of Ethiopia claims.to go back to the biblical "episode" between Solomon and the Queen of Sheba); and many of the inhabitants do not consider themselves purely African in the present "black" sense.

(b) Then down the *east* coast, covering: (1) Kenya and Uganda; (2) Tanzania, perhaps concentrating on the continental part of old, colonial German East Africa, later British Tanganyika; since the off-shore island of Zanzibar is (or, at least, *was*) historically somewhat oriented toward the Arab World and India; (3) for precisely the same reason the great island of Madagascar—the Malagasy Republic— might be limited to very brief mention in this particular unit; (4) Mozambique—the teacher is faced here with the problem of whether to switch across the continent to include the other huge Portuguese colony of Angola, or to omit Mozambique at that point and later return to it on reaching Angola in sweeping up the west coast—or to consider them entirely separately.

(c) Next the Union of South Africa, together with its three enclaves, Swaziland, Botswana (formerly Bechuanaland), and Lesotho (for-merly Basutoland)—and with the United Nations Trusteeship of South West Africa, which the Union oversees.

(d) Then up the east coast to include all or *some* of: (1) Angola (see comment above on Mozambique); (2) Republic of the Congo (for-merly Belgian Congo—Leopoldville); (3) Congo Republic (formerly French; capital, Brazzaville); (4) Gabon and Cameroon (mostly, along with the French Congo, Chad, and the Central African Republic, were part of French Equatorial Africa); (5) Nigeria (and Biafra); (6) the nations of "the Bulge": Dahomey, Togo, Ghana, Ivory Coast, Liberia, Sierra Leone, Guinea, Portuguese Guinea, Gambia, Senegal, and Mauretania; (7) A decision must then be made whether to switch back inland to include the former French colonies of Mali, Niger, Chad, and the Central African Republic; and the former British colonies of Rhodesia (formerly Southern Rhodesia), Zambia (formerly Northern Rhodesia), and Malawi (formerly Nyasaland).

A similar geographic approach would be to try to divide the entire sub-Saharan area into huge segments of East Africa, Southern Africa (not just the Union), West Africa, and Central Africa—giving less emphasis to the individual nation-states and concentrating more on each of these large segments. This approach may seem a bit contrived; yet, despite all the diversity in each segment, there are also some reasonably common themes of geography, economics, culture, and so forth.

2. Another Geographic Approach

This approach is also somewhat contrived—but perhaps more interesting to both students and teachers with a more scientific *geographic* leaning, would be simply to strike a line across the entire continent beneath the Northern tier and most of the Sahara at about 15 degrees north latitude, and then divide the area beneath the line into three bands of approximately 12 to 15 degrees latitude each. Thus, the class could sweep across the continent from coast to coast, studying in *each* band or strip the geography, the flora and fauna and other resources, and the people—along with their social and political organization. Of course, problems arise in this approach also because:

(a) The geography would not necessarily be uniform within each band, since climate, for instance, depends on altitude as well as latitude, and on other factors such as rainfall, prevailing winds, and so on.

(b) A look at any recent political map of Africa would show that in some cases these "bands" or strips would not conform to the northern or southern boundaries of currently established nation-states, but might cut right through the middle of some of them. However, it must likewise be recalled that these nation-state boundaries are themselves, in many cases, the artificial result of European colonial manipulations and compromises whereby the diplomats in various European foreign offices simply drew lines indiscriminately across maps in carving up the continent among themselves—often cutting right through tribal groups and ignoring subsistence areas, geographical entities, and the like.

(c) Such bands might be: (1) a Northern Tropical strip—from the Guinea coast on the west across to the Horn on the east coast. This would include the southern fringes of the Sahara and extend downward toward the equator; (2) a Central (or Southern Tropical) strip, along the equator and south of it, including most of Gabon, Zaire, Uganda, Kenya, and all of Tanzania; (3) Southern Africa, including most of Angola, the "former" Rhodesias and Nyasaland, Mozambique, and the Union's "conglomeration."

C. The Ethnic Approach

This approach would lean heavily on anthropology and would minimize colonial, political, and nation-state aspects; and it would concentrate on the great ethnic division groups: the so-called Negroids, Bushmen, Bantus, Pygmies, the white minority, and so forth.

D. The Samplings Approach

This might be very useful if class time were limited and might be along either of these two types:

1. *Nation-State Samplings*

Either by teacher choice or by class interests just a few might be chosen for careful study—perhaps formerly German and British Tanganyika (Tanzania) on the east coast, and formerly French Senegal on the west "Bulge" coast; plus possibly an inland, central nation as the Central African Republic, or Uganda, or Zambia (formerly British Northern Rhodesia).

2. *Tribal Samplings*

With some 400 tribal groups from which to choose, selection of only a few for study becomes quite random and possibly quite subjective as well. Purely for example only, one might mention the dominant Kikuyu of Kenya and the cattle-loving Masai near them; or the Zulu of the Union of South Africa, or the Hausa, Yoruba, or Ibo of Nigeria; or the Ashanti or Fanti of the Ghana area. Some of these are language as well as tribal groups, and the list is almost endless; but a sympathetic study and understanding of highly developed tribal life can be very rewarding.

E. The Topical Approach

This could cut across tribal, colony, and nation-state limits and cover a few *topics* of class interest. From among the many possible here are just a few examples:

(1) Relation of geography to life conditions

(2) Subsistence agriculture

(3) Degree of industrialization

(4) Inherent conflict between tribal life and the nation-state concept—and between rural and urban life.

(5) The music, art, and dances of Africa (very broad)

(6) Education, housing, and sanitation

(7) Life along the great rivers of Africa: Nile (upper Nile only if previously mentioned exclusion of northern tier is used), Congo, Niger, Zambesi, Volta, Senegal, Gambia, etc.

(8) The great lakes (Victoria and others), canyons (Rift Valley) and deserts (Kalahari) of sub-Saharan Africa

(9) The great variety of wild animal life: park reserves, safari hunters, poachers, conservation, etc.

(10) Diamonds, gold, and peanuts (called "groundnuts" in Africa)

(11) The whites in Africa—including, perhaps, such things as the former, irritating "Color Bar," as, for example, in the former east coast British colonies with such signs as: "Toilet for European Gentlemen," "Toilet for Asian (Indian) Gentlemen"—and often none for "African Gentlemen"! And the more recent reverse discrimination directed at East Asians by General Amin.

(12) Livingstone and Stanley

F. The Current Affairs Approach

Naturally, this would vary with the times. About two decades ago it would have focused on the independence movement, and a bit later on such personalities and events as the assassination of Patrice Lumumba, Moise Tshombe, the United Nations forces in the Congo; and the strange plane crash of United Nations Secretary-General Dag Hammarskjöld. In the late sixties and early seventies it might include: (1) civil war in Nigeria; (2) racial tension in Southern Rhodesia—unilateral independence, etc.; (3) the apartheid policy in the Union of South Africa; (4) current activities of African leaders of Africa, as Jomo Kenyatta of Kenya, Julius Nyerere of Tanzania, Milton Obote of Uganda, Kenneth Kaunda of Zambia, Leopold Senghor of Senegal, Haile Selassie of Ethiopia, and many others; (5) new hydroelectric power in Ghana from the Volta River dam; (6) Africans at the United Nations, etc.

IV. SOME GREAT CONCEPTS
THAT MAY BE EMPHAIZED

The most enlightened teachers with the most scientific knowledge to teach have sometimes been inhibited by popular disapproval of so-called controversial topics; but technology has now made the world so truly small and its problems so dangerously complex that the dedicated teacher must take the chance of teaching what science long has known, but which large segments of the people remain ignorant of—usually because of the stern resistance of powerful adult groups. One such topic is:

A. Evolution

As the result of a recent Supreme Court decision, it is not only permissible but also fairly safe to teach how the myriad forms of life came to exist on the earth. The majestic climb from primordial one-cell life to that of highly complex mammals is probably best left to the natural science classes, so the many millions of years of that development *prior* to the appearance of man will be omitted here except for the essential, general concept of *inherited mutations*—the little "accidents" in the reproductive process as unstable nature haphazardly, blindly experimented on billions of its early life forms, causing millions of mutations—some a hindrance, dooming the organisms to oblivion; others helpful in surviving in the rugged, primeval environment.

But the historically recent evolution of man (probably about two million years ago, and probably *in sub-Saharan Africa*); and the *even more recent* evolution among humans of very minor differences of absolutely no cultural significance, but about which some people get exercised, *is* the business of the social studies teacher. One of these is the degree of skin pigmentation.

1. *Skin Pigmentation*

A scientific explanation of the variety of human skin colors can be a very proper beginning for the study of Africa under present conditions. The following brief explanation may seem elementary to highly educated young social studies teachers, but literally millions of people (both black and white) do not understand it, and they desperately need to: Some even still cling to the old biblical curse placed on Ham by his angry father, as an explanation! So here is a proper and golden opportunity for the social studies teacher to "get it over" to students (by any method that works!) that *nobody* knows for sure what the skin color of the very earliest humans was—probably some neutral, dull shade, but *all* having within their skins, from their ancient past, a little melanin (black) and a little carotin (yellow) pigmentation.

At this point it is necessary to digress a bit to explain that vitamin D is very essential to good health, especially to the development of strong bone structure, and that one of the great sources of this important vitamin comes from the reaction of the skin to the ultraviolet light rays from the sun. But either too little or too much ultraviolet light can be very harmful. Along the equator, where the hot sun beats down fiercely from directly above, the ultraviolet rays are very strong; but far away toward the earth's poles, either south or north, (as in the Land of the Midnight Sun), these rays are very weak because the sun is farther away and down low and dim on the horizon. Thus, to be healthy and comfortable, people along or near the equator needed protection from too much skin-searing ultraviolet light—especially since they slowly lost most of their protective body hair—whereas those in the far north needed to soak up all of the scarce ultraviolet light that they possibly could.

Thus, skin color became very important—perhaps even a matter of survival under primordial conditions. It may be noticed even yet that in some families some of the children may be a bit darker or a bit lighter than the others; and so, as this trend continued over long periods, and as early humans slowly spread out all over the earth, accidental mutations gradually gave some of them more skin pigment thereby protecting them in regions where the ultraviolet light was very strong, helping them to be healthy and comfortable there—but not elsewhere. Conversely, those with gradual mutations toward less skin pigment could soak up needed ultraviolet light in the far north and be healthy there—but not along the equator. Those with the "wrong" skin in either place were less healthy, reproduced less, and slowly disappeared. Thus, through many generations of this kind of adaptation to their environment, some humans slowly became increasingly dark and others became increasingly light.

The *only* "pure lily-white" people are those very rare and unfortunate accidents of nature called *albinos,* who have no color at all in their skin, cotton-white hair, and pinkish eyes. They cannot tolerate the sun at all and are nearly blinded by bright light. They are very white, but also very unfortunate in this earthly environment. The average so-called whites are about 30 percent pigmented or colored, and thus can adapt fairly well to most parts of the globe. The difference between an absolutely white albino and the blackest African is a matter of *only* one twenty-fifth of an ounce of melanin in the skin; the others are all in between, with many average "whites" having some little spots of black melanin and yellowish carotin (freckles) in small clusters in their skin. Sunburn brings still more protective pigment to the skin surface; but unlike inherited mutations, this environmentally induced change does not last.

2. *Other Slight Human Differences of No Cultural Significance*

Other slight mutations may have helped or hindered early man, according to the environment; for instance, in hot areas the air is thin, and one must inhale a considerable amount of it to get enough oxygen. Thus, mutations toward wide noses and open nostrils may have been advantageous in very hot areas. Conversely, cold air is more condensed, more tightly packed with oxygen, but too cold to gulp into the lungs rapidly; thus, mutations toward long, slender noses and narrow nostrils could help warm the air as it entered the body. The tightly massed, kinky, black hair of some Africans probably protected the brain from sunstroke better than would have the straight, blond hair of, say, the early Scandinavians, for whom an excess of ultraviolet rays was no problem.

Still other slight human variations may have "just happened" without any particular relation to primitive survival—such as thick lips versus thin ones, black and brown eyes versus gray and blue ones, and the oval slant of Asiatic eye openings as opposed to those of other people. Some have even tried to argue that because many whites have high foreheads, they might represent a higher evolutionary stage than those peoples who more nearly resemble their ape-like ancestors; but there are many black people with high foreheads, and some whites with low, sloping ones. Neither skull shape nor size seem to have any relation to intelligence. Furthermore, this entire argument can easily be reversed; for example, most black people have very little vestigial body hair, whereas many white men, especially Mediterranean types, have much hair on their chest, shoulders, stomach, arms, and legs. Some black people have very full, turned-out lips, but apes have thin, tight lips, more like Nordic, white human types. Of course, none of this means that black people are more highly developed than whites; rather, it is impossible to prove the argument either way, so it is better just to accept racial variation and to realize that despite these variations, *all* humans are equally human.

B. The Term "Race"

It is rather unfortunate that people fell into the practice of using this term in referring to human beings, because to many unthinking people the word indicates vast, but untrue, differences, such as different "species"—or such differences as those between, say, horses and chickens! So, a course on Africa, dealing primarily with black people, is an excellent place to emphasize that there is only *one* human "race" in the genus Homo sapiens, and that man is its only species. Various scholars have long tried to divide this basic human species into subgroups, but without much success. At one time they tried using the "cephalic index," that is, the ratio of the width to the length of a cross section of the skull. Thus, Germans were said to have "round heads" and Italians "long heads"; but this soon proved untrue for the entire groups. One writer, Lombroso, even went so far as to try to classify people as artistic, scholarly, athletic, criminal, and so on, according to how far the ears were from the back of the head. Of course, none of this was accurate or scientific.

The most commonly used subdivisions in recent times are Caucasian (white), Negroid (black), and Mongolian (yellow). However, many very black people, such as Ethiopians and some of the people of India, have straight hair; long, angular noses; and thin lips; and they are considered to be Caucasians. Likewise, the black Bushmen and the Hottentots are not considered to be Negroes; and millions of Africans (the Bantu) are not black but dark brown. Occasionally one sees an obviously white person who seems to have what are regarded as Negroid features. But it should also be noted that Mongoloids are not very yellow and American "redskins" are not very red.

Still worse is the inaccurate use of such terms as, for example, "the English race," referring, of course, only to nationality; or perhaps "the Jewish race," referring to religion. Even learned college textbooks sometimes indulge in such nonsense as suggesting, for example, that someone was of "Egyptian blood," or "Indian blood," and the like. But all human blood is the same and may be safely transfused from any human to any other human—provided, of course, that the four basic blood types present in all groups are properly matched.

So, some anthropologists rather regret that they have been "stuck" with the popular use of the term "race" and are beginning to look for other terms, such as "stock," that would not imply vast and nonexistent differences. If the term "race" is used, it must be clear that it is only for convenience.

C. *Real* Equality

Another great concept that is important for students to understand is that true equality means that all groups are, not only equally *good,* but also equally *bad.* As one wag has put it: "Every group, including minorities, has a right to its fair share of bums." And this, of course, means a "right" to make their share of mistakes. Thus, if it comes up in class that Nigerians cruelly killed each other in a tragic civil war, it may be pointed out that a century ago Americans were doing the same thing; in fact, if casualties on both sides are compared, the American Civil War was among the most destructive the world had ever known up to that time.

If it is suggested that, with most of the colonial powers gone, the Africans are unable to govern themselves, because several new nations there have had civilian governments thrown out by military juntas and dictators, the teacher has only to point out the long history of this sort of thing in Latin America, Spain, Portugal, Greece, and other non-African places—to say nothing of those late dictators, Mussolini, Hitler, and Stalin.

If a bit of "personalism" and corruption such as that charged against independent Ghanna's first leader, Dr. Kwame Nkrumah, should come up in class, one has only to point to almost any daily newspaper at home for continuing examples of rigged bids, kickbacks, graft, and corruption among a few local, state, and even federal officials. However, it should be pointed out that American corruption hardly excuses its presence in Africa; this analogy merely indicates the universality of the phenomenon.

Even some seemingly trivial things sometimes need (under present conditions) objective teacher counterbalancing. For example, if a film, picture, or article used in class should, perhaps, show an occasional African with a ring in his nose, it can be pointed out that many American women have their ears pierced for earrings—in fact, some jewelry stores frankly advertise: "Free, sanitary ear-piercing with each purchase of our elegant earrings"!

If the same type of visual class material should depict Africans (usually men) in tribal dances doing things which American students might consider a bit silly, such as wearing elaborate head gear or face masks and leaping and twirling excitedly, it can be explained that these dances are serious, symbolic reproductions of tribal events, history, and folklore, far more meaningful to both participants and observers than much of the meaningless twisting, shaking, swaying, "grinding," and "bumping" of many popular American dances.

If the cosmetic practice of facial and body scarification (with its ancient social significance) in a few parts of Africa should come up, it can be at least partly equated with many Americans' obsession with fashion and fads—the ladies' dangerous elevated heels, the artificial eyelashes and eye shading, the wigs and exotic hairdos, the "hippie" unkempt look, and the leg-freezing miniskirt fad. In fact, Zambia has recently conducted a rather stern (and fairly effective) campaign against its young women wearing "indecent" miniskirts!

In summary, the point of all this is that the universal human weaknesses and mistakes of a few Africans (as well as different customs) can be freely admitted and discussed in class, *but* preferably only within the proper perspective of cultural differentiation that permits a discussion of universal and distinctive human characteristics.

Conversely, to be completely objective about this "equally good and equally bad" concept, the teacher might occasionally have to point out that there is also the other side of the coin, in which case the discussion is reversed and it has to be admitted that some *Africans*—for example, those who dealt in slaves—have been as bad as some whites.

1. *The Nefarious Slave Trade*

Certainly the whites deserve utmost condemnation for this cruel activity—one of the most evil episodes of their history. But some Africans themselves also participated in it. The white slave traders seldom had to forage far inland to capture their hapless victims first hand. On the contrary, they usually set up coastal trading posts and purchased the slaves from other Africans, some of whom seemingly had no qualms about capturing their own brethren (usually of other tribes) and bringing them in for whatever trinkets and other barter the whites had to offer.

2. *Warfare*

While the killing in wars among Western whites has undoubtedly been on a much broader scale than in Africa, there was considerable intertribal warfare among the Africans, with the usual wartime killing and injustice. A recent case in point is the extraordinary slaughter in the civil war in the Sudan.

3. *Colonialism*

Colonialism was not completely evil. It must be granted that the European colonial powers had little justification to have been in Africa at all, that they came there for greedy exploitation or for international prestige, and that they caused much injustice and practiced some cruelty. Still, some of them, particularly the British and French, did make positive contributions in such fields as education, sanitation, and (with the British) considerable tutorage of Africans for eventual democratic self-government on a national rather than on a tribal scale.

4. *Missionaries*

While they caused some conflict with the ancient, local religions, and some disillusion because of the "unchristian" behavior of some secular whites, and even a few pitched battles between new converts to Catholicism and Protestantism as to which had the "true" version of the new faith, still, some of them—albeit it is no longer the fashion to admit it—also made some helpful contributions, especially the few medical missionaries of the Dr. Albert Schweitzer type. Others established schools—of course, they were usually parochial and established for indoctrination; but they also contained some secular education, and many of the present generation of African leaders received their first formal, Western-type education in these institutions—later going on to universities either in Africa or abroad. Incidentally, when there was some white violence against the early efforts of the late Dr. Martin Luther King against segregation, an African visitor to the United States remarked that it seemed about time for Africa to send some missionaries here to teach Americans the meaning of brotherly love. At about the same time, an African graduate student was writing his doctoral dissertation on "Witchcraft in Medieval England."

V. SOME SUGGESTED "DOS" AND "DON'TS"

Years of experience in,teaching about Africa suggest the following advice to American secondary school teachers on a miscellany of topics, though there are many other important ones as well:

A. The Class Itself as a Resource

In the section of this text dealing with teaching about Latin America it was stressed that the presence of many students of Latin heritage in classes could be used as initial motivation, but this approach is *not* recommended in beginning a study of Africa. After all, the ancestors of black students were brought here forcibly, endured years of slavery, and were later subjected to all kinds of discrimination. It is one thing to begin a unit on Latin America by asking a student: "Pablo Gonzales, how did you get a Spanish name like that?" But it would be quite a different thing to begin a unit on Africa by asking a class member: "Dick Willis, how do you happen to be so black?" If the presence of some black students in a class has any motivation value, it will likely be obvious to all and will need no artificial introduction by the teacher—though this might not be the case in a school in Brazil, where skin color is hardly noticed. Of course, there probably will arise situations in which black students may proudly insist on, and enjoy emphasis on, their presence, but this would have to be handled very tactfully—even by a black teacher. In that case, the previous, motivating question might be impersonally and more acceptably worded as: "Why does it happen that some people have very pale skins and others very dark skins?" (p. 256).

B. The Word "Primitive"

It is suggested that the teacher avoid the word "primitive" in referring to tribal Africans; no one can objectively say what *is* primitive or what is "civilized." After all, what could be more primitive and uncivilized than the present possibility that a few "advanced" nations might annihilate all life on the earth in a nuclear holocaust, including millions of good, simple folk in their thatched huts all over the world who may never even have heard of the cold war. Norman Cousins, has said, paraphrasing an American Revolutionary War slogan: "This would truly be 'annihilation without representation' "! Many anthropologists now prefer the term "preliterate" to "primitive." But again, it is important to emphasize that "preliterate" does not have the derogatory connotation of lazy and that "primitive" has. Rather, it suggests a society that somehow did not (perhaps did not especially need to) develop a *written* language from their, perhaps, very highly developed oral language.

Closely related to this is the suggestion that it is probably better if the teacher does not use the term "natives" in referring to Africans. After all, one seldom refers seriously to the "natives of New York City's Fifth Avenue" or the "natives of California's Hollywood." Thus, some educated Africans feel that when the term is used by Europeans to refer to them, they intend, consciously or unconsciously, a sort of condescending meaning.

C. The Tribe

This almost unavoidable term must not be allowed to degenerate in students' minds into meaning a superstition-ridden bunch of "semi-savages." On the contrary, the tribe is usually a highly developed and complex organization of society, with customs (far more effective than laws) for dealing with nearly all of life's problems from birth to death. With its community activities and responsibilities, its customs are often very sensible and highly rewarding.

D. "Blacks" versus "Negroes"

Probably every group has the right to be called by whatever term it prefers, regardless of its accuracy. However, the word "Negro" simply means "black." In some languages—Spanish, for instance—there simply is no other precise, single word to use for either a completely black object or living creature except *negro*. It is easy to understand and sympathize with the current dislike of blacks for the term "Negro" because of its easy adulteration by whites into the undignified term "Nigger"; still, it must be remembered when using the term "black" that it is not always completely accurate, since the people of Africa are of many shades, ranging from brown to black. And wherever they have had prolonged contacts with whites, there have always emerged (despite alleged white antipathy!) mixed descendants, some of whom are far from black.

It is interesting to note in this connection that the custom in the United States of considering anyone with the slightest bit of black lineage to be a Negro is reversed in some nations, where the least trace of white lineage makes one white, no matter how dark he is. Interestingly enough, in some parts of colonial Latin America years ago, where wealth and social status were more important than skin pigmentation, a Negro who accumulated some wealth could purchase from the government a "Certificate of Whiteness," by which he became officially white, no matter how black he was, and could achieve certain positions legally open only to whites!

Closely related to this is the amusing incident some years ago in the Union of South Africa, when, rather than lose a very popular international athletic event, the government simply decreed that the Asiatic teams were not really "yellow-skinned" but, rather, were "temporary Caucasians." All of the above helps demonstrate the exaggerated trivialities associated with human differences. Perhaps one can be a bit more accurate by speaking of dark-skinned Africans as "African-Africans," of white Africans (of which there are many since colonialism) as "European-Africans," and of American "blacks" as "Afro-Americans."

E. What Is Beautiful?

Any such discussion of color might also be a good place for the teacher to work in the fact that what people consider to be beautiful or not beautiful is extremely relative: It is based on that to which they are accustomed. There can be little doubt that in their ethnocentrism many whites everywhere have automatically assumed that "white" was pretty and that "black" was not, as color related to people. Now some Africans, and some of African lineage elsewhere, are putting on a countercampaign that "black is beautiful." An interesting story to illustrate the relativity of both sides of this sort of thinking is found in the experience of the famous missionary, Dr. Livingstone. Not having seen a white man for more than six years, he was somewhat shocked when Stanley and his expedition "found" him at Ujiji in 1871—actually, he was not lost—that idea was an American newspaper publicity stunt. But the good doctor later admitted that the first sight of whites again sort of sickened him, actually nauseated him because they looked so insipid at first without any good, healthy-looking black color to which he was so accustomed. He added that they reminded him, somehow, of the little white grub worms one sometimes finds beneath a rock along a moist creek bank, and that it took him several months to become accustomed to the fact that it was perfectly acceptable to have a pale skin rather than a richly dark one.

A related, and perhaps ridiculous matter—which, hopefully, will not come up in class—is that of body odor. It is true that many whites, both in Africa and more particularly in the southern United States, who never knew any blacks except hardworking, sweaty fieldhands, without modern bathing and laundry facilities, got the idea that the blacks smelled differently—and that this, somehow, proved their differentness. If such speculation should come up in class, the teacher can be prepared to explain that all living organisms that excrete body wastes through the skin do give off a chemically induced odor, but that there is no particular "superior" or "inferior" sweat.

A rather cute story to illustrate the point of the "equality of odors" is that of a group of white missionaries in old China years ago, who wanted to have a joint meeting or convention. The only place large enough for the entire group to meet was the local Chinese temple, so they applied to the superintendent of the temple for permission to assemble there. The Chinese building superintendent replied that he was very flattered that they would honor his humble temple with their presence and that they were most welcome. He added that on the afternoon they wished to meet there was to be a Chinese meeting from 4:00 to 5:00 P.M. and that the missionaries could meet from 2:00 to 3:00 P.M. The latter said that this hour was a bit early for them and asked to meet from three to four, promising to get out promptly so as not to delay the four o'clock Chinese meeting. The superintendent politely refused, but the missionaries insisted and demanded to know why he refused them the later hour. Finally the Chinese gentleman explained, with elaborate apologies: "It embarrasses me very much to mention it, but, you see, to us Chinese you white people smell like sheep; so I have firm orders that any time you use our humble temple, I must have at least an hour to open all the doors and windows to air out the place thoroughly before the Chinese people arrive."

VI. SOURCES OF MATERIALS

Rather than repeat many details almost verbatim, it is urged that the reader see pages 242-244 about materials on Latin America; because, with the exception of books specifically on Latin America and specialized agencies such as the Pan American Union, virtually everything mentioned applies equally to Africa. In addition to the several suggestions there, the following might be added:

(1) Among the many specialized organizations now flourishing, a good one is The American Society of African Culture, 101 Park Avenue, New York, N.Y., which distributes exhaustive bibliog-

raphies. Another is The Afro-American Institute, United Nations Plaza, New York, N.Y.

(2) Among the many publishers now pouring out books on every aspect of Africa, Frederick A. Praeger, Publishers, 111 Fourth Avenue, New York, N.Y. 10003, seems to emphasize the area.

(3) Among the number of magazines on Africa now being published in the United States, a very good one is *Africa Report,* Suite 500, Dupont Circle Building, Washington, D.C. 20036.

(4) Among the many commercial firms engaged in business with Africa, one might mention the Farrell Lines (shipping), 1 Whitehall Street, New York, N.Y. 10004, which distributes free their *Africa News Digest.*

(5) Among the several brief *secondary textbooks* now available might be mentioned:

Belasco, Milton Jay, and Graff, Edward (both high school social studies teachers). *The New Africa, History, Culture, People* (Bronxville, New York: Cambridge Book Company, 1966), paperback, 154 pp.

Lengyel, Emil. *Africa, Past, Present and Future* (New York: Oxford Book Company, 1967), paperback, 154 pp.

For advanced senior classes, or for the teacher, from among the many college texts might be mentioned:

McEwan, Peter F. M., and Sutcliffe, Robert B. *Modern Africa* (New York: Thomas Y. Crowell Company, 1965).

Oliver, Roland, and Fage, J. D. *A Short History of Africa* (Baltimore, Maryland: Penguin Books, 1964), paperback.

Singleton, F. Seth, and Shingler, John. *Africa in Perspective* (New York: Hayden Book Company, 1967).

Wiedner, Donald L. *A History of Africa South of the Sahara* (New York: Random House, 1962), Vintage paperback.

(6) For purely anthropological material for advanced students, or for the teacher, among the many excellent ones might be mentioned:

Ottenberg, Simon, and Ottenberg, Phoebe. *Cultures and Societies of Africa* (New York: Random House, 1960).

CHAPTER XIII

Teaching About Asia

by Donald Johnson

I

On the bleak New England soil, many years ago, Governor Bradford predicted, "We shall build a city on a Hill . . . If God be with us, who can be against us?" To many of the founding fathers of the Republic, the American experiment was not only a national revolution but a model for the world. America saw itself as "chosen" and this assumption has tended to make education a homogenizing institution which perpetuates and passes on to the young what is essentially a northern European, Protestant, middle-class cultural ethic. This American mission continues to be an important factor in American education. It is so deeply rooted in our collective psyche, it will be difficult if not impossible to purge our national consciousness of it.

This sense of chosenness and mission to the world has tended to negate our realization of cultural pluralism. The idea of a wider cultural stream, fed by disparate but nonetheless valid racial, ethnic and class tributaries, has been a difficult concept to teach. Even in the teaching of American history, we have been slow to recognize the vast pluralism in our past; history texts illustrate a remarkable similarity in their stress of white, northern-European heroes, culture and achievement. It is even more difficult to change this emphasis when we are selecting and organizing a curriculum and a teaching methodology for the world beyond Europe.

Even though the discovery of the world beyond Europe is one of the great facts in modern politics, culture and education, the majority of schools are still working from texts and being taught by teachers who stress what is essentially Western civilization. Here again the model is essentially white, northern European, Protestant and middle class. When non-Western areas are included, they tend to be used as merely a stage on which the great drama of Western man is acted out.

In those schools where the world beyond Europe has been introduced, many large problems are yet to be solved. One problem is how to overcome the tendency many educators and teachers have of seeing Asia as part of the "non-Western world." Besides being imprecise, this label applies to a universe with the Western world at the center as the only criterion for the study of the remainder of mankind. As the Chinese scholar W. Theodore De Bary explains:

Non-Western civilization is essentially a negative concept, suggesting that the primary significance of civilizations outside Europe and North America lies in their difference from the West. Indeed, the seeming impartiality with which so many civilizations are thus equated (actually negated) tends to obscure the true proportions of their respective contributions. The positive significance of Asia particularly tends to be obscured when it is simply lumped together with other areas equally different from the modern West, which by implication becomes the norm for all.[1]

There is great temptation in this approach to use the post-Renaissance West as a model for the states of Asia. Implicit in this assumption is a value commitment to such products of the Western tradition as individualism, social mobility, the scientific method, and middle-class morality and behavior. In a widely used book entitled *West and Non-West,* the authors state in their introduction, "To understand the traumas and difficulties many of the emerging nations must pass through before they reach full *maturity,* let us look briefly at the way in which the Western world developed. . . ."[2] This metaphor seems to suggest that the Renaissance, the Reformation, the scientific and commercial revolutions, and the rise of national states experienced by the West since 1500 will inevitably be the script of the "emerging" nations. The tendency, of course, is to associate the good things—progress, development, stability—with the technological and economic sector of the society under consideration. As Edward Kracke explains, "In approaching any Asian civilization, the greatest difficulty seems to be that of overcoming our initial preconceptions concerning the bases of a civilization and its objectives, drawn from our Western experience." [3] The objectives of the social sciences must be related to value systems which are, after all, arrived at subjectively.

Another problem is how to overcome the consideration of Asia primarily as a problem in American foreign policy. The frequent assumption here is that Asia is worth studying because of its size and geography; hence, its importance to the West is essentially geopolitical. One Asian scholar, in decrying this approach, states:

> We must guard against the tendency to think of Asian peoples too much in terms of their direct effect upon our own lives. This was the great error of the pre-World War II period, which proved self-defeating insofar as it was preoccupied with surface phenomena and was unprepared to gauge the real depth and complexity of Asian reactions to the West.
>
> The purposes of a truly liberal or humanistic education will be served only if we accept the peoples and civilizations of Asia, not as factors in the Cold War or as means to some immediate practical end but because their experience in living together, what they have learned about life and what they have come to understand about the universe, is now seen as part of the common human heritage. They are to be studied, therefore, as people who can teach us much about ourselves, whose past can give us a new perspective on our own history, and whose way of looking at things challenges us to re-examine our own attitudes. [4]

If Asia is not viewed as "non-Western on the way to becoming Western" or as a means of enhancing the world prestige of America, it may be viewed as full of "poor, unfortunate people." This is in line with our missionary tradition: Asians were people who needed to be saved, if not from Satan, then at least from hunger, superstition, and primitive living. Thus teachers may stress famine in India, over-population in China, efforts to industrialize in Burma, and the high death rate in Indonesia. All these factors perhaps are true and should be considered in any study of Asia, but some balance should be struck between problems and the rich cultural achievements which deserve to be studied for their own sake.

These unspoken assumptions may easily color the entire presenta-tion of the civilizations of Asia. In a typical survey, present problems (and how the United States helps solve them) may be all that is considered. Economics and politics are stressed. Indian technological development, Japan's great "economic miracle," and Chinese com-munism may be the only factors many students will have studied about Asia in a short introductory course. The classical traditions of India, China, and Japan are often completely ignored. Because of the un-spoken faith in the causation of technology, the nontechnical aspects of Asian culture such as Buddhism, the Non-drama, and Chinese art may be either completely ignored, downgraded as unimportant, or pre-sented as obstacles to progress. For example, a young teacher in New York City was assigned to teach a lesson on: "How Hinduism Is Holding Back India." The assumption contained in that approach is startling.

An equally serious problem in the consideration of Asia is the temptation to approach it as the panacea for all the West's problems. Some of the more critical students who are questioning the basis of Western culture look to Asian culture, particularly to Asian philos-ophy, much as Rousseau regarded the American Indian. To this type of student, Hinduism and Buddhism are humane, sophisticated religions not associated with materialism and imperialism. Thus, everything Asian becomes good and beautiful because it is "not West-ern" (or what their parents have handed down to them). This overly romantic view can be nearly as disastrous as the opposite belief that the West embodies all civilization. This romantic approach is not new in the West's relations with Asia. In the nineteenth century, men like Emerson and Whitman tried to project into Hinduism a notion of self-fulfillment that simply was not there. The desire to find a psychological escape from the burden of present reality may always be a temptation. In a problem-filled contemporary society, this wish may be greatly increased, and Asia offers a splendid area for escape. A responsible teacher must discourage such flights of fancy and help youngsters to realize that achieving nirvana is not similar to a high on marijuana or LSD, that Yoga cannot be mastered in a week, or that classical Hinduism and Zen do not offer avenues to individual fulfillment of a personal ego.

Thus, the teacher of the world beyond Europe must conceptualize Asia on its own terms, must put American relations with Asian countries in their proper perspective, must realize Asians are more than unfortunates to save, and must guard against romanticizing the Asian experience.

How an individual teacher organizes his course on Asia and what method he chooses to use to present the material will be largely determined by that teacher's own philosophy of history and the social sciences. Among the basic philosophic questions that must be resolved are: Whether the individual postulates a *linear* view or a *cyclical* concept of history, and how he stands on the *uniqueist* versus the *universalist* view of culture.

The linear view of history holds that all previous historic development was but a prelude to the ever greater and more sophisticated society of which it was to become a part. This view is generally associated with progress in man's affairs. Though there may be temporary interregnums of backsliding, on the whole the line moves over the millennia upward to "better things." High priests of this history have been Hegel, with his world spirit coming to fruition by the process of dialectic, his descendant Marx, the American anthropologist Lewis Henry Morgan, the philosopher Herbert Spencer, and a host of others. One may choose to put the classless society, liberty culminating in political democracy, material prosperity, or any political or economic system that has the commitment of the particular author or philosopher at the pinnacle of man's development. It is perhaps coincidence that all these linear theories have arisen in Western civilization. It is a further irony that Western civilization is usually held to be the acme of man's development—the exquisite product of man's total efforts at perfection. In this scheme, China, India, and Japan are seen as stepping stones to understanding a higher civilization. The value in studying them is in seeing them as links in the process of development and not in understanding them as self-contained cultures worthy of study on their own merits.

The cyclical view conceives of civilizations rising and falling in great cosmic arcs much like the birth, life, and death of individuals and the ebb and flow of the seasons. The cyclical views of such historians as Spengler and Toynbee have gained wide attention in modern scholarship and perhaps have ameliorated somewhat the implicit ethnocentrism of most linear views of history. In addition, these cyclical conceptions serve to provide a historic framework for the notion of cultural relativity that has gained much credibility among anthropologists such as Ruth Benedict.

However, even these cyclical theories rest in the context of closed systems characteristic of much of Western thought. For the Christian, all men are conceived in sin and were redeemed by the sacrifice of Christ. The cyclical view often holds the Good News of God is for all men, even though some have not yet heard the Word. Similar beliefs are held by both Muslims and Jews, at least insofar as the correctness of their theology is concerned. On the other end of the spectrum are those who have replaced the God of our fathers with the machine and the theology of technology. This orthodoxy insists that all of man's great achievements have been rooted in technological breakthroughs. Thus, man emerged from hunting into agriculture and later into the industrial age. Consequently, all societies are either underdeveloped-agricultural or developed-industrial. Whether chosen by God or blessed by the machine, the Western industrial states, in these thought systems, stand in the forefront of man's achievement and bear the message of truth for all who would heed it. Thus, whether one opts for the linear view of historical development or for the cyclical model, it must be kept in mind that both these philosophies of history are products of Western scholarship and tend to diminish the historical importance of the great Asian civilizations.

The modern social scientist has contributed much to the diminution of the more blatant misconceptions of some of these historic generalizations. He, more than anyone in the postwar world, has contributed to the idea that men everywhere have had much in common at all times of history. Thus there has been a growing movement, stimulated by the social sciences, to accentuate these common problems, institutions, and social structures whether in the West or non-West. One could argue that we have come full cycle from Hegel and other nineteenth-century historians to another model based on the universality of man's behavior and evolution. The archetype of this new social science model is Daniel Lerner's structure, set forth in *The Passing of Traditional Society*.

The assumption in this approach is that all societies, like most individuals, experience more or less the same growing processes; these can be analyzed as phenomena in themselves and do not require deep and sophisticated knowledge of the culture and tradition of individual societies. Professor Lerner explains:

> Our data on 73 countries, distributed over all the continents of the earth, indicate that many millions of individuals everywhere are in the same position. This further suggests that the model of modernization follows an autonomous historical logic—that each phase tends to generate the next phase by some mechanism which operates independently of cultural or doctrinal variations.[5]

According to Professor Lerner's model, societies such as China, India, and the other states of Asia are passing, or are about to pass, through three distinct phases of growth toward modernization. Each will experience urbanization, literacy, and media and political participation. In this analysis, all societies tend to be either traditional or modern. In this approach to Asia, data would be used from all societies in an effort to understand the *process* of modernization and the societal changes which accompany that process. The cultural uniqueness of a Japan, an India, or a China is subordinated; their cultures become case studies for the application of social science efforts at universal principles of change and growth.

The goal of these "universalists" is to create a genuinely worldwide study of man in all his cultural settings. The use of Asia in this social science approach provides additional data for generalizations made on a grand scale and may also suggest fallacies in these generalizations that will become modified in the light of new information from societies outside the West. A leading anthropologist of this school maintains that:

> One ironic consequence of the growth of non-Western studies has, in fact, been to downgrade the importance of the distinction between "Western" and "non-Western." For this particular way of dividing the world has little theoretical significance in any of the disciplines, old or new. On the contrary, just as comparative philology and historical linguistics brought Sanskrit and the languages of North India closer to those of Europe, so may the newer comparative studies discover new sources of affinity between Western and non-Western people. In that case, non-Western studies will be significant, not because they specialize in the exotic and unfamiliar, but because they help fill in the specific content and color of the blurred contours of a human nature that is universal.[6]

In contrast to the universalist are those who believe in the uniqueness of individual cultures. They are usually area-studies specialists who have spent many years involving themselves in the affairs of one great civilization. They tend to stress the original contributions, the unique institutions, and the cultural mix that constitutes each of the great Asian civilizations.

For the uniqueist, time and effort are best spent analyzing and studying a single civilization in depth and attempting to relate the disparate parts of the civilization into an organic whole which is more than the sum of the parts. One scholar suggests that "If we can confine ourselves to penetrating as deeply as time allows into one civilization, and try to get beyond generalizations to the details that give them color and reality, we are on the way to understanding other civilizations as well. . . ." [7]

If such a single-civilization approach is used, it must further be decided which of the social sciences and humanities will serve as the major focus of the study. One Indian scholar goes so far as to suggest that the use of social science disciplines be completely disregarded for a study of India. Instead, he proposes what he terms "a self-image approach." Professor Potter describes this method as "An effort to see how the people of a given culture view themselves and their surroundings, rather than using the categories of any one discipline or of Western values in studying an Asian civilization." [8] Professor Potter, in arguing for this approach, points out that it provides ample opportunity for the reading of materials written by the people of the civilization under study and that it offers an assessment of the civilization based on the values of the civilization rather than on a particular discipline or on our own values.

Thus, we have at least two dichotomies to deal with. Are the societies of Asia to be treated as a part of a greater historic drama culminating in the "Rise of the West"? Does each great civilization proceed through the organic cycle of rise and fall within the context of its own norms and culture? In our treatment of Asian social institutions are we to stress the societies as exemplars of a greater universal culture dealing with such phenomena as Japanese feudalism, Chinese court life, and Indian village organization as case studies to support larger social science generalizations? Or are we to plunge our students into the cultural uniqueness of Indian, Chinese, Japanese, and Indonesian societies, stressing the peculiar characteristics of such processes and structures as caste, Hinduism, scholar gentry, and face?

It is within this framework that a philosophy of teaching Asian civilization must be forged. Our answers to these questions will dictate our use, and meaning, of such frequently used terms as "modernization," "underdeveloped," "evolving," "backward," "catching up," "Westernization," and numerous others. Are the nations of Asia now experiencing the social transformation roughly equivalent to the last four hundred years of Western history, or is their experience qualitatively different? Should the peculiar life-style and cultures of Japan, China, and India be stressed, or should they be used as case studies for the wider application of certain universal processes? Each teacher must resolve these questions in his own way.

Most likely each teacher will have his own orientation in this debate. Whichever approach is used, each has a value; neither emphasis makes any claim to infallibility. The unique and universal schools of thought may be combined without doing violence to the methodology of either. A teacher may want to stress the transition of the societies of Asia and use the model of "Traditional and Modern" and still attempt to teach the uniqueness of the Japanese character, the Indian mind, and the Chinese world view. A tension between the poles of uniqueness and universalism could serve to stimulate much thought by students who are studying Asia. A class might want to accept Professor Lerner's model of modernization as a hypothesis and attempt to prove, disprove, or modify the hypothesis in light of data collected from one specific Asian society. Students might come to understand what Professor Reischauer meant when he observed that modernization does not mean the end of a nation's unique culture. Mr. Reischauer cited the propensity of the modern Japanese to retain their traditional group loyalties, formalism in social relations, and interest in classical cultural forms such as music and drama even as they were "becoming modern."

Once the teacher or curriculum builder answers some of these questions and faces the many problems involved in creating an authentic course of study on Asia, he must decide when the material should be offered. He must decide if the work on Asia is best handled as a separate course or should be included in the larger framework of a world history course. If the latter approach is taken, the rather tenuous (and perhaps false) notion of East and West would seem to be broken down. Asia would find its rightful place in *world* history; Asian literature would be included in literature survey courses; art and music from the Orient would be part of any art-appreciation course. Ideal as this approach is, world history, art, music, and literature teachers are probably neither willing nor equipped to incorporate Asian studies into their existing surveys. Because of this, Asian studies will have to be offered either as a senior elective or included as a part of the ninth- or tenth-grade course on world cultures.

As a prerequisite to a better understanding of Asian civilizations, it would be of great value if Western civilization (what we have called world history) could be studied first. In many schools, this would mean shifting the present tenth-grade Western civilization course to the ninth grade. Unless we understand the assumptions of the Western tradition and how these forces developed and shape our present life, it is doubtful that we can understand a culture which stresses other aspects of human behavior. Furthermore, having analyzed our own tradition, a comparative study can be made between our institutional structure, value system, and history and that of the major Asian societies. As Professor De Bary has said, in regard to Asian studies, "We are Americans; we start from there or we make a false start." [9]

When we study Asian cultures, we will probably find out more about ourselves than about Asians. However, if we do not know our own traditions, it is doubtful whether we will even know what to look for in another society.

As we approach the study of Asia—as part of a larger study of world civilization, as a special course, or as part of a course—we should keep several concepts in mind. These may help keep us from relying on our often ethnocentric yardsticks for evaluating other civilizations; they may also be a way to cut through much that could be misleading about our traditional studies of Asia.

First, there may be no such thing as "Asia" if we are thinking of it as a culturally homogeneous area. This immediately removes from our vocabulary such clichés as the "Asian mystique," the "Oriental mind," and the "inscrutable East." The Muslims are a vital part of Asian civilization, but they have considerable influence also in the Mediterranean basin and in Africa. In many ways, Europe has as much or more in common culturally, linguistically, and ethnically with India than India has with China. Perhaps even the philosophy of Confucius is closer to the pragmatism of Charles Peirce than to his supposedly Asian brother Sankara. Certainly Tokyo resembles San Francisco more than it does a farming village of Thailand or Pakistan.

Second, abstract thought (a Western concept) tends to be defined in behavioral terms in Asian societies. Whereas the Greeks sought truth and knowledge for their own sakes, and created the Western discipline of philosophy, there appears to be no such division among thought, speculation, and behavior in India and China. In both the Chinese cultural area and the Indian cultural area there is a tendency to use ideology—what we term philosophy—for practical life ends. Thus, a study of philosophy *and* religion in China and India may be altogether misleading. While we have become accustomed to neurotic psycho-therapists or ethics professors who beat their wives, the Chinese would tend to define Christian ethics by the actions of those professors, and the Indian would define parliamentary democracy by the life-style of the British in India. Professor Edward Conze, a long-time student of Buddhism, calls this phenomenon "pragmatic metaphysics." Professor Paul Mus believed that both Chinese and Indian philosophy are inseparable from the daily behavior that is observable in these cultures.[10]

Third, many Western scholars have tended to overemphasize the sacred and philosophical books of Asian cultures. This is probably because the major Western religions are scripturally based. In studying about India, we have emphasized such works as the *Bhagavad-Gita*, the *Upanishads*, and commentaries of Sankara. For China, we have perhaps placed too much emphasis on the court and gentry and on the Confucian philosophy which underlay that strata of life. Recent scholars, particularly anthropologists, are making us more aware of the "little traditions" largely contained in the village structure of Asia. Any teacher should be careful to balance his offerings between the great classical traditions of India, China, and Japan and the lives and culture of the ordinary people in those societies. This new stress on the common people is part of a larger move in cultural analysis. It strives to ameliorate the dominance of official, high-status histories and to give credit to popular culture, mass movements, and thought not necessarily systematized by great thinkers.

Fourth, there is a great heterogeneity of the societies of Asia. Now that American studies in high school are becoming increasingly aware of the pluralism that has always been present in American society, a fine opportunity for comparison of this factor with the same reality in Asia is presented. Certainly China had more disparate elements to blend into a society than has the United States; the constant infusion of new racial, ethnic, and linguistic groups into Indian society is one of the most significant aspects of that nation's history and helps account for her unique institutional structure. Perhaps Japan alone among major Asian countries has had a homogeneous human group with which to forge a culture. Again, Japan's experience would offer fruitful comparison with China and India as well as with the United States.

Fifth, none of the societies in "Asia" have developed in isolation. Constant contact with the other civilizations has been an important theme in Asian life. Commenting on this point, Professor McNeil has stated:

> ... I do suggest that contact with alien ideas and manners provided the mainspring for historical development through most of the recorded past. Without such contact ... men would not have been stimulated to change their ancestral patterns of life. ... If this be so, it should be possible to interpret the history of the world in terms of the successive manners in which men of alien cultures come into contact with one another.[11]

This stress on cultural contact and interchange significantly modifies Arnold Toynbee's interpretation that great civilizations develop and fall in near-isolation. Tracing the spread of a particular idea, art form, or custom can be fascinating detective work and often gives a human dimension to an otherwise abstract notion. For example, the influences of Greek art in North India; Buddhism in China and Japan; Buddhist architecture and religions in Europe; Persian and Turkish influences in Europe, India, and China; and the impact of the West in Asia are only a few of the many possibilities such an approach suggests.

METHODOLOGY

The basic methodology for a study of Asia should be no different from that used to study any other area. We begin with the students' frame of reference in mind, we emphasize process and concepts rather than facts and recall and we employ inquiry wherever relevant and possible. Because, in a study of Asia, students are being asked to deal with subject matter and life-styles which likely are quite alien to them, it is especially important that their frame of reference always be kept in mind. The teacher should always be aware that his students need to be standing on familiar ground before they undertake to analyze a culture that is distant and different from their own. At the same time, students must not be allowed to carry with them the unconscious yardsticks they have accumulated through the years: They must not categorize, evaluate, and classify other societies on the basis of progress, technology, and humanism.

The most effective way to achieve a balance here is to use the comparative approach to Asian cultures. Comparative history and studies is gaining in scholarly reputation and practice. Psychologically, the comparative approach offers the young student a means of identification; his Indian, Japanese, and Chinese contemporaries offer different answers to the same basic questions of life and illustrate other forms of social organization. At the same time, the comparative approach builds on concepts, processes, and knowledge already learned by the students. As one advocate of comparative studies explains:

> In much the same way, the approach to a foreign culture could profit from just such contrastive studies. They would highlight the points of difference between certain aspects of Western and the particular non-Western culture to be studied and also permit one to take advantage of whatever points of similarity do exist. There are, for example, likenesses between baroque and certain types of Far Eastern literature and art, and certainly an experience of the one provides an entry to the understanding of the other. Similar observations might be made about the picaresque tale of Renaissance Europe and Japan, or between some aspects of early Christian and African art. From these similarities, one can proceed to the more definitely marked contrasts.[12]

Assuming that students have had some experience with their own tradition, comparison can easily be made between the Greek epics such as the *Iliad* and the Indian *Ramayana;* between the political science of Kautilya and the *Panchtantra* and that of Machiavelli; between the creation stories of the Vedas and those of the Bible and the Koran; and the speculations in the *Upanishads* and Lao-tzu and those of Kant, Spinoza, St. Augustine, and Martin Buber.

Because of the exposure of most American children to a constant flow of information and impressions from television movies and magazines, it can be assumed that many of them will already have some impressions of Asian societies. They may think of the Indians as being very religious and are certain to be aware of caste and cows without having any depth knowledge of either. They may have images of the Japanese as being overly efficient or of bowing all the time and inundating the world with transistor radios. They may think of the Chinese as gentle laundrymen or as Communist monsters bent on destroying them. These impressions are bound to be present even when they are not realized by those who hold them. Even scholars who have spent many years dealing first hand with the peoples, culture, and traditions of Asia are prone to this tendency. Harold Isaacs has shown us in his *Images of Asia* that among the 181 Americans whom he polled, all of whom were Indian and Chinese scholars, a great many biases were apparent. Mr. Isaacs does feel somewhat optimistic about the possibility of going past the "scratches on the mind" and reshaping our opinions and stereotypes. He suggests that:

> The problem for every man, be he Chinese, Indian or American, would still seem to be to try to know the nature of this process, to sort out the sounds and distinguish among the sights, to understand their effects in his own mind and in the minds of others. It is at least barely possible that this knowledge can help make the new relationships, the new assumptions, the new images a little less unflattering to themselves and to human society.[13]

These scratches on our minds may be both a curse and a blessing. If we use the inductive approach, they may serve as hypotheses from which to launch into the study of the Asian societies. "Is Hinduism essentially otherworldly?" "Is Japanese industrialization related to their historic character?" "Does traditional Confucianism conduce to an acceptance of Marxism?" may serve as points for intensive research. Even such stereotypes as the sacredness of the cow, the hold of caste, the apathy of the Indian peasant, or the corruption of Vietnamese officials may serve as hypotheses for further study rather than as assumptions the teacher must indoctrinate or refute.

In developing a methodology for Asia, it is strongly suggested that the social sciences be liberally supplemented with materials and skills from the humanities. One problem with much of the material being published on Asian societies is its emphasis on social science concepts at the expense of a humanistic emphasis. This approach is unbalanced, and it leaves out materials and approaches which encourage student empathy and identification. Both the social science process and humanistic studies can easily be synthesized by selecting material from the indigenous literature, art, music, and philosophy. This synthesis will allow students the opportunity to have perceptive kinds of experiences as well as those associated with conventional conceptual learning. In short, the cerebral process must be supplemented with more visceral learning opportunities.

Drawing on the humanities also provides a direct and dramatic kind of motivation for the introduction of an Asian culture. Most students will be able to distinguish the difference between the music of a koto, a sitar, and a trumpet. They also will feel the difference in style and organization of the music of India, Japan, and the United States without having had any training in the field. Most students can see the difference between the architecture of the Greek Parthenon and the Indian Temple at Madurai without having studied art. All kinds of guesses and impressions can be gathered from a class simply by allowing students to think out loud while looking at Asian art or listening to its music. Again, these impressions may serve as *hypotheses* for further study.

Literature, especially, is of great use in teaching about Asia. For example, if social change is to be taught, use Chekhov's *The Cherry Orchard*, Osamu Dazai's *The Setting Sun*, John Hersey's *A Single Pebble*, Han Suyin's *Love Is a Many-Splendored Thing*, or Neela Padmanabhan's *The Generations*.

Literature is available for virtually any phase of Asian life. It offers a firsthand impression of the feeling of the age or the place. Most any concept of the social sciences—enculturation, urbanization, nationalism, religious reformation, ethnic rivalries—may be taught through literature without losing the nature of the process being taught. There is perhaps no more vivid picture of Togagawa Japan than Oliver Statler's *Japanese Inn,* or no more moving an account of the partition of the Indian subcontinent than Khushwant Singh's *Train to Pakistan.* Geography, history, and anthropology can become much more alive when taught through literature. Reading the last chapter of Vyankatesh Madgulkar's *The Village Had No Walls* is a far more real introduction to the importance of the monsoon in India than the standard pulling down of the map and ensuing discourse on wind currents and rain patterns.

It would be ideal if the cooperation of the music, art, and English departments could be solicited in the teaching of Asian culture. But that seems to be more a future possibility than a present reality. Until that time, the social studies teacher should not fear to use art, literature, and music even though he himself is not expert on these subjects. The mere exposure of students to these art forms will often interest them in doing further study. The excellent films produced in Asia should also not be overlooked as teaching aids. Both Japan and India rank among the top three film producers in the world. What these two cultures have to say about themselves through films is often more profound than any textbook can be. *Chushingura* and *Pather Panchali* are musts for anyone who would understand India and Japan. Films of this sort may serve as final summation of the unit or course or equally well as an introduction to the study of the cultures.

Peoples Republic of China

American students who undertake the study of the Peoples Republic of China face several factors which may obfuscate their vision. For two decades public debate has raged over such questions as: "Who lost China?" "Should the Communist regime be recognized?" and "What is the most effective American policy toward this largest nation in the world?" Any course on China is likely to be framed within the emotional context of these questions. The American temptation is to overly stress the Communist period in Chinese history and to consider the society primarily as a major "problem" of United States foreign policy.

The Chinese concept of time could serve to place the twenty-five year period of Communist government in the proper light. Several years ago, at a conference on the teaching of Asia, a professor from Taiwan was admonishing a group of American teachers for not teaching more about China. Piqued at this advice, one American teacher, in a rather harsh voice, asked: "What is being done in Chinese schools about American history?" "Oh," replied the Chinese professor, "we don't do much with current events in our schools."

The Chinese, unlike the Indians, have been great historians; history plays a major part in the world view of the Chinese people. Traditionally, they wrote their history dynasty by dynasty; the present dynasty would write the history of the previous dynasty. Built into this concept of history was a hesitation about commenting on anything so contemporary as the last twenty years. If American teachers could teach this long, sweeping concept of time and history, the Communist period would of necessity fall into perspective, and the American propensity toward present-mindedness might be tempered.

Important as history is to the Chinese world view, it is doubtful that any teacher will want to take a straight historical approach to the over 3,000-year tradition of China. To teach Chinese history the way it was written, dynasty by dynasty, would soon involve young students in an encyclopedic web of confusion which would probably turn students away from China as the memorizing of soliloquies turned generations away from Shakespeare. If a straight historical approach is used, it would be best to stress what Professor Arthur Wright terms "nodal points or formative experiences." Mr. Wright selects nine such experiences in Chinese history:

A. The period of genesis: the emergence of distinctive features of a Chinese civilization in the Shang;
B. The later Chou viewed as a "classical age";
C. The unification of state and culture: the founding of the Chinese Empire by the Ch'in, consolidation and development by Han;
D. The first experience of dismemberment and foreign invasions, cultural and political, c. 300-589;

E. Unification: a new centralized empire and its culture—Sui and T'ang, 589-750;

F. The breakdow of the second imperial order and the beginnings of the new society and culture—late T'ang, Five Dynasties and Sung; proto-modern China;

G. The first experience of total conquest and of incorporation in a large world-empire: the period of Mongol domination, the brutalization of politics, and the evolution of mass culture;

H. Reassertion of Chinese control over state, society, and culture: the Ming. The failure of creativity. With apologies to Toynbee, "abortive effort to revive the ghost of the T'ang oekumene";

I. The second total conquest, continuation and atrophy of Ming institutions and cultures under a Manchu-Chinese dyarchy.[14]

To this list should be added the breakup of the dynastic system, the impact of the West, and the birth and growth of Chinese communism.

A much preferred entry into the study of China would be the rural scene in both its classic and revolutionary forms. Plunge the student into a real slice of Chinese society: a changing agricultural life and the function of a modern Commune. The student can then have the opportunity to identify with real people as they act out events in their lives. The rural setting will provide the opportunity of meeting a China of change at the basic level of society as well as a road back into an analysis of classical Chinese society. The intermixture of traditional forms with the modernizing process as evidenced in the setting of the countryside will also illustrate the complexity of social change and help avoid the simplistic view of old being replaced by new without synthesis.

Fortunately there is an abundance of good sources on this phase of Chinese culture. Jan Myrdal's *Report From a Chinese Village* and his later *The Revolution Continued* offer the student an opportunity to visit with real people in one village over a period of a decade. C.K. Yang's *Chinese Village* is also valuable. *Fanshen* by Harold Hinton and Jack Chen's *A Year in Upper Felicity* are examples of sources which will present the organization and function of a rural Commune in a sympathetic way.

The use of Felix Green's series of films *One Man's China* is a well proven inside look at life on a rural commune.

As one looks back into China's rural past from the Communes of the present, basic classical values can be introduced. The desire for sons, the authoritarianism of the male, the respect for age and the farmers feel for nature should be introduced here. The Confucian doctrine of five relationships should also be included. The division of the family land among the sons, as opposed to the Western European system of primogeniture, should be included. It is the basis for the fragmentation of the land in modern China and is useful background for understanding the Communist attempts to consolidate land holdings into larger farms.

Whether through history or through the village, the teaching of China should include the understanding of several concepts that could underlie the entire time spent on the civilization.

First, it should be kept constantly in mind that China, like India, is too large and too diverse to refer to with any facile generalizations; all the generalizations will have major exceptions. Great size, diversity, and pluralism are all factors of the Chinese population and culture. From the desert peoples and Muslim influences of the West to the dry wheat-growing areas of the north to the rich, wet rice lands of the south there are great differences in life-style, economic structure, and culture. New influences from peoples from north and central Asia, bringing customs from the Middle East and even Europe, have further contributed to Chinese pluralism. The Chinese racial stock may lead the outsider to assume a remarkable homogeneity. However, this homogeneity is soon disproved; closer anthropological inspection reveals a mixture of many diverse strains of hair color, nose shape, and facial structure.

It is within this great heterogeneity that the basic consensus of Chinese culture must be analyzed. The important concept here is the creation of a remarkably stable synthesis from diverse elements and its continuity through Chinese history. It would be important to deal with this philosophic synthesis and to stress the syncretism of Chinese culture. A comparison with the Western propensity to exclusiveness and dualism would be natural here. Whereas American students will be inclined to posit either/or choices for major questions, the Chinese mind has successfully integrated most opposites into its philosophic system. This provides an opportunity to discuss Buddhism in its Chinese setting. As Chinese scholars made their own translations of the Indian Buddhist texts, many modifications and changes were made so the foreign ideology would fit into an organic Chinese setting. (Comparisons between this adaptation and the later adaptation of Marxism-Leninism to a Chinese environment would be a subject for fruitful analysis.)

Another conceptual framework which should serve as a guide to the study of China is the culture's propensity for an anthropocentric view of reality. In most of Chinese thought, "man as the measure of things" would stand as a basic criterion. Unlike Indian thinkers, who devoted much time and energy to the metaphysical realm of investigation, the Chinese mind tended to deal with secular matters and human relationships. In the Chinese language structure, *man* is usually the subject *who has* ideas and *for whom* abstractions exist. The language also reveals an emphasis on the concrete as opposed to the abstract, with concern for nominalism and not for the sweeping generalities one finds in other languages.

The penchant for concreteness in thought and philosophy may be traced in part to Chinese character writing. The language has also been very important in building a common culture and in passing on the Confucian ethical system. Though few students are likely to want to exert the time and discipline to learn this difficult language, they can be introduced to some of its assumptions and structures by comparing it with English. Students can look in their language for nonphonetic, semantic symbols such as Arabic numerals, italics, proofreaders' marks, and so on. From this insight into character writing, students may be asked to create their own ideographs. They can be shown some simple Chinese characters such as the sun and moon, together standing for bright, or two women under one house standing for trouble. From ideographs, students may go on to learn about calligraphy, painting, and even the magical aspects of the construction of ideography and the *I Ching,* which is so popular in the United States.

The basic conservatism, exaltation of antiquity, and esteem for a hierarchical system of relationships should also guide the teacher in the organization of the study of China. After the competition of the "hundred schools of philosophy" and the short experience with legalism, in early history, the Chinese, after the triumph of Confucianism, have exhibited a remarkable tendency to use traditional orthodoxy as a basis for all decisions and as a model for life. This would imply a strong emphasis on the Confucian system in any study of China. Certain excerpts from the Analects should be available for students to read first hand. From these sources and some of the commentaries, students may see the implications of the philosophy for daily life, the formation of government, and the establishment of social institutions. A good project would be to have students create a Confucian social system for the class or school to see how it actually works when applied. It may be particularly interesting to compare Western ways of dealing with the phenomenon of the "generation gap" with the Confucian way of dealing with such a problem. The current Cultural Revolution may be better understood as an effort at radical change when placed in the context of the traditional Confucian system.

Despite some claims that the rise of communism has destroyed Confucian influences, it is likely that such a formative experience in the collective tradition of a people cannot be obliterated by edict, revolution, or a society convulsed with change. As C. P. Fitzgerald's work has shown, Confucianism continues to be a great influence in modern China. In the Confucian tradition, the student can see the propensity for secularism and the importance of ideology in the life and in many of the ethics long associated with Chinese culture. Professor Fairbanks has written of the importance of Confucianism in Chinese history:

if we take this Confucian view of life in its social and political context, we will see that its esteem for age over youth, for the past over the present, for established authority over innovation, has in fact provided one of the great historic answers to the problem of social stability. It has been the most successful of all systems of conservatism. For most of two thousand years the Confucian ideology was made the chief subject of study in the world's largest state; nowhere else have the sanctions of government power been based for so many centuries upon a single consistent pattern of ideas attributed to one ancient sage.[15]

Another concept central to an understanding of China is the great sense of harmony of nature which existed in the minds of Chinese men. Since ancient times, the idea of *T'ien* has been conceived in relationship with man. This is closely related to natural law that was so much a part of the Western Enlightenment. During that period, many European thinkers looked to China as a classic model for a society based on nature and on man's understanding of natural law. The idea that man should follow his true nature has been stressed in much of Chinese philosophy and has been a guiding principle in the formation and evolution of the culture.

It is important for students to realize that Chinese society has, traditionally, really been two societies. One is the traditional village, where over 80 percent of the population have lived. The other is the society of the walled cities, where the merchants, scholars, and officials have lived. To understand this second society, an understanding of the gentry class would be most important.

The Chinese gentry class came to power partly because of its larger landholdings. However, the important means to "leap through the eye of the needle" and become a member of this class was through the complex examination system with degrees and positions conferred upon those who excelled. This group of civil servants made Chinese society unique, and the system must be studied on its own terms, since few of the generalizations of the feudal system seem to fit. Students may want to try and grasp what the examination system meant. Make up a few tests that would be equivalent to what would have been given in traditional China. A test based on the memorization of the entire Old Testament as well as all the commentaries on it might be comparable.

The concepts of the gentry, bureaucracy, and the examination system should go hand in hand with an understanding of the classic Chinese government and the concept of dynastic cycle. An excellent discussion of this can be found in John Meskill's *The Pattern of Chinese*

History, Cycles, Development, or Stagnation. Many selections from this pamphlet may be read by students or interpreted by the teachers.

The remarkable continuity and stability of the historic Imperial system of China—the longest in man's history—should be appreciated. This is even more impressive when the vast diversity that makes up China is kept in mind. The study of this stability offers an opportunity for American students to look at a historical case study of the building and maintaining of a pluralistic society. This is a challenge of immense proportions for contemporary American society; it is well within the frame of reference of most students.

Finally, there remains the impact of the West on China. In presenting this subject, the teacher must not overemphasize Occidental influences. Recent scholarship suggests that Asian societies were in a great state of internal flux and change at the time Western contact was first made; the radical changes in Asia in the last century and a half must not be construed to have been caused exclusively by Western contact. The meeting of the two cultures can be a fascinating topic of study for high school students. The crisis of contact between the northern European culture and the black African and Afro-American cultures in this country can be an effective comparison. Missionary diaries and Chinese accounts of the Jesuits and other Europeans make fascinating reading; they offer splendid opportunities to study and to analyze what happens when cultures meet.

In dealing with communism in the Peoples Republic, the teacher must make a genuine effort to present the possibility of the continuance of much of the classical culture within modern China and yet introduce students to the changes and achievements of the revolution. The study of the essentially Western ideology of Marxism-Leninism as it is being adapted to a Chinese setting is a fascinating case study in intellectual history, cultural diffusion, and ideological adaptation. Recent books such as Peter Seybolt's *Through Chinese Eyes,* and Schell and Schurmann's *China Reader* stand out among the numerous student sources on modern China. No school library should be without *China Reconstructs* and *China Pictorial,* both of which are published by the Peoples Republic. Of course, these magazines are geared to present the point of view of the Peoples Republic in much the same way as

Chamber of Commerce journals would present the United States. Nonetheless, they offer so many opportunities to see and hear China from inside that they are essential adjuncts to any sources for students of modern China.

Like all great cultures, China offers material for a lifetime of study. As the teacher selects materials for a few weeks, or perhaps a semester, of study by high school students, it is hoped he will keep these important conceptual ideas in mind. By the end of the study, perhaps the students will have fulfilled the criteria set by Professor Fairbanks for anyone who hopes to obtain an adequate understanding of China:

> Today, if we in America are to discharge the responsibilities which attend our power, we must know not only the conditions in which the Chinese find themselves under Communism but also their traditional patterns of response and aspiration, their mode of action when moved by hope or fear, their channels of expression for ambition, jealousy, pride, or love, their standards of the good life, of duty among friends and to the state, of loyalty to persons and to ideals. We can truly understand Chinese events and relate ourselves to them with wisdom only when we have become sophisticated as to Chinese motives.[16]

Japan

The use of Japan in the study of Asia provides the teacher with several outstanding opportunities to break stereotypes concerning Asia and to utilize a comparative approach to area studies. Japan alone among the Asian nations has experienced rapid industrialization, and it ranks today as one of the world's great economic powers. A study of how this happened is essential in any study of Asia. It will illustrate graphically that the industrial revolution is not the monopoly of Western man. At the same time, it will serve to show that a society outside the Western world can certainly modernize without forsaking its traditional culture and way of life. Japan's experience in the nineteenth and twentieth centuries, as a parliamentary system was established and a rapid industrialization took place, offers great possibilities for comparison with China's experience during the same period and also with Germany and Italy, which had some of the same problems and phases of development.

The study of Japan also offers the teacher a perfect opportunity to analyze the process of cultural diffusion. Two great cultural transformations have been the formative experiences of Japanese history. The first was the contact with China, which began in the sixth century when Japan began to participate in the Chinese culture area. This great cultural impact was felt first at the capital and among the intelligentsia. It filtered down to the most remote Japanese village until, by the thirteenth century, Buddhism had had an impact on all levels of society; and by the eighteenth century, most Japanese families were living according to Confucian patterns of relationship.

The second great cultural diffusion and synthesis was, of course, Japan's experience with the West in the nineteenth century; the effects of this are still being worked out today.

In both instances of foreign impact we have a similar Japanese response: the ingenious selection of the most attractive and functional elements of the alien culture and the process of ingestion and adaptation to the native Japanese style and culture.

If Chinese society has already been studied, as it should be *before* an examination of Japan is taken up, the institutions and culture forms evolved in classical China may now be analyzed in a Japanese setting. The Chinese political system stressed that the emperor was only the temporary possessor of the mandate of heaven, who could be overthrown if he failed to manifest moral leadership. In Japan the emperor came to be regarded as being divine in his own right and was the symbol of the state. This view of the divine ruler, with few exceptions, continued through all subsequent Japanese history until modern times. The Chinese idea of a scholar gentry, which composed the ruling bureaucracy in Japan, became modified and was reincarnated as the "soldier administrator"; and later as the samurai. Again, the neo-Confucianism used to philosophically cement the bureaucracy of the Southern Sung dynasty in China became in Japan the guilding principle for centralized feudalism of the Tokugawa period. As Buddhism from India was modified to suit the Chinese landscape‚ so, too, Chinese Buddhism was adapted to the Japanese culture force. Here Buddhism blended with the native Shintoism to form a unique, more optimistic, more natural religion not duplicated anywhere in the world. The Zen of the Japanese is as unique to that culture as is the tea ceremony, the flower arrangement, the art, and the literature it helped produce.

Similarly, the Meiji restoration offers another case study in cultural borrowing and transformation of Japanese society. Japan's efforts and great success in this sphere might well serve as a basis of comparison with the efforts at modernization other Asian states have made. The differences in degrees of success could serve as hypotheses for further research. The rise of the constitutional system, the evolution of the Japanese corporation, and the development of an army and navy and a new educational system all are institutions which deserve attention from students of modernization. Like all other Asian societies, Japan offers ample opportunity to study traditional and modern forms of society and culture. Books such as *The Makioka Sisters* by Junichiro Tanizaki well illustrate the rapidity of change in recent Japan and the social crisis that trails in its wake even in a single family. From the conflict of change students will want to go back in Japanese history to examine the traditional pattern of living, if possible back into the Heian period, or, if not, at least to an analysis of life in the Tokugawa period. For the better students, *Japanese Inn* is an excellent introduction to this period, as is the play *Chushingura*, which is also a magnificent movie that depicts the code of the samurai in feudal Japan.

From the Tokugawa style of life may be extrapolated many features of the Japanese character and style to be explored. These characteristics can be illustrated through the comparative method, using Chinese culture and the life-style of American high school students as a basis for the comparison. The tendency of the Japanese to be ambiguous about their own culture and foreign influences is a good point to contrast with the Chinese idea of themselves as unquestionably superior and the center of the civilized world. This ambiguity may also be useful as a partial explanation of Japan's great ability to change and innovate in its national life. It may well explain the nation's self-consciousness in confronting the outside world and the eagerness with which the Japanese have sought to be accepted and praised by foreign peoples.[17]

A discussion of the seeming paradox of the intense Japanese feeling of emotionalism expressed in literature, art, theater, and festivals, combined with an almost stoical external appearance in public relationships, would also be of interest to high school students. This balance between emotionalism and outward stoicism and control of emotions could be compared with the Puritan ethic in America and the attack on that lack of outer warmth by so many of today's questioning youth.

In the midst of the contemporary attack on many aspects of Western rationalism by members of the younger generation, it would seem timely to raise the thesis of F. S. C. Northrup in *The Meeting of East and West*. He maintains that Eastern civilization is essentially aesthetic in contrast to the West's emphasis on theoretical and rational means of discourse. If there is truth in this generality, the teacher will want to draw heavily on Japanese poetry, graphic art, literature, and drama if students are to get the cultural story as perceived by those who made it. Any study of Japan that left out haiku and tanka poetry, the No drama, Kabuki plays, and landscape art would fail completely to capture the inner spirit of the people that is essential for the giving of life and spirit to the often dry bones of social science processes.

The observation that the Japanese are not religious is a cliché, which, like many others, is without foundation in fact. The synthesis of indigenous and imported religious beliefs and customs again makes for a uniquely Japanese institution. The ancient rites of Shinto historically have withstood the onslaughts of Buddhism, Confucianism, and Christianity. The constant force of Shinto has given Japanese religion a perennial flavor of connection with nature and supplied the abstractness of Buddhism with native myths, heroes, and traditions, as well as serving as a vital force to national unity and identification. A study of Zen would also be essential not only for an understanding of a driving spirit in Japanese life but because it has had such an impact on modern American life in philosophy, art, theater, and pop culture. Probably many high school students have already read Alan Watts and Hermann Hesse on their own. Thus, motivation may already be present for a deeper study of this important religion, which could serve as an understandable entry into the complex religions of Asia.

If comparative studies work on the ideological level, the study of Japan offers a fine opportunity to open up the comparison between living in a guilt-ordered society, which most American children are accustomed to, and a shame-control society, which is more basically Japanese. David Riesman's thesis in *The Lonely Crowd* may be introduced in some way to show the types of control that stem from inner direction and outward group pressure. Not only would this be an interesting approach to the study of Japanese concepts like face, hara-kiri, the pressure of college admittance, and success, and even an analysis of the language, but it would also serve as a basis for discussion as to whether Americans were ever really inner directed or whether shame has always and still does play an important role in our own forms of social control.

Professor Hajime Nakumara suggests in his *Ways of Thinking of Eastern Peoples* that the Japanese, in addition to the characteristics already mentioned, have a propensity to accept the phenomenal world as absolute, to stress group relationships at the expense of the individual, and to exhibit a marked indifference to the exact logic of Western scientific philosophy. Any of these subjects would make fascinating study and suggest comparisons with all sorts of Western subjects and with American national characteristics.

If the concept of nationalism is a topic of study for Asia, Japan can figure prominently. The impact on total Asian consciousness resulting from Japan's dramatic showing in the Russo-Japanese War cannot be stressed enough. Throughout China and India nationalist leaders pointed to this event as an important step toward parity with the colonial powers which dominated Asia. Also, Japan's national identity, successfully manifested throughout its history as a unified national state, provides an excellent case study in the rise of a national state outside Europe.

A study of the rise of the Japanese military in the 1920s and 1930s would give students a chance to examine the process of political polarization, and this phenomenon could be contrasted with events in Germany and Italy in a similar period and with developments in the

United States in the 1850s or even with what is happening in America today. The postwar period is filled with interesting aspects worthy of study. Again, cultural contact and diffusion are natural. The result of the American occupation, the change in physical structure of the people, the new fads of baseball and Western music, the embracing of the age of electronics would all be fruitful subjects of research. The rise of a feeling of passivism, the disillusionment of losing the war, and the changes in family and social structure are all well presented in contemporary novels such as Junichiro Tanizaki's *The Makioka Sisters,* and *Some Prefer Nettles,* Yasunari Kawabata's *Thousand Cranes,* and *Fire on the Plains.*

The economic recovery of Japan may be used as a case study in the flexibility, adaptiveness, and energy of the traditional Japanese culture and could be compared to the aftermath of the great earthquake in 1923, the opening of the country in 1854, and the years following the Korean tragedy in the sixteenth century.

Whatever aspects are selected and whatever approaches are used, the honest teacher must not fail somehow to rid his students of a likely notion that Japan is nothing more than a carbon copy of China or of the West. Phrases like "the Great Britain of Asia" or "the Prussia of Asia" must be discouraged. Whatever else Japan is as a culture, it is like all great nations: unique. As former Ambassador Reischauer has so well stated:

> It can be argued that, in almost every phase, Japanese culture differs more from other cultures than, say, the cultures of Germany, Persia, or Siam from those of their respective neighbors. Japan's graphic arts, her industrial arts, writing systems, poetry, prose styles, drama, culinary arts, domestic architecture, clothing, political and social institutions, and even her religions and philosophy show, for better or for worse, a distinctiveness that few if any other lands can boast.[18]

India

For the average Western student, the study of India may be the most difficult of any Asian nation. Certainly, no culture form is more unlike the ethic of American life than traditional Indian society. Perhaps no people in man's history have spent so much time probing the mysteries of the soul, the nature of the universe, and other metaphysical questions as have the Indians. Probably no society has been less interested in these matters than the American. In addition, Americans probably hold more stereotypes and generalizations about India than about any other nation. For many students, studying about India means looking at subjects like poverty, sacred cows, peasant apathy, and the obstacles Hinduism presents to modernization.

India does offer much valid data about modernization and social change, but to confine the study of the country to that sphere does a great disservice to truth. There exists no country in the world with a richer and more productive civilization than India. As one of the early cradles of man's civilization, it deserves the same lofty place in the galaxy of historic luminaries as Mesopotamia, Greece, and Egypt.

It would perhaps be possible to study modern Western civilization without reference to its philosophy, but it is hard to imagine any legitimate course on India that leaves out its rich and variegated philosophy. Hinduism, Buddhism, and Jainism have been—and are—a vital part of the basic fabric of Indian life, and they underlie and shape so many of the art forms, institutions, and life-styles of the people that any study of India which excludes them is merely an empty vessel. Remembering the vast differences in belief and practice that exists in India, what are some of the concepts which, because of their influence, historic continuity, and manifestation in everyday life, deserve to be taught?

The first such concept is the idea of the oneness of all things. As all spokes meet in the hub of the wheel, so do all discrete phenomena blend into the oneness of reality. To define this oneness as God is to perhaps confuse rather than to enlighten. The oneness is more *the* ultimate mystery than it is a personalized deity. In fact, even the gods, such as Shiva, Vishnu, and the others, are subject to the one and are less than it. The one is not a creator-god standing outside the universe, but rather an immanent and all-pervasive force that is both outside and inside and from which all things spring and to which they ultimately return.

Moksha is certainly an important concept to deal with early in a study of India. Since *moksha* means to be released from the eternal round of births and rebirths—released from the clutches of the phenomenal world—into, or back to, that oneness—*moksha* could be described as death everlasting. This idea as the major aim of life could be compared with the view of most students—likely they will believe in a life geared to personal fulfillment, and, if they accept a heaven, it will be a place for eternal life.

From *moksha,* one could move to the concepts of *karma* and *samsara.* The law of *karma* is the moral balance which is worked out over a period of many lifetimes. There is always a balance between good and evil; the deeds of one life are carried forward, in a process of moral bookkeeping, to the next existence. If one does one's duty well in this life, future lives may be lived at higher levels of existence until one is finally released from all births and deaths. *Samsara,* the process of births, deaths, and rebirths, is known variously as transmigration and reincarnation.

Understanding the four ends of life—*kama, artha, dharma,* and *moksha*—is essential for an understanding of India; it would also serve to clear up the misconception that Indians are obsessed with things mystical and otherworldly. *Moksha,* the fourth end of man, has already been defined. This release from life comes after one has achieved the other three ends of life *(trivarga).* *Kama* and *artha* can be grasped easily by high school students. *Kama* is roughly equivalent to the pleasure principle. One must be careful not to let the Puritan tradition interpret this concept as merely sexual pleasure as found in the *Kama Sutra. Kama* includes love, art, music, and the good life in general. *Artha,* the power principle, includes political and financial success. In our society we are inclined to elevate these two ends as the supreme goals of man; the rich, the powerful, and the playboy are all familiar figures to us. Students will be interested to read how these concepts are manifested in Indian sources.

Dharma is the remaining end of man; no concept is more basic to an understanding of Indian life. The word may be translated as duty, as adhering to one's own attribute, or as the cosmic order of the universe. In daily behavior, *dharma* means to be, to the best of one's ability, what one is born to be, whether butcher, baker, candlestickmaker, wife, or husband.

Once students understand *dharma,* it would be logical to discuss two of its forms: *asrama dharma* and *varna dharma.* In *asrama dharma* is found the Indian evolution of life-stages—student; householder; forest dweller; and, finally, *sanyasin,* or holy man. For each of these four stages of life there is a *dharma.* A student must remain chaste and devote himself to his guru; a householder must practice *kama* and *artha* and perform all the duties of husband and father and endure all the worries of living in this world. When one's eldest son is old enough to assume the duties of the household, the individual leaves all secular things behind (traditionally by going to the forest) and devotes himself to the final end of life—*moksha.* The usual means one uses for this is Yoga—the discipline with which a seeker of the One attempts to rejoin the Godhead or oneness of all reality. (Students will be interested in this concept and some of the variety of yogas, but they should not be inundated with all the varieties and details.) After achieving this end, the individual may return to society as a "holy man," but he is no longer a personality; rather, he is a symbol of the extinction of the ego and the unity of all life.

The other form of *dharma* is *varna dharma,* one form of what is known as the caste system. In this *dharma,* one performs the duties appropriate to the caste into which one is born—whether Brahman, Ksyatria, Vaisya, Sudra, or outcaste. Social mobility is not the aim here; the aim is performing the tasks of whatever position one is born to. (Historically, there has been mobility among these *varnas,* and the teacher should be careful not to overemphasize the *varna* system and make it synonymous with the caste system.)

These are the important concepts that should be considered in the study of India. They offer a framework for comparison with

Western values and with the students' own philosophies of life.

One of the best ways to teach these concepts is through the use of metaphor. If the metaphor of God as creator serves to picture the Western view of God, the idea of God as a player in a drama would serve for the Indian idea of divinity. The God force may be manifest in many deities—Vishnu, Shiva, Kali, Krishna, and a host of others—but the central truth is that the God force is merely playing a part in the world in the form of one of these deities, much as members of the class might be assigned parts in a production of *Hamlet*. The idea of God *in* the play as opposed to our idea of God *outside* and *controlling* the world is very important and very difficult to conceptualize. It requires illustration from art, sacred literature, and dance as well as examples from the daily round of life.

The model of a game is another useful device for teaching Indian philosophy. One might start a discussion about sports and games and their playing rules. Football, basketball, baseball, chess, or Monopoly would be good examples. In each game or sport, the student could explain the rules, what is allowed, what is not. Students will easily see the foolishness of asking how many touchdowns Babe Ruth made or how to checkmate Boardwalk. Each game has its own rules of play and goals or means of winning. Once this idea is understood, it can be applied to world views—the aims of life in different societies. Each society has its rules of laws and its own ends for which the people live. When a student asks such questions as "Doesn't caste inhibit social mobility?" or "Doesn't Hinduism inhibit personality fulfillment?" the teacher can reply by asking: "Doesn't tackling a man stealing second base lower his foul shot average?"

From here, one can determine that the goal of the Indian game of life is to seek release from life, which is suffering (not cure the suffering; that's a Western goal). *Moksha* may be postulated as the end zone. The four *asrama dharmas* may be likened to the four quarters of a football game, each with its own rules and requirements. One must first be a student, then a householder, then go to the forest, and finally become one with God. The basic rules of the game may be aims of life—*artha, kama,* and *dharma.*

In the study of these concepts, students should be allowed to read some of the original sources, which, if chosen with care, can easily be understood by teen-agers. Excerpts from the *Arthasastra* of Kautilya and tales from the *Panchatantra* are ideal for teaching the concept of *artha*. Some contemporary material should also be brought in to illustrate the workings of *artha*. The toy fish which eats smaller fish, Herblock cartoons, and most any election campaign will provide ample contemporary material on the subject. For *kama* the teacher may not want to go directly to the *Kama Sutra*, although no doubt many high school students are reading it on their own. Certain Krishna Bhakti poetry, classical dance, and selected sculpture all provide materials useful for teaching the art of pleasure.

The concept of *dharma* lends itself well to the metaphor of the game. One could use chess (which, incidentally, is a game of Indian origin) to teach *dharma*. Simply challenge someone to a game and at the first opportunity move one of your pawns down and capture your opponent's king. When he complains of this irregularity, reply that your individual wishes made you want to make that move. It can easily be conceptualized from this tangible illustration what happens to the game when one does not move in the realm of one's given responsibility. The same idea could be illustrated by postulating a lineman in football who wanted to carry the ball and countless other examples in games and sports. The aim here is to illustrate the basic rule of the game of life in India—to do one's duty and to do it well.

Karma and *samsara* can be illustrated through the use of a drama club. It is clear that members will have different parts to play as different plays are produced. The parts will be assigned on the basis of how well the individuals played their parts (fulfilled their *dharma*) in the previous plays.

All these concepts can and should be taught through the use of Indian literature and selections from the classical scriptures. Carefully selected, they are not above the level of comprehension of high school students. Both modern Indian literature in translation, or that written originally in English, abound with manifestations of these concepts, and many of the books can be obtained in this country in paperback. The *Ramayana,* the *Bhagavad-Gita,* the *Panchatantra,* and the *Jataka* tales are in paperback and are available in translations that can be read and comprehended by high school students.

If only a short time is available for the study of India, the best place to begin is probably the village and its daily round. Recent anthropology has done a noteworthy job in providing a number of village studies which are both scholarly and interesting. William and Charlotte Wiser's *Behind Mud Walls,* among others, offers a wealth of information in an interesting presentation. On a fictional level, Vyankatesh Madgulkar's *The Village Had No Walls,* Premchard's *Godan,* Thukashi Pillai's *Chemmeen,* Bibhutibhushan Banerji's *Pather Panchali,* and Raja Rao's *Kanthapura* are excellent impressions of village life.

If the study begins with village life, it is important to have students attempt to *induce* the major religious beliefs from reading the selections on the village. The concepts of *karma, dharma,* reincarnation, *kama* and *artha* are all there if one only will look; they make more sense when presented in a life-situation than as a philosophical system. One could begin with village or traditional life and then, using the same materials, go back over them for religious insights and analysis.

But what about history? In a short study of India, it is a mistake—no, it is impossible—to try to cover the entire four thousand years that constitute Indian history. This approach becomes mere chronological survey, and concept is sacrificed for coverage once the goal is to go from Mohenjo-Daro to the Green Revolution. It would be far better to weave the past and present together to form a comprehensible pattern: the Harappan civilization and the Aryan invasion and its effects, Asoka, the classical Gupta age, and the Muslim invasions as they apply to an understanding of contemporary India.

The British period in India may provide a good opportunity to deal with colonialism and racism. Two excellent sources for this period are Christine Weston's *Indigo* and E. M. Forster's *A Passage to India;* most students will find Rudyard Kipling's *Kim* enjoyable as a good adventure story as well as being useful as a study of the pursuit of two of the aims of life: *artha* and "going to the forest." Let students draw parallels between conversations between Indian and English in *Passage to India* and between blacks and whites in America today.

The national period is a good place to show the pluralism of India. Look at the biographies of some of the great leaders, like Tilak, Ghokale, Gandhi, and Nehru. These will show the wide spectrum of national goals that characterized the nationalist movement. It could serve to correct the mistaken assumption that Gandhi and his non-violence was the only method in the Indian nationalist movement.

The chance for comparative studies abounds no matter what aspect of India is being studied. Students are generally fascinated with discussions of the position of women and with comparing arranged marriages with "love marriages." Arranged marriages must be taught with objectivity; it is a social system which may be as successful as our own. It has worked for centuries, and divorce is almost unknown in India. There are colorful accounts of this form of marriage in Bhabini Bhattacharya's *Music for Mohini,* Kamala Murkandaya's *Nectar in a Sieve,* Thakashi Pillai's *Chemmeen,* Ruth Jhabvala's *Amrita,* B. Rajan's *The Dark Dancer,* and some of Tagore's short stories. Again, the students could induce something about *dharma* and the aim of life from a consideration of this subject.

Caste is another institution which can be done on a comparative basis. Too often we think of caste as a deadly social problem, unique to India. Caste is a functional social institution in India's tradition, and it has counterparts in other societies, even our own. It is an organic institution which has been modified constantly over its long history.

There is much debate among scholars over what caste is. About all they can agree upon is that caste is an endogamous group, that is, one in which people socialize only with members of their own group. Some hold that *varna* originally meant color, but it may also have meant appearance; thus, it cannot be said with certainty that the *varna* system resulted from the subjugation of the dark Dravidians by the light-skinned Aryans. Other scholars stress the Jati system, explaining that a caste is basically an occupational group. Some, like Professor Iwarti Karve, maintain that caste is basically a blood-related extended family. The average high school teacher should not try to be too definitive about caste and its origins. The important thing is for students to get a feel of caste and how it is manifest in Indian society. The best, unselfconscious presentations are in Premchund's *Godan (Gift*

of a Cow; as it has been translated into English) and *Chemmeen.* Raja
Rao's *Kanthapura* is also good. If the teacher wants to get the students
angry at what was the outcaste's lot, have them read Anand's *Untouch-
able.* Books like Zinken's *Caste Today* are also readable and helpful
accounts of caste. It would not be out of the question to bring in *Beyond
the Melting Pot* or any analysis of ethnic, class, or religious identification
in America as counterparts of caste. Although one cannot move out of
one's caste (you can move up or down *as* a caste) but one can leave a
labor union, the analogy is instructive. Labor unions, police forces, and
other occupational groups in America are, in many cases, dominated
by a single ethnic group and may be likened to certain caste organizations. Caste may also be examined as a method a pluralistic society
uses to find a place for, and to keep peace between, the hundreds of
different groups that compose it.

Whichever aspects are selected by the teacher for a study of India,
the richness and productivity of Indian culture should be emphasized.
The all-too-often-held stereotype of a primitive culture held back by
caste, cow worship, and the superstitions of its religion must be dis-
pelled above all.

Many theologians will agree that Hinduism and Buddhism represent the most sophisticated philosophic systems in world history. H. G.
Wells has called Asoka the greatest ruler who ever lived. Even in
science and mathematics, long held to be the strong points of the West,
Indian civilization has made significant contributions in the discovery
of zero, and in the fields of astronomy and technology.

Any organization of the India curriculum should stress these historic
facts and the richness of the culture. An exclusive attention to economic growth, modernization, and the social and political problems
that beset this largest of the world's democracies would be a violation
of any commitment to truth.

NOTES

1. Theodore de Bary and Ainslie T. Embree (eds.), *Approaches to Asian
   Civilization,* New York: Columbia University Press, 1964, xiii.

2. Vera M. Dean and Harry D. Harootunian (eds.), *West and Non-West: New Perspectives,* New York: Holt, Rinehart and Winston, Inc., 1963, p. 4.

3. As quoted in Milton Singer, "The Asian Civilizations Program at the University of Chicago," Eugene P. Boardman (ed.), *Asian Studies in Liberal Education: The Teaching of Asian History and Civilizations to Undergraduates,* Washington, D.C.: Association of American Colleges, 1959, p. 26.

4. de Barry and Embree, *op. cit.,* ix.

5. As quoted in *ibid.,* p. 230.

6. Milton Singer, "The Social Sciences in Non-Western Studies," Donald N. Bigelow and Lyman H. Legters (ed.), *The Non-Western World in Higher Education,* Philadelphia, 1964, The Annals of The American Academy of Political Science and Social Science, Volume 356, p. 26.

7. Edward Kracke as quoted in Milton Singer, "The Asian Civilizations Program at the University of Chicago," *op. cit.,* p. 26.

8. Karl Potter, "The Self Image Approach," de Bary and Embree, *op. cit.,* 273.

9. Speech given at the Conference on the Conversation of the Disciplines, State University of New York at New Paltz, October 11, 1968.

10. Paul Mus, *Asia,* New York (Winter), 1966, p. 13.

11. William McNeill, *Past and Future,* Chicago: University of Chicago Press, 1954, p. 13.

12. Albert Marckwardt, "The Humanities and Non-Western Studies," *The Non-Western World in Higher Education,* Bigelow and Legters (eds.), *op. cit.,* pp. 52 and 53.

13. As quoted in Dean and Harootunian, *op. cit.,* 443.

14. Arthur Wright, "Chinese History for the Undergraduate," de Bary and Embree, *op. cit.,* pp. 6-7.

15. John K. Fairbank, *The United States and China,* New York: Viking Press, 1968, p. 52.

16. *Ibid.,* p. 10.

17. For a discussion of this phenomenon see Edwin Reischauer, *The United States and Japan,* New York: Viking Press, 1968, pp. 108-115.

18. *Ibid.,* p. 105.

CHAPTER XIV

Ethnocentrism and the Social Studies

by Donald Johnson and Leon Clark

ME AND THEE

All social studies, perhaps, should begin with self-studies. If we ask questions about ourselves—before asking questions about the world—we will find answers that have profound implications for everything else that follows.

We will find, for example, that students already have answers about the world. They will "know" that one God is better than many, that one wife is better than two (at least at the same time), that private property is better than communal property, that a nation is better than a tribe, and that the rest of the world would be happier if it were more like us. In short, we would find that students are ethnocentric. They believe that *our* way is *the* way, that what is right for us is right for everybody.

Ethnocentrism, of course, is universal. Everyone begins life in a particular culture, learns how to behave in that culture, and will probably continue throughout life to view reality through the spectacles of that culture. There is nothing inherently wrong with this type of acculturation. Without it we would fail to learn the rules of behavior; we would be lost. We would be disoriented in our own culture, and we would probably lack any perspective for viewing other cultures. After all, we have to begin somewhere. But to impose our rules on others—to assume everyone wants to see life the way we do—is an injustice to other human beings. Moreover, it is a false assumption that distorts reality; it undermines any hope for objectivity in social studies.

Perhaps the most obvious distortion created by ethnocentrism is the division of the world into two parts: superior and inferior. Not only is this simplistic, but it is humanly degrading. Naturally, our culture, the right culture, is superior and all other cultures are inferior. This follows automatically because we set the "standards." Like Professor Higgins in *Pygmalion* (who wondered why women can't be like men), we feel a little disappointed but quite pleased. Hence, Africans are backward because they do not have atom bombs, and Indians are stupid because they do not eat beef. We forget, of course, that Nazi Germany was very "forward" when it came to bombs, that many Americans do not eat pork, and that others do not eat meat on certain days. It is interesting—and also revealing—that we do not criticize the Indians for not eating spiders. Why?

At the same time, ethnocentrics (as we might call them—us) seldom look at some of their own problems and see how they fail *even in their own terms.* Tom Wicker of the *New York Times,* writing about "The Underdeveloped U.S.A.," points out:

> The nation has the wealth, the science, the technology, the energy to do virtually anything it has to do. The apparatus so quickly put together to place a man on the moon almost surpasses belief. Yet, it has sickening racial problems, an antique rail system, horrible slums, shocking poverty, inadequate schools, overloaded hospitals, water unfit to drink and air so foul its largest cities may literally choke. It is simply not organized to do what its resources and energies make possible, and it shows no particular will to reorganize itself or even to recognize the need. That can only mean an underdeveloped society, whether in Togo, Chad or the U.S.A. *(New York Times,* "News of the Week" section, December 4, 1966)

Or, as comedian Dick Gregory says, "You have to hand it to the white man. Who else could find an island in the Pacific where there is no poverty, no crime, no war, plenty to eat, lots of leisure time, warm human relationships—and call it backward." It is easy to lose perspective. We are all caught up in our own world. Recently, for example, a movie house hired two Mohawk Indians to stand in front of the theater to publicize a western movie. The Indians, of course, were dressed in ceremonial garb.

A well-meaning lady approached one of the Indians and said, "You are a real Indian, aren't you."

"Yes, madam, I am."

"Well, how do you like our city?" inquired the lady.

"Oh, fine," said the Indian, "and how do you like our country?"

Even scholars who are professionally concerned with suspending culture-bound judgments have to watch out for culture bias in their views. A few years ago, for example, an anthropologist friend was out driving with a colleague from Korea. He happened to pass through a ghetto area that had just experienced a riot. The streets were cluttered with mattresses, broken chairs, smashed television sets, and other debris. The American exclaimed, "Isn't that terrible!" The Korean said, "How wealthy these people must be if they can afford to destroy so much." Both men looked at the same reality, but they saw different things.

Another American professor had a similar experience, this time in India. He had heard that an American Peace Corps volunteer had recently arrived in a nearby village, so he went out to pay him a visit. Arriving at the village, he met a local leader and the two of them walked to the outskirts of town where the Peace Corps boy was helping to build a road. As they approached the work site, they both noticed the Peace Corps boy immediately; he stood out from the rest of the workers, not only because he had blond hair, stood six feet two inches, and weighed 240 pounds (about double the Indian workers), but also because he was working at such a furious pace. The American professor turned to his Indian guide and said, "Boy, look at him work. He's really pitching in." The Indian leader simply responded: "Imagine how much food he must have to eat to work like that." Again, these men saw the same reality, but what they thought about it was different. (Or did they see the same reality?)

These stories about American professors—both highly trained in cultural analysis—illustrate how difficult it is to get out of our "cultural bag," so to speak. American students, we can assume, are even more culture bound. In fact, a recent study conducted by Project Africa shows clearly the challenge facing social studies teachers. The study, which involved thousands of students across the nation, attempted to find out what seventh-grade students and twelfth-grade students thought about Africa. As might be expected, both groups held many negative stereotypes. In fact, their attitudes were virtually identical. "To American seventh and twelfth graders, Africa south of the Sahara seems to be a primitive, backward, underdeveloped land with no history—a hot, strange land of jungles and deserts, populated with wild animals such as elephants, tigers, snakes and by black, naked savage, cannibals, and pygmies" (Beyer and Hicks, *Africans All,* New York: Thomas Crowell Co., 1971 [Teachers Guide] 1967). The only difference between the seventh graders and the twelfth graders was this: The seventh graders were not sure of their images (they were ready to be convinced otherwise); the twelfth graders were convinced they were right. In other words, seventh graders were still educable, while the twelfth graders were almost beyond the point of change. American education, then, had not only failed in five years to rectify these false, negative impressions, but it had actually reinforced them.

Students come to school with these attitudes; it is where they are. Hence, any course on world cultures must begin here. It must try to break down ethnocentrism, to help students escape their superior-inferior characterization of the world. Until this is done, there is little hope of developing an appreciation for other cultures and other times. This first step, however, may be the most difficult, for the very air we breathe is laden with ethnocentric elements. Not only do individual parents and other adults pass on their own cultural biases, but the mass media perpetuate and promulgate the general rather than the enlightened attitudes of the culture. If it isn't Tarzan on television, it is a cannibal cartoon in a magazine. The films, too, in their attempt to succeed commercially, pander to the public, emphasizing the most sensational aspects of most subjects.

Not long ago, for example, a documentary film called *Africa Addio* was making the rounds of local theaters. It dealt with the violence in Africa immediately following independence, which, by creating instant nations, led to political instability. In short, the makers of the film—who also produced the sensational *Mondo Cane*—scoured the African continent to film as much violence as they could find. Naturally, they found plenty, as they could on any continent.

A paperback version of the film also appeared. It contained a generous selection of blood-and-gore stills from the film, plus 70,000 words of background text to deepen viewers' and readers' understanding of "the bloody birth pangs of Africa." Both film and book, according to the *Saturday Review*, were disfigured by an "overweening preoccupation with violence." Obviously, such books and films reflect the cultural bias, the ethnocentrism, of the Western world. They also perpetuate this bias by influencing young people. The question, for teachers, is how to counteract such sensationalism—how to add some balance—or, at the very least, some critical examination of the issues.

In a sense, films like *Africa Addio* are blessings in disguise. They represent such obvious and concrete examples of stereotyping that teachers can grab hold of them and use them as points of entry into the larger area of ethnocentrism which so pervades one way of looking at the world that we often miss the subtlety of its influence. Perhaps the best way to begin a world cultures course is to look at the way Americans see the world. A teacher might begin, for example, by discussing a biased cartoon, a news story, a television program, or, as in this case, *Africa Addio*. It would be pointless, however, for a teacher to stand up and say: "Class, this is only one side of the story." The film has already indicated the contrary, and no teacher can compete with that. Besides, the film has reinforced a stereotype that was already there.

It would be equally fruitless to point out that America left thousands of slaughtered Indians in the wake of its nation-building. After all, that was more than a century ago—a very dim past for students who were born after the Korean war. Moreover, the white man in America, as Hollywood has shown time and time again, was forced to kill to survive; he was not "naturally violent" like the "primitive" Indians (and Africans). In other words, the notion of violent, barbaric Africa is so much a part of our culture that no simple pronouncements will change the minds of students. Something else is needed.

ROLE-PLAYING

One answer, perhaps, lies in some sort of role-playing, a technique for creating gut-level experiences, which in turn help to internalize learning. After all, our biases and prejudices lie deep, and if we hope to ferret them out, we have to "get down there." In the case of *Africa Addio,* the teacher might begin the class by asking the students to imagine they are movie-makers, bent on showing as much violence in America as possible. Ask the students: "What scenes or events of the past three or four years would you include in such a film?"

The students would very likely begin with the student occupations of university buildings—followed by the invasion of club-swinging police. Or they might show the riots in Detroit and Newark; or the "busting" of innocent bystanders at the Democratic convention in Chicago. The next scenes could include the assassination of President Kennedy, and finally the funeral procession of Martin Luther King as it marches through the superimposed background of a Ku Klux Klan cross-burning ceremony.

The class might then compose a sequence of "representative" shots from various aspects of American life: City life would be represented by a gang war; romance by a rape; journalism by the front page of the *National Enquirer;* justice by a montage of gallows and electric chairs; "entertainment" by a scene from a horror movie, or a closeup of a right cross staving in a boxer's face; and literature by Truman Capote's *In Cold Blood.*

The final "truth" of America, of course, might be represented by the napalm burning of Vietnamese children.

As the students give their ideas for "good" shots, one student could write them on the board. After about five minutes, there should be an impressive list of gruesome images.

By this time, of course, the foundation has been laid for the real point of the lesson. After a pause—long enough to allow the students to run down the list—and a question ("How accurately would this film depict the real America?" or "What is wrong with this picture of

America?"), the class may begin exploring questions of sensationalism, misrepresentation, commercialism, and so forth.

Implicit throughout the discussion, of course, will be the comparison with *Africa Addio.* In fact, the title should be put on the board so the two "films" are constantly paired in front of the class. It would also be a good idea to have the students give a name to their own film. Some clever student is bound to come up with an apt alliteration, such as "America Amok."

The point that such films are misleading has now been made, but the class should not end here. The next series of questions and the next class discussion might go something like this:

Who, throughout the world, would feel most offended by "America Amok"? (Americans). Why? (Because they wouldn't want their country seen in such a poor and false light.) Why wouldn't other people also see the faults of this film? (They might not know enough about America. They might not see these isolated events in their entire context.) How much do Americans know about Africa and the African context?

The class discussion now returns to Africa and *Africa Addio.* The students quickly see that just as outsiders might not know enough about the total complexity of America, Americans may not know enough about the complexity of Africa. And just as Americans do not want to be misunderstood, neither do Africans.

It follows, of course, that (1) there is a need to study a country or continent to really understand it, and (2) the only way to understand it is to see it from the inside, to see it contextually.

At this point, the class is ready to begin a serious study of other cultures. At least the students are more aware of the gaps in their present understanding and are therefore motivated to move beyond "themselves." Of course, our study itself must be free of ethnocentrism, and not only the personal biases we have developed but the larger historical biases that the entire Western world is saddled with. As Ruth Benedict has pointed out, we tend "to identify our local ways of behavior with behavior [in general], our own socialized habits with human nature." In other words, our own ethnocentricity leads us to make assumptions, consciously or unconsciously, about what is true and factual about civilization. This happens even when we have become sensitive to our personal value judgments.

Look at the anthropological scale most world history teachers, or teachers of teachers, use for judging the development of a culture. In the first place, they "know" man develops in a linear progression. They "know" man starts out as a savage, learns to use fire, eat fish, employ a bow and arrow to kill, and then develops pottery, evolving all the time to higher (better) level of barbarism. He then learns to domesticate animals, or irrigate his crops, and smelt iron ore; he is progressing (improving) to the higher level—civilization, which is achieved when man has a written language.

In this approach, technological development—man's rational abilities applied to solve a tangible problem—is the sole measure of society's development (improvement, advancement, worth). This materialistic, technological criterion leads to such phrases as the "underdeveloped world" and "primitive tribes"; it leads to such questions as "Will China catch up to the West?" "Will Nigeria make it?" We are using this approach even when we do not realize we are technological determinists. Give a class a list of terms such as: Tanzania, Eskimos, France, West Germany, Ghana, Indonesia, Japan, Trobriand islanders, Navaho Indians, India. Ask them to group them in as many categories as they wish and to label their categories. Our ethnocentric, technological determinist bias is at the base of a grouping that puts France, West Germany, and Japan as developed states; India, Ghana, and Indonesia as underdeveloped states, and the rest as primitive groups.

Would our extraterrestrial visitor to the world be hunting for arrowheads or stone tools to judge the people he sees? Might he not as just well look for art or for forms of mystical expression? It is hard for us to give up technology, however, for our own culture comes out with a high rating when it is used. Man's ability to subdue nature for his own end is a paramount value in our culture. Would it not be fair, then, to determine what the paramount values of other peoples are and then evaluate them by their own standards? Do you judge a football player by how well he plays basketball or a golfer by the quality of asphalt on his course?

Technological determinism goes even deeper, however; for many of us believe it is the sole cause of man's development and that every social arrangement depends upon it. This belief in technological causation tells us that, as man's technology develops, his economic institutions will progress and that these two material factors will then effect changes in the political institutions and in the ideals and values. Artistic, religious, and political contributions become the result of technological innovation. Witness our belief that democracy is a product of middle-class behavior, that the Protestant Reformation was in essence an economic movement, and that gunpowder destroyed feudalism. Now Marshall McLuhan has tied the entire history of man to changes in technological methods of communication. It is small wonder we have concentrated on technological manifestations of a culture if in them lie the origin of all constructive social change. But would our space traveler see it this way? Might not he believe a country's values determined its technological development? Even that man's creativity produced technology?

This technological criterion and causation mind set is one reason why adding facts about other peoples onto an existing study of the world may lead to graver misunderstandings than plain ignorance does. Given this bias, when I learn that Chinese refuse to build railroads across ancestral graveyards or that American Indians do not subdue nature, I would have to conclude the Chinese and Indians are backward and superstitious (inhibitors of technological advance). Were I starting with American Indians, however, and my criterion for cultural advance is their value in harmony with nature, then American bulldozers and insecticide plants might be seen as evil and dangerous (destroyers of harmony).

When the political scientists help us ask political questions about peoples, they exhibit their own form of ethnocentrism. Here, they "know" that man's political institutions develop from a clan, to a tribe and finally up to the nation-state—the highest, Hegel would have us believe, form of political organization. They "know" a tribal grouping is simple and primitive (inferior); they "know" a nation-state is complex and advanced (superior). Is it any wonder the political scientist finds trouble dealing with a tribal community as a unified, highly developed political and social system? If they have any time to give to such a society, they approach it only as a stepping stone toward greater things (the nation-state).

Finally, the historian—and through him most of what we have called "world history"—falls into his own ethnocentric traps. Because of the dominance of Western power in modern times, he assumes the evolution of Western society since the Renaissance is the inevitable script that the "non-West" is to follow. Certainly the West has played a significant part in modern history. But does the supreme power (technological dominance) of the West during this period mean it also has manifested the supreme cultural achievements in all fields since 1500? It may be fair to say that Westernization is technological advancement, but how a non-Western society lives through the twentieth century (modernizes) may not be based on Western models. Could a society choose not to make an atom bomb?

The present power dominance of the West may be what tends to make the historian feel that all progress and achievement is contained in a linear pattern from Egypt through Greece and Rome to modern Europe and America. The historian may "know" that present Europe and America are the most highly developed manifestations of man's achievements and therefore believe it is important to spotlight how man achieved this height—thus, he teaches Western civilization. While all students should be encouraged to see the development of that peculiar character and civilization which we call Western, and which may be based on technological development, they must *not* be allowed to use it as a criterion or even as a model for understanding the rest of the world.

At the same time, we should not allow America's "official" view of the world, that is, our foreign policy, to dominate our approach to other cultures. Not long ago, for example, a superintendent of schools telephoned a prominent cultural agency to inquire about an in-service course the agency was offering on the cultural and social aspects of Asia. The superintendent was most anxious to have a number of his teachers attend the course because his school system was in the process of incorporating Asia into the social studies curriculum. His one reservation, however, was that the course was not going to cover Russia. "How can you teach about Asia without teaching about Russia?" he asked. "After all, the hammer and sickle hang over the heads of all Asians." It may be true that communism is a threat to most Asians, although this point is debatable (certainly Asians do not see communism the same way Americans do), but whether it is true or not is unimportant. The main point, of course, is that Asian culture can certainly be studied without discussing Russian communism. Surely, no American would say it is important to study Chinese ideology to understand American culture. Our beliefs and practices have value in and of themselves. The same is true of Asia. To see another culture in the light of one's own foreign-policy interests is to see it from an ethnocentric point of view. This can have the effect of distorting reality and dehumanizing people, of transforming concrete aspirations into abstract ideologies.

One helpful tool the historian can employ to get out of this ethnocentric way of viewing history is to see any particular event in time from another's perspective. The Indians hardly mentioned the invasion of Alexander; the Chinese Emperor looked upon the visit of Marco Polo as hardly an earth-shaking event; to the citizenry of central Africa, Stanley and Livingstone were hardly the central theme of African history and to the eleventh-century Muslims the European Christians were less developed invading imperialists bent on conquering Islamic homelands.

Westerners write about the present period as the Atomic Age (technology again); for millions of Africans and Asians, the period might more aptly be labeled "The Death of Colonialism." How would the ancient Egyptians describe the Exodus? What was the Persian view of their wars with the Greeks? What view did the Aztec, the Hindu, the Chinese have of Cortes, Robert Clive, and Simon D'Andrade, respectively? How would the English write about the American Revolution, the Germans about World War I, the Chinese about the Open Door Policy and the Opium War, the Indians about Churchill, the Mexicans about the Mexican War, the Afro-Americans about slavery? These are but samplings of the type of approach that it is possible to take for any event which affected a large segment of the world's people. You make them up. Today teachers can easily secure the necessary primary documents to give students the view "from the other side of the bridge." Start with textbooks from other countries. American Indian societies and Afro-American societies are "telling it as it was" from different perspectives.

It is only as we become free from our own ethnocentric biases, both personal and scholarly, that we will, in Tom Paine's definition, be "educationed"—that is, be able to transcend our own time and place. And it is in that transcendence that our own time and place becomes comprehensible, "as the view of the mountain is clearer from a plain."

There is little question about the urgency with which our professional historians and other leaders call upon the schools to reorder their priorities in teaching world history. Hajo Holborn, Yale professor and former president of the American Historical Association, has called for the construction of a universal history, the placing of man in the midst of his total social environment. In his presidential address before the Historical Association in 1967, he said we must "transcend the limitations of our own station in time and space and become aware of our full potential. . . . Aiming at the highest historical truth, we shall fortify our courage to be free."

Former Senator J. William Fulbright has gone even further, claiming that international understanding is man's only hope of survival and that education is the best means of achieving that understanding. In a speech—now famous—delivered to the Swedish Institute for Cultural Relations in Stockholm Fulbright envisioned a new kind of international relations, one based on human understanding and empathy rather than on national self-interest and power struggles. The only way to avert self-destruction, he said, was to build a new world order through education. "My theme is the contribution of education, particularly international education, toward restraining the competion of nations."

The major problem we face, according to Fulbright, is "the irrational inversion of priorities as between human and national needs." He points out that "nations have always tended to give primacy to

their roles as powers while neglecting their responsibilities as societies."
This situation, he feels, cannot be tolerated if man hopes to survive.
"The irrationality of unrestrained national rivalries make it desirable
to develop new concepts of the national and of international relations;
the danger of universal destruction makes it absolutely essential."

While admitting of no ready answers—"we cannot put the atomic
genie back into its bottle"—Fulbright does believe there is hope—"and
that hope consists primarily in the promise of education. . . . What we
can do, through the creative power of education, is to expand the
boundaries of human wisdom, sympathy and perception. Education is
a slow-moving but powerful force. It may not be fast enough or strong
enough to save us from catastrophe, but it is the strongest force
available for that purpose, and its proper place, therefore, is not at the
periphery but at the center of international relations."

If the answer is education, the question is what kind of education.
Fulbright offers three broad recommendations.

First, "we must seek through education to develop *empathy*, that rare
and wonderful ability to perceive the world as others see it."

Second, we must develop a sense of objectivity; that is, we must
overcome any narrow ethnocentrism that allows us to think we are
always right and others always wrong. Here again, Fulbright feels,
"Education is the best means—probably the only means—by which
nations can cultivate a degree of objectivity about each other's
behavior and intentions. It is the means by which Russians and
Americans can come to understand each other's common aspirations
for peace and for the satisfactions of everyday life."

Third, we must learn to convert nations into peoples and to translate
ideologies into human aspirations. It is not surprising that Fulbright,
whose name signifies this country's most famous exchange program,
would make a specific recommendation here for educational exchange.
In Stockholm he said, "Educational exchange can turn *nations* into
people, contributing as no other form of communication can to the
humanizing of international relations. Man's capacity for decent
behavior seems to vary directly with his perception of others as individual humans with human motives and feelings, whereas his
capacity for barbarism seems related to his perception of an adversary

in abstract terms, as the embodiment, that is, of some evil design or ideology."

In conclusion, Fulbright summarized his position by saying: "If international education is to advance these aims—of perception and perspective, of empathy and the humanizing of international relations—it cannot be treated as a conventional instrument of a nation's foreign policy. Most emphatically, it cannot be treated as a propaganda program designed to improve the image of a country or to cast its current policies in a favorable light. . . . The purpose of international education transcends the conventional aims of foreign policy. This purpose is nothing less than an effort to expand the scope of human moral and intellectual capacity. . . . Far therefore from being a means of gaining national advantage in the traditional game of power politics, international education should try to change the nature of the game, to civilize and humanize it in this nuclear age." The first step in this educational process, of course, is self-examination. Until we uncover our own ethnocentricism, we will never be able to perceive the world from the perspective of others; until we escape the confines of narrow self-interest, we will never be able to study man in global terms. In short, the first step of social studies education is synonymous with the Greek dictum for all education: Know thyself.

CHAPTER XV

Measurement and Evaluation

Elazar J. Pedhazur

When description gives way to measurement, calculation replaces debate.

S. S. Stevens

Measurement in education is a controversial subject among educators and laymen alike. Measurement has no place in education, claim some, because education is an art, not a science. Measurement in education is meaningless, maintain others, because in the process of applying it one loses sight of the "whole child" and deals instead with fragments which have no meaning and are of no consequence. Then there are those who claim that the important educational outcomes are intangible and can therefore not be measured.

While the above arguments may be representative of a general opposition to measurement in education, one also encounters arguments dealing with specific issues, such as the effect of testing on learning minutiae and conformity to solutions deemed correct by the teacher rather than creativity in proposing alternative solutions to the same problem. Measurement, it is claimed, discriminates against the disadvantaged and the culturally deprived, who are not test oriented and make no efforts to exhibit their "true" ability and knowledge when subjected to testing.

These are some of the arguments that are marshaled against measurement in education. The reader could probably offer a list of his

323

own. The fact, however, is that most of the arguments are irrelevant or emanate from an incorrect application or misinterpretation of measurement. Take, for example, the argument about the loss of the "whole child" in the process of measurement. It stems from a lack of understanding that one never measures an object but only an attribute or attributes of an object. Being interested in one attribute does not always necessitate awareness of others. Being interested and measuring the weight of students does not necessitate measuring their mental abilities, unless one is interested in studying the relation between weight and mental ability. If information about other attributes is important for the interpretation of a given attribute—as is often the case in education—one can and should measure the pertinent attributes. Still, one is not measuring the "whole child" but rather some of his attributes.

When confronted with a group of students, the teacher is engaged in a process of assessment which, more often than not, is impressionistic. While treating measurement with distrust, the teacher may have no reservations about describing one child as bright and another as dull; one as imaginative and another as pedestrian; one as highly motivated and another as lacking motivation. The disturbing fact is that in many instances such descriptions are drawn on the basis of flimsy, questionable, or irrelevant evidence.

Since assessments are being made and will have to be made as long as educational decisions are to be made, the question is not whether to measure or not to measure, but rather what to measure, how to measure, and how to use the results of measurement. Measurement, properly applied, can serve as a tool, as evidence collected in a specified manner for use in the process of decision-making and assessment of the educative process.

Even teachers who employ some measuring instruments tend to view the purpose of measurement solely or mostly for the assignment of grades. This is unfortunate, since measurement has, or should have, a much wider role in education. For it to be used to the utmost advantage, measurement should be an integral part of the educative process. It is one of the important means of assessing the effectiveness of teaching; it can serve as a reinforcer of learning in much the same manner as a programmed instruction does; it can be useful in making predictions in selection and guidance. In sum, measurement is not an end but rather a means in the broad spectrum of education in which the effectiveness of programs and methods is to be assessed; in which individual differences in ability, motivation, interests, attitudes are to be assessed and considered so as to make the educative process best suited and most effective for a given individual or group.

Just as it is inconceivable to approve of a teacher who does not know his subject matter, so should it be inconceivable to approve of a teacher who lacks the knowledge to measure his students so as to be better able to suit his teaching to their abilities and needs, and to assess the effectiveness of his teaching.

Needless to say, one cannot do justice to as wide a subject as measurement within the confines of a single chapter. There are available several good texts of varying degrees of sophistication to suit almost any level of knowledge. A selection of such texts is given in the bibliography. The present chapter is written with the intention of providing the reader with an introduction to some of the basic principles of measurement. More specifically, since this book is directed to social studies teachers, achievement testing, primarily by teacher-made tests, will be discussed. Other areas of measurement, no less important than achievement testing, will not be dealt with, because of space considerations.

Understanding measurement and some facility with its techniques, even on an elementary level, requires some knowledge of statistical concepts. In order not to break the continuity of the presentation and at the same time to provide the reader who has no background in statistics with the basic rudiments necessary for the understanding and application of the materials presented in this chapter, the statistical concepts are presented in an appendix to the chapter. The reader who lacks background in statistics is advised to refer to the appendix whenever necessary.

Basically, the chapter deals with the following topics: (1) Definition and Levels of Measurement; (2) Some Characteristics of a Measuring

Instrument; (3) Some Principles of Test Construction; (4) Analysis and Interpretation of Test Data; and (5) Some Statistical Concepts.

DEFINITION AND LEVELS OF MEASUREMENT

"Measurement is the assignment of numerals to objects or events according to rules" (Stevens, 1951). The use of the term "numerals" rather than "numbers" in the definition is meant to convey the idea that a symbol is being used and that the symbol does not, under certain circumstances, imply a quantity. If, for example, we decide to assign the numeral 1 to all males and the numeral 0 to all females, 1 and 0 serve only as symbols, or numerals. Note that by assigning numerals to males and females according to rules, which in the present case need not be spelled out in detail, we have achieved measurement—admittedly, at a crude level, but it is still measurement. In fact, categorization is the crudest level of measurement. It is referred to as *nominal measurement* or *categorical measurement*. Married, single, divorced is another example of this level of measurement, as is categorization according to race. Whenever we categorize, the assignment of the numerals is quite arbitrary and could therefore be replaced by another set of numerals without any change in meaning.

The second level of measurement is reached when the numerals assigned to a set of objects indicate a rank order of the objects. If, for example, one assigns numerals to one's students by ranking them on a given attribute, say height, and assigns a 1 to the tallest in the group, 2 to the second tallest, and so on, *ordinal measurement* will have been employed. Note that, after having assigned the numerals, one can say only that student number 1 is taller than student number 2; one cannot specify by how much he is taller. In fact, in the case of height, a loss of information is incurred by the conversion of the measures into a rank order. As a rule, one should not settle for a lower level of measurement when a higher level is available or attainable.

When the numerals assigned to objects enable one to make statements about the distances between one numeral and another, one is operating on the level of *interval measurement*. An example of interval measurement is the thermometer. One may state that 20° is as far from 40° as is 60° from 80°. Note, however, that one may not say that 40° is twice as hot as 20°. The reason is that we are dealing with an arbitrary zero point, which in the Centigrade scale has been set at the point when water freezes. It is important to bear in mind that in educational measurement we are not as yet able to reach the interval level. At best we reach a quasi-interval level. Take, for example, a test in social studies consisting of sixty multiple-choice items where each correct answer is scored 1 and each incorrect answer is scored 0. If Tom achieved a score of 20, John a score of 40, and Jim a perfect score of 60, one may say that John has surpassed Tom by the same number of points as he was surpassed by Jim. But it is in most cases not correct to say that the achievement manifested by the 20 points from 20 to 40 is similar to the one reflected by the differences between 40 and 60. The only safe statement one may make is that Jim ranks first in achievement on the present test, that John is second, and that Tom ranks third. These considerations bring into focus an important principle in measurement, referred to as *isomorphism*. Basically, isomorphism means that the relations between the numerals assigned to objects reflect the relations between the objects. If one rank orders students on height but assigns the numeral 1 to the third in height, numeral 2 to the shortest, numeral 3 to the tallest, and so on in a random fashion, the numerals do not reflect the relations between the students in height. The most important point about this principle is that when one has scores from a group of students on an achievement test, the scores should reflect, at least, the rank order of the students on achievement in the subject tested. This point is related to validity and reliability, which will be discussed later.[1]

The fourth and highest level of measurement is the *ratio* level. This level is achieved when one deals with measures which have an absolute zero, such as measures of height or weight. When one deals with such measures, it is possible to make statements of ratio, such that ten is twice as much as five, or that Tom is twice as tall as Jim. Note that in educational measurement we do not reach this level at all.

In summary, one should be cognizant of the method one assigns the numerals and interpret the results of his measurement within this context. Caution in this regard will protect one from gross misinterpretations of test scores.

SOME CHARACTERISTICS OF
A MEASURING INSTRUMENT

There are a number of characteristics of a measuring instrument that one can consider. One can discuss, for instance, the cost of a test, the time it takes to administer, and so forth. The two most important characteristics, however, are validity and reliability. It is therefore to these aspects that we shall devote our attention.

Validity

Unlike the physical sciences, the treatment of measurement in the social sciences is characterized by a great deal of concern about validity. This concern stems from the nature of measurement in the social sciences, which is mostly indirect. On the basis of responses to a given set of items, or on the basis of a sample of behaviors, an inference is made about a given attribute. In most cases one is not interested in the individual's responses to a given set of items per se, but rather in the inferences that can be made on the basis of the responses. A teacher who is interested in his students' achievement in social studies may construct a sixty-item multiple-choice test and, on the basis of their responses to the items, make an inference as to their achievement. The underlying assumption is that the items the teacher has written are representative of the kind of achievement he is interested in measuring. Or, if a teacher wants to measure the social attitudes of his students, he may administer an attitude scale and, on the basis of their responses, describe some students as liberals and others as conservatives. His conclusions necessarily depend on the kind of items he has used, believing that they tap the dimensions of liberalism and conservatism. To the extent that this assumption is questionable, his conclusions may be erroneous.

The selection of items or behaviors to represent a given dimension is basically a problem of validity. Generally speaking, validity raises the question whether a test is measuring what it purports to measure. To the question of whether or not a given test is valid, there is no adequate answer. One must specify the validity for what and for whom. A test may be valid for one purpose and not for another. A test in social studies consisting of items dealing with knowledge of facts only may be valid for measuring knowledge of facts and not for measuring applications of principles in social studies. Furthermore, the test may be valid for a seventh-grade and not for a tenth-grade class. Validity is not an attribute which is either present or absent in a test; rather, validity is a matter of degree.

Three kinds of validity are identified (APA, 1974), depending on the purpose for which the instrument is being used. When one is interested in assessing the degree to which an individual has acquired a certain amount of knowledge in a given area—as in tests of achievement—one is concerned mainly with *content validity*. If, on the other hand, one uses an instrument to predict an individual's present or future performance on a task other than the one measured by the test—as in aptitude testing —one is mainly concerned with *criterion-related validity*. The third kind of validity—*construct*—is of primary concern when one is interested in assessing the degree to which an individual possesses a given attribute, as is the case in the measurement of attitudes. Note that it is the purpose for which the instrument is used which is critical. The same instrument may conceivably serve more than one purpose, though probably with differential effectiveness.

It should be recognized that the assessment of the validity of an instrument used in a course in social studies cannot be divorced from the explicit and implicit goals of such a course. In fact, it is only with the goals in mind that one may attempt to determine the degree to which the instrument measures them.

Needless to say, there is no universal agreement as to the desired goals of courses in the social studies. While some teachers emphasize factual knowledge, others are concerned with the ability to seek and organize information. While some teachers maintain that the most important goal is the ability to solve social problems, others maintain that the most important goal is the learning of values and attitudes which will be manifested in the student's behavior outside of the confines of the school, not only during his school year, but throughout his life.

Ebel (1960) reports of a conference of social studies teachers in which a variety of goals were indicated and which he believed to fall under three major headings: (1) knowledge and understanding; (2) attitudes, values, and feelings; (3) intellectual skills.

No instrument can measure with equal effectiveness all these goals. Furthermore, it is impossible to construct an instrument that will exhaustively measure even one of the goals mentioned. One can, at best, attempt to define some desired objectives and proceed to construct an instrument to tap them. The first prerequisite for the construction of a valid measure is a clear definition of the objectives. Lacking a clear definition of an objective precludes the possibility of assessing it regardless of how desirable it is deemed to be. Consider, for example, "good citizenship," which most social studies teachers will probably agree to be one of the desirable outcomes of a course in social studies. What does "good citizenship" mean? It probably means different things to different people. It is conceivable that one may come up with some behavioral manifestations of "good citizenship" and still fall very short of conveying the meaning and flavor of the concept.

In the area of social studies, one is concerned mostly with either construct or content validity.

Construct Validity. When one is dealing with attitudes, values, feelings, and the like, one is primarily concerned with construct validation. That is, one asks: To what extent does an individual possess a given attitude or value? This kind of validity is probably the most difficult to demonstrate, and it requires, among other things, a thorough understanding of measurement, research design, and the philosophy of scientific inquiry. In the present chapter, one can only recommend some of the more accessible and easier sources which deal with one aspect or another of attitudes and values.

Attitudes and values are of major concern for the social psychologist. Textbooks in social psychology generally devote a major portion of the presentation to theories of attitudes and attitude change as well as to some approaches to the measurement of attitudes (e.g., Krech, Crutchfield, and Ballachey [1962]). Fishbein (1967) has compiled a very good selection of readings in the theory and measurement of attitudes. Some of the popular methods of attitude measurement are discussed and demonstrated by Edwards (1957). A wide selection of attitude scales compiled from various sources will be found in Shaw and Wright (1967). Each scale is accompanied by general information, specific measurement information, scoring procedures, and recommended use. Values and their measurement, as well as their relation to beliefs and attitudes, are discussed by Rokeach (1968, 1973).

Most of the sources cited thus far deal primarily with the measurement of the verbal expression of attitudes and values. The complex problem of the relation between verbal expression and behavior is of great importance. Efforts to measure attitudes in behavioral settings attempt to cope with some aspects of this problem. For a summary of multiple approaches to the measurement of attitudes, see Cook and Selltiz (1967). Some novel approaches may also be found in Webb *et al.* (1966).

Content Validity. When, as in achievement testing, the question whether a test measures a specific content is raised, one is dealing with content validity. Here, too, the first prerequisite is to define the area; the special emphases; and the relative importance of learning factual materials, principles, and the like. These will, of course, vary with the kind of subject matter one is dealing with, the level of the students, and the particular orientation of the school and the teacher. An excellent analysis of educational objectives and approaches to measuring them can be found in Bloom *et al.* (1956), and Bloom *et al.* (1971), which includes a chapter on evaluation in the social studies.

Having decided about the specific goals, content, and emphases, the process of studying the content validity of a test is basically judgmental. One studies the test to see whether the kind and proportion of items included correspond to one's blueprint. In other words, if one wishes, for example, to have a test in which only 10 percent of the items deal with knowledge of facts, one will not accept a test as valid if the items dealing with knowledge of facts is far exceeded. The same procedure is followed in other categories. In each case, one must not only decide whether the proportion of items in a category is acceptable, but also whether the items test the kind of materials one wishes to test. The ability to assess the applicability of a given set of items depends, among other things, upon the individual's knowledge of the subject matter being covered as well as upon his general knowledge of test construction.

The teacher who seeks a test in social studies may either choose from a wide variety of published tests or construct one himself. Even though the published tests have the advantage of being constructed, generally, by a team of people who have a good deal of knowledge in measurement or by people who have the benefit of consultation by measurement experts, such tests may not be suited to the specific needs of a teacher. A commercial test attempts generally to satisfy a wide variety of needs and may thus not satisfy adequately one's specific needs. It is probably most useful when one wishes to compare one's class with a given norm.

The best source for guidance in choosing a published test is Buros's *Tests in Print* (1961). This book provides brief information about over 2,000 tests in print. What is more important, *Tests in Print* serves as an index for five volumes of *Mental Measurement Yearbooks*, edited by Buros. In the *Yearbooks* pertinent information is given for each test, followed by one or more critical evaluations by experts in the field. Probably the most useful volumes are the most recent *Yearbooks* (1966, 1972). Note that these *Yearbooks* are not covered by *Tests in Print*.

Another source of information about published tests in the social studies is Peace (1965).

The most meaningful measurement of achievement is still the one constructed by the teacher to reflect the special emphases in the curriculum and abilities to be fostered. Needless to say, to construct an appropriate test the teacher needs to have a good deal of background in the area of measurement and test construction. The remainder of this chapter will deal briefly, and, of necessity, superficially, with some of the elements involved in constructing and evaluating a test.

Reliability. The usefulness of a measure depends on, among other things, its reliability. To the degree to which a measure has low reliability—is not accurate—one's decision on the basis of its use may turn out to be quite erroneous. If, for example, a test in social studies is used for the assignment of students to one of several sections differing in the level of sophistication with which the subject matter is studied, one should be reasonably sure that the scores on the selection test are dependable. In the event that the scores are not accurate, students may be assigned to sections which are not the most suitable for them.

Accuracy, dependability, consistency, and repeatability are some aspects of the general question of reliability of a measure. Probably no other concept in measurement has received a more elaborate and a more mathematically sophisticated treatment than reliability. What follows is an intentional oversimplification for the purpose of enabling a reader who has little or no background in statistics and measurement to employ some of the notions of reliability.

Important as reliability is, however, one should recognize that it is a necessary but not a sufficient condition for the validity of a test. That is, if a test has low reliability, if it does not measure accurately, it cannot be valid. But having a high degree of reliability does not necessarily demonstrate that the test measures what it is purported to be measuring. All that is being indicated by high reliability is that the test is measuring something accurately. That "something" may be entirely different from what the test constructor thinks that it is measuring.

Unlike the measurement of length or weight, for example, where one can apply the measure repeatedly to the same object in order to determine the accuracy of the measurement, one cannot follow such a procedure in most educational and psychological measurement. When responding to the same measure again the individual is not the same person anymore. He has undergone a certain amount of change, some of it by virtue of having responded to the measure in the first place. Rather than applying the same measure several times to the same individual, the reliability of a measure is being assessed by administering it to a group of people and studying, for example, how consistent their performance on one form of the measure is with their performance on another form of the same measure.

In order to be able to understand and employ the notions of reliability, one must have some knowledge of statistics, particularly the concept of correlation. Without an understanding of the concept of correlation, one cannot understand and interpret reported reliabilities or attempt to estimate the reliability of one's own test. The reader who lacks statistical background is advised to turn now to the statistical appendix and, after some mastery of the material presented there, resume the reading about reliability.

There are several approaches to the estimation of the reliability of a measure. We cannot deal here either with all the approaches or with their theoretical and practical implications. We shall, instead, present, by way of illustration, two approaches and then concentrate upon an approach which is probably the most useful and easiest to employ in the estimation of the reliability of a teacher-made test.

Test-Retest Reliability. If one administers a test to a group of students and after a brief interval, say three to ten days, again administers the same test, one is in a position to compute a correlation coefficient between the scores on the two administrations. The higher the coefficient of correlation, the more it essentially indicates that the rank-ordering of the students as a result of the first administration of the test is similar to the rank-ordering of the students as a result of the second administration of the test. It indicates, for example, whether the student who ranked first on the first administration also ranked first, or ranked close to first place, on the second administration, and so forth for the rest of the students. When the estimate of reliability is accomplished by a test retest method, it is referred to as a *coefficient of stability.*

The estimation of reliability by a coefficient of stability is generally not a desirable procedure, since it is quite possible, for example, that students will remember the answers they have given on the first administration and will mark the same answers during the second administration. This may lead to a spuriously high correlation and thus to a misleading conception of the reliability of the test. If, on the other hand, the interval between the two administrations is long, say several months, real changes in knowledge among students may have occurred and thus possibly lead to a low correlation between the two administrations. Note, however, that this does not necessarily mean that the test has a low reliability, but rather that the rank-order is not maintained because of actual changes in the students' knowledge.

The test-retest procedure is therefore not recommended in most situations. The reason it is presented here is to illustrate the basic procedure which is common to other methods of reliability estimation.

Equivalent Forms Reliability. If instead of administering the same test twice, one administers first Form A of a test and then an equivalent Form B of the test, one is in a position to compute a correlation coefficient between the two forms. Such a coefficient is referred to as a *coefficient of equivalence.* This is probably the best approach to the estimation of reliability, but it involves the construction of two equivalent forms, a task which a teacher will generally not undertake in view of the complexity of preparing two equivalent forms. Some test publishers provide several equivalent forms which are useful not only for the estimation of reliability but also, for example, in assessing gains when Form A is given before a study unit and Form B at its conclusion.

Split-Half Reliability. As a substitute for computing a reliability coefficient by correlating the scores of individuals on two alternate forms of a test, the teacher may split a test in two halves and compute the correlation between the scores of individuals on the two halves (we shall see later that a correction is necessary).

Basically, what is being proposed is to treat one test as being composed of two equivalent parts. It is obvious that there are any number of ways in which a test can be split into two halves. If one has no obvious method of making the two halves equivalent (e.g., on the basis of the kinds of items used), it is proposed to split the test into one half consisting of the odd items, the other half of the even items. This procedure is referred to as the odd-even reliability, which is one of the variants of the split-half reliability. Before proceeding with an illustration, it should be noted that this method is applicable for power tests only. That is, one can use this method if at least 90 percent of the students have had a chance to attempt all the items in the test. If speed is an important element in the test (this is not the case in most achievement tests), this procedure should not be applied.

In Table 1 are depicted scores of fifteen students on a ten-item test. (In an actual situation, one will have more students and more items. The larger the number of items, the more reliable the test will be.) Each item is scored 1 if it is answered correctly and 0 if answered incorrectly. The score of a student is the number of items he answered correctly. This is the general procedure one follows in scoring an achievement test. Some people recommend, however, the use of a correction for guessing. Without going into the pro and con arguments for the correction for guessing, it is recommended that it not be used; instead all students should be encouraged to make an intelligent guess when they are in doubt about an answer. Scoring the number right when such instructions are given will result in the same rank-ordering of students that will result after a correction for guessing is made.

Looking now at Table 1, we have for each individual a score on each item. We can find each individual's total score on the test simply by counting the number of items he answered correctly. By the same method we can determine his scores on the odd items and on the even items. Referring to Table 1, student A, for example, has a total score of 10; his score on the odd items is 5, and his score on the even items is 5. Student I, on the other hand, has a total score of 6; his score on the odd items is 5, and his score on the even items is 1. This was done for all students and is reported in the last three columns of Table 1.[2]

Table 1

STUDENTS	ITEMS												
	1	2	3	4	5	6	7	8	9	10	odd	even	total
A	1	1	1	1	1	1	1	1	1	1	5	5	10
B	1	1	1	1	1	1	1	1	1	0	5	4	9
C	1	1	1	1	1	1	1	1	0	0	4	4	8
D	1	1	1	1	1	1	1	0	0	0	4	3	7
E	1	1	1	1	0	1	0	0	0	0	2	3	5
F	1	1	1	1	1	1	1	0	0	0	4	3	7
G	1	1	1	0	1	1	1	0	1	1	5	3	8
H	1	1	1	1	1	0	0	0	0	0	3	2	5
I	1	0	1	0	1	1	1	0	1	0	5	1	6
J	0	0	1	0	1	1	1	0	1	1	4	2	6
K	0	0	0	1	0	0	0	1	0	0	0	2	2
L	1	1	1	1	1	1	0	0	0	0	3	3	6
M	0	0	1	1	0	0	1	1	0	1	2	3	5
N	1	1	1	1	1	0	1	0	0	1	4	3	7
O	0	1	1	0	1	1	1	1	1	0	4	3	7

In Table 2 we provide the calculation of the mean (X), the standard deviation (s) and the correlation coefficient between the odd and even items (r_{oe}).[3] The correlation between the odd and even items (r_{oe}) is .296. If one considers one half of the test as equivalent to the other half, this correlation coefficient may be considered an estimate of the reliability of a test consisting of five items (half the test). But we are interested in the reliability of the entire test, in the present case, the reliability of the ten items. Spearman and Brown have developed a formula which enables one to estimate, on the basis of a computed reliability, what will be the reliability of a test increased or decreased in size. For the present case, we want to estimate the reliability of a test double in size. The formula for this special case is:

$$r_{tt} = \frac{2r_{\frac{1}{2}\frac{1}{2}}}{1 + r_{\frac{1}{2}\frac{1}{2}}}$$

where r_{tt} = reliability of the test; $r_{\frac{1}{2}\frac{1}{2}}$ = the correlation between the two halves of the test

For our figures:

$$r_{tt} = \frac{(2)\,(.296)}{1 + .296} = .456 \text{ or } .46$$

The odd-even reliability corrected by the Spearman-Brown formula is .46.

When reporting a reliability coefficient one must also report the method by which it was estimated, because the different approaches to the estimation of reliability address themselves to different sources of errors (e.g., errors due to bias in item selection, errors due to temporary changes in the individuals taking the test). Consequently, different approaches to the estimation of reliability tend to yield different values. For a discussion of sources of errors and their relation to the estimation of reliability, see, for example, Thorndike and Hagen (1969).

The procedure outlined above applies not only to tests in which the items are scored 1 and 0, but to any system of item scoring. For example, in an attitude scale where one responds to an item on a five-point scale from very unfavorable to very favorable, one can find the subjects' scores on the odd items and on the even items and proceed to compute the reliability coefficient as outlined above.

In concluding this rather superficial treatment of reliability, some comments will be made as to its desired magnitude. Realizing that the reliability coefficient indicates how accurate a test is, one would of course want a coefficient as high as possible, one that is as close to 1.00 as possible. In practice, one may settle for different levels of reliability, depending on the purpose for which one uses the test scores. If one uses an instrument for certain research purposes which are exploratory in nature, one may accept a reliability of about .50 or even lower. If, on the other hand, one uses the test for important individual decisions, it is essential that it have a reliability in the .90s. For teacher-made tests, one would aspire to construct tests having reliabilities of about .70 and above.

Serious issues of reliability, such as the relation of reliability to the variability of the group, to the size of the test, and to the standard error of measurement, cannot be discussed here. The interested reader is referred to any of the measurement books cited in the bibliography.

SOME PRINCIPLES OF TEST CONSTRUCTION

When a teacher contemplates the construction of an achievement test, he must decide whether he wants an essay test, an objective test, or a combination of both. The reader is probably familiar with some of the controversy that surrounds this important issue, which cannot be discussed here due to space considerations. What will be offered, instead, are some specific recommendations for the construction of objective and essay tests.

Objective Tests. An objective test is one consisting of items about which competent judges agree about the correct answer. From the variety of objective-type items, the matching and the multiple-choice item are probably the most useful for testing in the social studies. While the former has limited use for certain types of material, the latter is quite versatile.

Prior to deciding what kind of items to use, it is necessary to define

Table 2
Calculations of $\bar{X}$, s, and r_{oe} for the data
given in Table 1 [4]

STUDENTS	ODD	ODD^2	EVEN	EVEN^2	ODD × EVEN	TOTAL	TOTAL^2
A	5	25	5	25	25	10	100
B	5	25	4	16	20	9	81
C	4	16	4	16	16	8	64
D	4	16	3	9	12	7	49
E	2	4	3	9	6	5	25
F	4	16	3	9	12	7	49
G	5	25	3	9	15	8	64
H	3	9	2	4	6	5	25
I	5	25	1	1	5	6	36
J	4	16	2	4	8	6	36
K	0	0	2	4	0	2	4
L	3	9	3	9	9	6	36
M	2	4	3	9	6	5	25
N	4	16	3	9	12	7	49
O	4	16	3	9	12	7	49
Σ:	54	222	44	142	164	98	692

$$r_{oe} = \frac{N \Sigma OE - (\Sigma O)(\Sigma E)}{\sqrt{N\Sigma O^2-(\Sigma O)^2}\,\sqrt{N\Sigma E^2-(\Sigma E)^2}}$$

$$\bar{X} = \frac{98}{15} = \underline{6.53}$$

$$= \frac{(15)(164) - (54)(44)}{\sqrt{(15)(222)-(54)^2}\,\sqrt{(15)(142)-(44)^2}}$$

$$s = \frac{\sqrt{N\Sigma T^2 - (\Sigma T)^2}}{N}$$

$$= \frac{2460 - 2376}{\sqrt{3330-2916}\,\sqrt{2130-1936}}$$

$$= \frac{\sqrt{(15)(692) - (98)^2}}{15}$$

$$= \frac{84}{\sqrt{414}\,\sqrt{194}} = \frac{84}{(20.35)(13.93)} = \frac{84}{283.4755}$$

$$= \frac{\sqrt{10380-9604}}{15}$$

$$= \underline{.296}$$

$$= \frac{\sqrt{776}}{15}$$

$$= \frac{27.8568}{15} = \underline{1.86}$$

clearly the objectives of the test. This relates to the topic of validity discussed above. Unless the test constructor prepares a blueprint indicating the specific content to be covered, the kind of competencies to be tested, and the degree of emphasis each will be given, he cannot proceed to construct the test.

Having decided on the objectives, the test constructor can proceed to decide what kind of item will be best suited for a given objective and how many items of each kind are needed.

It is always advisable to prepare a larger number of items than the number contemplated for final use, since in the process of editing and assembling the test some items may be deemed lacking or inappropriate in the general context of the test.

The mechanics of preparing items, editing, assembling the test, and building a test-item file will be facilitated if each item is written on a separate index card. Following this procedure, one can shuffle items and reshuffle them to come up with what one considers the most desirable grouping and order. Any information gathered about the item can be entered on the card for future reference in constructing a new version of a test in a given area.

The Matching Item. In this type of item two columns are provided, and the students are required to match items from one column to items of the other. This type of item is particularly suitable for testing knowledge of events, personalities, geographic locations, dates, and so on.

Some of the principles to be followed in constructing such items are:

1. The matching items should not exceed ten or twelve in a column. If one desires to test more information, it is advisable to construct several matching items.
2. One column should include more items than the other in order to reduce the chance of guessing by the process of elimination.
3. The items in each column should be homogeneous in content. If a column consists, for example, of a name of a capital, a name of a river, a name of a product, a name of a king, and so on, it is conceivable that one could successfully match the items while knowing very little of the subject matter.
4. It is advisable to arrange the items in each column in some

logical order. Dates, for example, should be arranged in chronological order; names, in alphabetical order; and so on.

5. It is quite acceptable that a given item in a column serve as a match for more than one item in the other column. When this is the case, the instructions should clearly indicate that.

Multiple-choice Items. The notion that the multiple-choice item lends itself only to the testing of facts and figures is entirely erroneous. The degree to which the multiple-choice-item tests more than recognition of factual material depends on the ingenuity and sophistication of the test constructor. Multiple-choice items have been used, among others, for problem solving, inferences about cause-and-effect relations, application of principles, and the like. In the area of social studies, one may, for example, introduce a map, a graph, a political cartoon, a picture, an excerpt, followed by a set of multiple-choice items. The items may call for comprehension, interpretation, inferences, planning, and the like. When the materials presented are new to all students, the teacher can assess whether, and to what extent, transfer has taken place. Are the students, for example, able to apply principles they have learned to new situations? Are the students able to derive a principle on the basis of the material provided? Can the students solve a social problem they encounter for the first time? The possibilities of such testing are almost limitless.

Some principles of multiple-choice item writing are given below. For a comprehensive treatment of this subject see, for example, Gerberich (1956), Berg (1965), Ebel (1965), and Engelhart (1966).

1. Even though some people recommend the writing of five-choice items, it is rather difficult to write four plausible distractors. The teacher is therefore well advised to limit his items to four choices and, when necessary, to three, rather than to include alternatives which are so obviously wrong that they do not serve as distractors at all.

2. One of the choices must be clearly the best, while the others should seem plausible to students not familiar with the material.

3. The stem should be written in clear and succinct language. Test for one idea at a time.

4. All the alternatives should fit the stem grammatically. When necessary, the stem should be written to accommodate different grammatical structures in the distractors.

5. The alternatives should be of about the same length. The inexperienced item writer tends to make the correct alternative longer, thus providing a clue.

6. The correct alternative should be placed randomly about an equal number of times for each possible choice.

7. It is recommended that alternative "none of the above" or "all of the above" be used sparingly, generally, only when one wishes to introduce some variation.

8. Ask for the "best" answer when some of the alternatives are partially correct.

9. Avoid providing a clue to the answer of one item by the wording of another item in the test.

It is recommended that the test constructor take the role of the student and respond to the items after the test has been assembled. In addition to providing him with a general review of the test, it may alert him to ambiguities, repetitions, or other deficiencies which may have eluded him when he dealt with one item at a time.

Essay Tests. The proponents of essay tests maintain they they are superior to objective tests because they call, among other things, for organization of materials, for recall rather than recognition, for inferences and creative contributions on the part of the respondent.

It has been argued, on the other hand, that essay tests have generally very low reliabilities, owing to the subjectivity of the scorer, questionable validities, and to the limited sampling of content. Low reliability of scoring essay tests has been demonstrated in numerous studies as well as in numerous anecdotes. For example, the *New York Post* (July 23, 1966) relates in a dispatch from Manchester, England, that five medical students in Manchester University set out to test their examiners by handing in "identical answers to the school's pathology exam." The five papers fared quite differently with the examiners. One student failed, three passed, and one passed with first-class honors.

The above is not meant to discourage the use of essay tests but rather to emphasize that when used, essay tests require a great deal of thought in the preparation stage, and a great deal of thought and effort in the evaluation and grading stages. The teacher who dreams up some questions on the way to his classroom will, most probably, end up with a very poor test, which may not be salvaged regardless of the efforts expanded in assessing the answers. Some recommendations for the preparation and scoring of essay tests follow. For a more detailed treatment of the subject see, for example, Stalnaker (1951), Ebel (1965), and Gronlund (1965).

1 Ask thought rather than fact questions. If you wish to test for facts, the objective test is more suitable and affords a possibility of a much wider sampling of content.

2 Structure the question by asking for the treatment of specific issues and aspects rather than those of a global nature, which will of necessity turn out to be ambiguous and thus render an evaluation of answers impossible.

3 The best method to determine whether the question is appropriately structured and whether it addresses itself to the issues you wish to test is to write a model answer. This will almost always result in necessary revisions of the question.

4 Rather than giving a global scores to the answer, assign score to parts of the answer on the basis of your model answer and the emphases you are seeking. When you plan to give differential weights to answers or parts of answers, the students should be informed of the system of scoring.

5 When the essays are meant to test achievement for the purpose of grading, do not allow for options from among a larger number of questions, since this may be akin to administering several different tests which may not be comparable.

6 When evaluating a test, do not look at the name of the student; thus, you will decrease the danger of the "halo effect."

7 Read and score one answer for all students and then proceed to the second, rather than reading consecutively all answers for a given student. This procedure will afford you a more appropriate frame of reference in comparability of scoring. It will also further decrease the danger of the "halo effect."

8 Errors in spelling, grammar, punctuation, and the like, should be corrected but not considered in scoring, unless they are an integral part of the test.

9 To assess the reliability of your scoring, you could score the tests twice, allowing for an interval of a couple of days between the first and second scoring, and then compute a correlation coefficient between the two sets of scores. Such a procedure may serve as an eye-opener.

The above are just some of the procedures to follow in order to make an essay test more meaningful. It is unfortunate that some teachers use essay tests with very little forethought and planning and exercise very little care and discipline in assessing them. Unless properly employed, it would be better not to resort to essay testing at all.

An essay may be used for tapping attitudes, prejudices, values, and the like. When used for such purposes, the essay should not be graded. The question or the topic should be phrased in a manner which will best elicit responses in the areas which are of particular interest to the teacher.

ANALYSIS AND INTERPRETATION OF TEST DATA

Having constructed and administered a test, the teacher must carefully analyze it. Provided the test was constructed on the basis of clearly defined objectives, the teacher may use the test data to detect areas of strengths and weaknesses for the class as a whole and for individual students. The findings will thus serve as an indication for whatever remedial work is necessary and as a basis for the planning of future study units.

It should be borne in mind that high or low performance by the entire class is not in and of itself sufficient cause for satisfaction or alarm. It is conceivable to write a test on which even the least informed and able students may achieve high scores, or to write a very difficult test on which even the most informed and able students will achieve low scores. The teacher must have in mind what he wishes his class to know and attempt to construct the test accordingly.

When the test is to serve also as a means of discrimination between students, its reliability should be relatively high. Low reliability will result when there is very little variability among the scores. This will happen either when the items are generally too easy or too difficult for the group.

As a first approximation to the assessment of the performance of the group on a test, one can study the relation between the mean to the number of items in the test. Dividing the mean by the number of items in the test will provide an index of the difficulty of the test as a whole. If this index is low, for example, .20, it indicates that the test was too difficult for the class. If, on the other hand, the index is too high, for example, .90, it indicates that the test was too easy. It is generally desirable to achieve an index between .60 and .70.

Item Analysis. A more thorough analysis of the test will be achieved by various techniques of item analysis, two of which will be briefly described here.

(1) Item difficulty. In order to determine the level of difficulty of an item, one divides the number of students who answered the item correctly by the number of students who attempted the item. Such an index may thus take values from .00 to 1.00. If, for example, none of the students answered the item correctly, the item difficulty index is .00. If, on the other hand, all students answered the item correctly, the item difficulty index is 1.00. Note that the higher the index, the easier the item.

Items which are too easy or too difficult contribute very little to the reliability of a test. Test constructors recommend that for a four-choice item, which is not corrected for guessing, the item difficulty be about .75. This does not mean that one should eliminate items that differ greatly from this index. In the last analysis, it is the judgment of the teacher which is most important. Other considerations, particularly validity, may dictate that the item be retained regardless of its level of difficulty.

(2) Item discrimination. It is also revealing to consider whether the item discriminates between the more informed and the less informed students. This can be accomplished by the use of an item-discrimination index. For this purpose, one rank orders the test papers from the highest to lowest and composes two groups, a high and a low group. There are various alternatives for composing two such groups. One

may, for example, take the top 25 percent and the bottom 25 percent. In the case of the average-sized classes, however, this will result in very small groups. In most cases, it is probably best to split the class at the median so that the top 50 percent will constitute the high group and the bottom 50 percent the low group. The index of discrimination is computed as follows:

$$\text{Discrimination} = \frac{\text{Number correct in high} - \text{Number correct in low}}{\text{Number of students in either group}}$$

If, for example, one has fifteen students in the high group and fifteen students in the low group, the index of discrimination for an item which ten students of the high group answered correctly and five students of the low group answered correctly is .33.

$$\frac{10-5}{15} = \frac{5}{15} = .33$$

Note that an index of .00 indicates that the item does not discriminate at all between the high and the low group. An index of discrimination having a negative sign indicates that more students of the low group were able to answer the item correctly. One should study such an item for possible ambiguities which may have led to such a pattern of responses. It is not necessary to discard such an item. One may change part of it in order to eliminate the ambiguity. When used again one, will note whether the item has a positive discrimination index as a result of the change.

It is recommended that items have indices of discrimination of .10 and above. But, as in the case of item difficulty, the discrimination index should not serve as the sole criterion for retaining or discarding an item.[5] There is a relation between the index of item difficulty and that of item discrimination. Very easy or very difficult items, for example, have low indices of discrimination.

Interpretation of a tests score. The score that a student gets on a test, be it the number of items he answered correctly on a multiple-choice test or the score assigned him by the teacher on an essay test, is referred to as a raw score. Two broad approaches may be taken when interpreting a raw score: 1) comparing it with a criterion of performance deemed desirable or indicative of mastery in a given area; 2) comparing the score with scores of other students who have taken the test. Tests constructed for use according to the first approach are labeled criterion-referenced tests, while those constructed for use according to the second approach are labeled norm-referenced tests. The history of measurement has been dominated by the norm-referenced approach. It is only in the last decade that psychometricians have begun to pay serious attention to criterion-referenced tests. Consequently, guides for the construction and analysis of such tests are not well developed. The classical approach to test construction and analysis (for example reliability and item analyses as discussed in this chapter) was developed within the framework of norm-referenced tests and does not apply equally well to criterion-referenced tests. Often it does not apply at all. Discussions pertaining specifically to the role of criterion-referenced tests in instruction, as well as principles for the construction, analysis, and interpretation of such tests may be found in Block (1971, 1974), Gronlund (1973), and Popham (1971). The discussion that follows deals with the interpretation of scores on norm-referenced tests.

Different types of norms have been developed. The use of a specific type of norm and norm group depends on the goals of the person or institution administering a given test. Grade and percentile norms, for example, are used for the purpose of interpretation of scores on standardized tests. A given school system may develop its own norms—in many cases it will be well advised to do so.

Probably the best method for interpreting scores on teacher-made tests is to convert them into standard scores. A standard score is defined as follows:

$$z = \frac{X - \bar{X}}{s}$$

where z = standard score; X = raw score; $\bar{X}$ = mean; s = standard deviation

Converting a set of scores to standard scores results in a distribution of scores that has a mean of zero and a standard deviation of one. For the purpose of illustration, suppose that on a given test the mean is 84 and the standard deviation is 6. Shown below are some raw scores on such a test and how they are converted into standard scores.

Raw Score	Computation	z score
84	$\dfrac{84-84}{6}$	.00
82	$\dfrac{82-84}{6}$	−.33
87	$\dfrac{87-84}{6}$	+.50
78	$\dfrac{78-84}{6}$	−1.00
90	$\dfrac{90-84}{6}$	+1.00

Note that when a raw score is the same as the mean (84), the corresponding z score is .00. When a raw score is 6 points below the mean (78), the corresponding z score is -1.00. The sign of the z score is very important. A minus sign indicates that the score is below the mean of its group, while a plus sign indicates that it is above the mean of its group.

The virtue of z scores is that they afford comparisons not only between individuals on a given test, but also within individuals across different tests. Given below are means and standard deviations of a class in history and geography, as well as raw scores for two students, Tom and John, on the two tests:

History	Geography
$\bar{X}$: 61	$\bar{X}$: 49
s: 5	s: 4
Tom 58	50
John 67	54

In order to interpret the scores we first convert them to z scores. The conversion is given below:

raw score	*History computation*	*z score*	*raw score*	*Geography computation*	*z scores*
Tom 58	$\dfrac{58-61}{5}$	$-.60$	50	$\dfrac{50-49}{4}$	$+.25$
John 67	$\dfrac{67-61}{5}$	$+1.2$	54	$\dfrac{54-49}{4}$	$+1.2$

Note that while Tom has a higher raw score in history, his performance in geography was really much better (a z score of $+.25$ in geography as compared to a z score of -.6 in history). John, on the other hand, has identical z scores on both tests. Comparing John's scores with Tom's scores, we find that his performance in history is superior by 1.8 z scores as compared to a difference of .95 z scores in geography.

For the purpose of grading, teachers generally use a student's score on several tests. It is incorrect to take an average, or in some fashion weight the raw scores. Such a procedure does not take into account the relative performance of the student on each of the tests. One should first convert all the scores to z scores and then proceed to take an average or weight them in a fashion one prefers. For procedures of converting z scores to scores that are unencumbered by negative signs and fractions, also for weighting standards scores and assignment of grades, see Ebel (1965).

CONCLUSION

This chapter has presented an introduction and some basic orientations and procedures in the area of measurement. This should by no means be construed as a substitute for a more thorough treatment of the subject. In fact, if this chapter serves to stimulate the reader to further study the area of measurement, it will have accomplished its main purpose.

STATISTICAL APPENDIX

This appendix deals with some basic statistical concepts necessary for the computation of reliability as well as the interpretation of test data. The statistical concepts presented here are the mean, the standard deviation, and the correlation coefficient. Since the main purpose of this presentation is to learn to compute and interpret these measures, it was decided to use small numbers so as not to becloud the presentation with extensive computations. It should be realized that though the numbers used are not representative in scope and magnitude of what one encounters with actual test data, the techniques apply to any set of numbers.

The Mean

The mean is the arithmetic average which we so frequently use in various fields and therefore requires no elaboration here. In the case of test data, we add up all the scores and divide by the number of people in the group. It is advisable, however, to present here the conventional symbols and the formula used for the computation of the mean. Many people become uneasy when the need arises to deal with symbols and formulas. To some, symbols and formulas actually seem unnecessary, confusing the issues. It should be recognized, however, that the use of symbols and formulas simplifies rather than complicates a presentation. What must be said in so many words, which may be misinterpreted or misunderstood, can be stated clearly and succinctly by a symbol or a formula.

We shall present symbols and formulas as the need arises. For the purpose of computing the mean we define the following symbols:

X = a raw score on a measure.

Σ = the sum of. Whenever Σ precedes a symbol, it indicates to sum all the values that symbol represents. For example: ΣX means sum all the X's.

In a class of 30 students, each student's raw score is symbolized by an X. ΣX will mean the sum of the 30 raw scores.

N = number of subjects in a group.

$$\bar{X} = \text{mean} = \frac{\Sigma X}{N}$$

Note that the formula for the mean states that one sums all the X's (all the scores in the group) and divides by N (the number of people in the group).

The Standard Deviation

Knowing the mean of a set of scores provides one only with partial information about the group. Various combinations of scores may yield identical means. Look, for example, at the three sets of scores below:

I	*II*	*III*
1	4	10
2	4	8
3	4	4
4	4	2
5	4	2
6	4	1
7	4	1
$\Sigma X = 28$	$\Sigma X = 28$	$\Sigma X = 28$

$$\bar{X} = \frac{28}{7} = 4 \qquad \bar{X} = \frac{28}{7} = 4 \qquad \bar{X} = \frac{28}{7} = 4$$

Note that the while the means are 4, the sets of scores that yield these means are quite different from each other. In order to describe a set of scores appropriately, we need, in addition to the mean, a measure of variability. We need a measure that will show the spread of the scores around the mean. Note, for instance, that in set II there is no variability. All the scores are 4.

One of the most useful measures of variability is the standard deviation. We define the following:

x = a deviation = $X - \bar{X}$. A deviation is defined as the raw score minus the mean.

s = standard deviation = $\sqrt{\dfrac{\Sigma x^2}{N}}$. The standard deviation equals the square root of the sum of all the deviations squared divided by the number of the deviations. Note, again, how more succinct is the symbolic presentation compared to the verbal statement.

Let us take set I and see what the computation of the standard deviation entails.

(1)	(2)	(3)
X	$x = X - \bar{X}$	x^2
1	-3	9
2	-2	4
3	-1	1
4	0	0
5	$+1$	1
6	$+2$	4
7	$+3$	9
$\Sigma X = 28$	$\Sigma x = 0$	$\Sigma x^2 = 28$

$$\bar{X} = \frac{28}{7} = 4 \qquad\qquad s = \sqrt{\frac{28}{7}} = \sqrt{4} = 2$$

In column (1) we have the raw scores for seven individuals. $\Sigma X = 28$. $\bar{X} = 4$. In column (2) the deviations from the mean were computed. For the first score, for example, we have $1 - 4 = -3$, and so on. for all the scores. We could add all the deviations and divide by the number of deviations in order to determine how, on the average, the scores deviate from the mean. But note that $\Sigma x = 0$. The sum of the deviations from the mean is always zero. In order to eliminate the minus signs we square each deviation. These are found in column (3). $\Sigma x^2 = 28$.

We can now take the average of the squared deviations and then take the square root of that average, thus getting the standard deviation.

$$s = \sqrt{\frac{\Sigma x^2}{N}} = \sqrt{\frac{28}{7}} = \sqrt{4} = 2$$

You may wonder what this value means. By itself it means very little. It becomes meaningful in a comparative sense. Let us assume that we have the following statistics for three classes A, B, and C.

	A	B	C
N:	30	30	30
$\bar{X}$:	60	60	60
s	5.73	11.35	2.89

Note that the three classes have identical means, but the scores in class C are the least variable around the mean, while the scores in class B are the most variable. Put in other words, we may say that class C is the most homogeneous of the three, or that class B is the most heterogeneous. Class A is more heterogeneous than class C and less heterogeneous than class B.[6]

The calculation of the standard deviation presented above is misleadingly simple. What happens, for instance, when the mean is a fraction and one decides to round at a given number of decimals? The computation becomes quite cumbersome and the result is inaccurate, the degree of inaccuracy depending at what decimal place one rounded the mean.

The demonstrated calculation of the standard deviation is therefore not recommended in most cases. It was presented to illustrate the logic behind the concept of the standard deviation. For computational purposes, it is suggested that we use a formula that employs the raw scores only. In raw scores:

$$s = \frac{\sqrt{N\Sigma X^2 - (\Sigma X)^2}}{N}$$

Even though this formula uses only raw scores, it is an algebraic identity of the formula that uses deviation scores. That is:

$$s = \sqrt{\frac{\Sigma X^2}{N}} = \frac{\sqrt{N\Sigma X^2 - (\Sigma X)^2}}{N}$$

The raw-score formula looks more complex and demanding, but it is in fact easier to use and is more accurate when rounding is introduced in the calculation of the mean.

Before demonstrating the use of this formula, note the difference between ΣX^2 and $(\Sigma X)^2$. ΣX^2 means square each X and then sum them all. $(\Sigma X)^2$ means sum all the X's and then square the sum. In other words, ΣX^2 is the sum of the squares, while $(\Sigma X)^2$ is the square of the sum.

Let us use this formula to compute the standard deviation for set I.

X	X^2	$N = 7$
1	1	$\Sigma X = 28$
2	4	$(\Sigma X)^2 = 784$
3	9	$\Sigma X^2 = 140$
4	16	
5	25	
6	36	
7	49	
ΣX: 28	ΣX^2 140	

$$s = \frac{\sqrt{(7)(140) - 784}}{7} = \frac{\sqrt{980 - 784}}{7}$$

$$= \frac{\sqrt{196}}{7} = \frac{14}{7} = 2$$

Note that the standard deviation is 2, the same result obtained by the previous method. It is true that with the present figures the first method seems easier, but with actual test scores the second method is preferable. When doing computations, it is recommended that you use tables of squares and square roots which can be found in most statistics books. Better yet, one can obtain an inexpensive calculator that has the capacity to square numbers, extract square roots, and accumulate numbers in memory. Try to calculate the standard deviation for set III above (the answer is: 3.34). Note that a standard deviation is reported to two decimal places. Now try to calculate means and standard deviations for some actual sets of test scores from your classes.

Correlation

There are various kinds of indices that are used to describe the relation between two variables. The index that we are going to use is the Pearson Product-Moment Coefficient of Correlation, or, briefly, Pearson r. This coefficient can take values from .00 to 1.00. That is, when there is no relation between the two variables, the coefficient is .00. If, on the other hand, the correlation between two variables is perfect, that is when on the basis of knowledge of a value on one variable one can make a perfect prediction as to what the value on the other variable is, the correlation is 1.00. The correlation coefficient is reported to at least two decimal places. The closer the value of Pearson *r* is to 1.00, the stronger the relation between the variables.

The correlation coefficient may also be positive or negative in sign, depending on the kind of relation that it describes. If an increase in the value of one variable is associated with an increase in the value of the other variable, the sign of *r* is positive. If, on the other hand, an increase in one variable is associated with a decrease in the other variable, the sign of *r* is negative. In the present context we need not be concerned with negative correlations.

The symbol for the correlation coefficient is usually written with subscripts to indicate what the variables are. For example, $r_{xy} = .62$ means that the correlation between *x* and *y* is .62. The symbols *x* and *y* may stand for any two variables. In the present case, *x* may stand for I.Q. and *y* for scholastic achievement (by the way, this is about the magnitude of relation between I.Q. and achievement generally encountered). One may use any set of subscripts to identify the variables. If, for example, one reports the relation between performance on form A and form B of a test in a social studies, one may write r_{ab} instead of r_{xy}, or any other subscript which ones deems more appropriate.

Before proceeding with the method of calculation, it is important to note that a correlation coefficient can be computed for a group only and not for a single individual. Furthermore, each member of the group must have two measures, one measure on X and one measure on Y. The formula for computing *r* is:

$$r_{xy} = \frac{N\Sigma XY - (\Sigma X)(\Sigma Y)}{\sqrt{N\Sigma X^2 - (\Sigma X)^2}\ \sqrt{N\Sigma Y^2 - (\Sigma Y)^2}}$$

Note that this is a raw-score formula, using only raw scores in the computation. The computation of r_{xy} will now be illustrated with a small set of numbers.

X	X^2	Y	Y^2	XY
1	1	2	4	2
2	4	4	16	8
3	9	6	36	18
4	16	8	64	32
5	25	10	100	50
ΣX:15	ΣX^2:55	ΣY:30	ΣY^2:220	ΣXY:110

In order to compute the relation between the set of X and Y scores, one needs the following values (to plug into the formula): ΣX; ΣX^2; ΣY; ΣY^2; ΣXY, and N. Note that the first five values were computed in the table. N is the number of students, or the number of pairs of scores; in this case, 5. Note carefully that though there are 10 scores in the table they come from five individuals, each having a score on X and a score on Y, and therefore N is 5 and not 10.

Applying the formula:

$$r_{xy} = \frac{(5)(110) - (15)(30)}{\sqrt{(5)(55) - (15)^2}\ \sqrt{(5)(220) - (30)^2}}$$

$$r_{xy} = \frac{550 - 450}{\sqrt{275 - 225}\ \sqrt{1100 - 900}}$$

$$= \frac{100}{\sqrt{50}\ \sqrt{200}} = \frac{100}{\sqrt{10,000}} = \frac{100}{100} = 1.00$$

$$r_{xy} = 1.00.$$

There is a perfect correlation between the two sets of scores. Look at the scores and you will see that this is so. Actually, $Y = 2X$. When, for example, $X = 4$, $Y = 8$. We can make a perfect prediction from Y to X or from X to Y.

X	X^2	Y	Y^2	XY
1	1	4	16	4
2	4	2	4	4
3	9	6	36	18
4	16	8	64	32
5	25	10	100	50
ΣX:15	ΣX^2:55	ΣY:30	ΣY^2:220	ΣXY:108

We take now the same set of numbers and make one change as indicated in the table, switching 2 and 4 in the Y column.

It is obvious that the only column affected is the XY. All the rest will have the same values, since it makes no difference whether, for example, one squares the number 2 first and adds it to the square of the number 4, or vice versa.

Applying the formula again:

$$r_{xy} = \frac{(5)(108) - (15)(30)}{\sqrt{(5)(55) - (15)^2} \; \sqrt{(5)(220) - (30)^2}}$$

$$= \frac{540 - 450}{\sqrt{10,000}} = \frac{90}{100} = .90$$

$$r_{xy} = .90$$

The switching of two numbers reduced the relation from 1.00 to .90. It should be noted that because we are dealing with five pairs only, switching two numbers results in so noticeable a change. Within a larger set of pairs there will be more stability.

You can now practice easily the computation of r by changing the order of the numbers in the X or Y column, or in both. As long as you use the original numbers, the only column that will change is XY. You will therefore always have the same denominator (100), while your numerator will change.

When computing, remember that multiplication precedes subtraction. You therefore should first multiply N by ΣXY; multiply ΣX by ΣY, and only then subtract the latter result from the former. This rule, of course, also applies to the operations in the denominator.

When dealing with large scores, one may simplify the computations by a process of coding. One form of coding is subtraction of a constant from all the scores in a column. It is not necessary to subtract the same constant from the scores in both columns. One may subtract one constant from the X column and another from the Y column. One useful procedure is to subtract from all scores a round figure closest to the lowest scores in the column. For instance, in the following sets of scores, one may subtract 110 from each score in column X and 100 from each score in column Y (100 from each score in both columns, or any other score) and compute the correlation coefficient.

X	Y
110	105
111	102
114	108
112	107
116	102
111	106
113	109
118	112
115	111
120	114

The result will be the same as when one uses the original scores.[7] Compute r with the original scores and then by subtracting some constant(s) from the scores in either or both columns. (Answer: $r = .67$.)

NOTES

1. While we cannot demonstrate that educational measurements have the properties of an interval scale, we act as if they did when analyzing and interpreting them. Practical as well as statistical considerations have shown that the relaxation of the requirements works. In the section dealing with standard scores, for example, we set the mean of the group as the arbitrary zero and treat the scores as if they were on an interval scale.
2. For the purpose of computing the reliability, one does not need to first display the item scores as we have done in Table 1. Just as one generally counts for each student the number of items answered correctly to determine his total score, so one can count and record for each student the number of correct answers to the odd items and the number of correct answers to the even items. Odd plus even, of course, equals the total score for a given individual.
    The display of item scores in tabular form is helpful when one engages in certain aspects of item analysis, a topic we shall discuss briefly later.
3. The $\bar{X}$ and s of the test should always be computed. We shall show later how they are used in the interpretation of test scores.
4. See statistical appendix for explanations of $\bar{X}$, s, and r, and computational examples.

5. Educational Testing Service, Princeton, N.J., has published a *Test and Measurement Kit,* which is supplied free on request. This is a set of booklets dealing with various topics in measurement, among which are: *Making a Classroom Test, Selecting an Achievement Test: Principles and Procedures, Multiple-choice Questions: A Close Look,* and *Shortcut Statistics for Teacher-made Tests.* The last mentioned outlines very useful and simple procedures of items analysis which can be performed in class involving the students in the process.

6. When the scores on a test are normally distributed, or approximate a normal distribution, the standard deviation can be used for purposes of interpretation in conjunction with the properties of the normal curve. Such matters are beyond the scope of this presentation. The interested reader will find a treatment of this aspect in almost any elementary statistics book. See, for example, Peatman (1963) and Popham (1967).

7. Coding by subtraction will also leave the standard deviation unchanged. Therefore, if you have to compute a standard deviation for a set of large scores, you may subtract a constant from all the scores and compute the standard deviation for the set of coded scores.

BIBLIOGRAPHY

Adams, G. S. *Measurement and Evaluation in Education, Psychology, and Guidance.* New York: Holt, Rinehart & Winston, 1964.

Ahmann, J. S., and Glock, M. D. *Evaluating Pupil Growth.* 3d ed. Boston: Allyn and Bacon, 1967.

American Psychological Association. *Standards for Educational and Psychological Tests.* Washington, D.C.: American Psychological Association, 1974.

Berg, H. D., ed. *Evaluation in Social Studies.* Washington, D.C.: National Council for the Social Studies, 1965.

Bloom, B. S., *et al. Taxonomy of Educational Objectives.* New York: David McKay, 1956.

Handbook on Formative and Summative Evaluation of Student Learning. New York: McGraw-Hill, 1971.

Block, J. H., ed. *Mastery Learning.* New York: Holt, Rinehart and Winston, 1971.

——— ed. *Schooling, Society, and Mastery Learning.* New York: Holt, Rinehart and Winston, 1974.

Buros, O. K. *The Fifth Mental Measurement Yearbook.* Highland Park, New Jersey: Gryphon Press, 1959.

———. *Tests in Print.* Highland Park, New Jersey: Gryphon Press, 1961.

————. *The Sixth Mental Measurement Yearbook.* Highland Park, New Jersey: Gryphon Press, 1966.

————. *The Seventh Mental Measurement Yearbook.* Highland Park, New Jersey: 1972.

Cook, S. W., and Selltiz, C. "A Multiple-Indicator Approach to Attitude Measurement," *Psychological Bulletin,* LXII (1964), 36-55.

Ebel, R. L. "The Problem of Evaluation in the Social Studies," *Social Education,* XXIV (1960), 6-10.

————. *Measuring Educational Achievement.* Englewood Cliffs, New Jersey: Prentice-Hall, Inc., 1965.

Edwards, A. L. *Techniques of Attitude-Scale Construction.* New York: Appleton-Century-Crofts, 1957.

Engelhart, M. D. "Exercise Writing in the Social Sciences." In A. Anastasi, ed., *Testing Problems in Perspective.* Washington, D.C.: American Council on Education, 1966. Pp. 153-64.

Fishbein, M., ed. *Readings in Attitude Theory and Measurement.* New York: John Wiley, 1967.

Gerberich, R. J. *Specimen Objective Test Items.* New York: David McKay, 1956.

Gronlund, N. E. *Measurement and Evaluation in Teaching.* New York: Macmillan, 1965.

————. *Preparing Criterion-Referenced Tests for Classroom Instruction.* New York: Macmillan, 1973.

Krech, D., Crutchfield, R. S., and Ballachey, E. L. *Individual and Society.* New York: McGraw-Hill, 1962.

Noll, V. H. *Introduction to Educational Measurement,* 2d ed. Boston: Houghton Mifflin, 1965.

Peace, B. A. Bibliography of Social Studies Tests. In H. D. Berg, ed., *Evaluation in Social Studies.* Washington, D.C.: National Council for the Social Studies, 1965. Pp. 230-47.

Peatman, J. G. *Introduction to Applied Statistics.* New York: Harper and Row, 1963.

Popham, W. J., ed. *Criterion-Referenced Measurement.* Englewood Cliffs, New Jersey: Educational Technology Publications, 1971.

————. *Educational Statistics.* New York: Harper and Row, 1967.

Rokeach, M. *Beliefs, Attitudes, and Values.* San Francisco: Jossey-Bass, 1968.

————. *The Nature of Human Values.* New York: Free Press, 1973.

Shaw, M. E., and Wright, J. M. *Scales for the Measurement of Attitudes.* New York: McGraw-Hill, 1967.

Stalnaker, J. M. "The Essay Type of Examination." In E. F. Lindquist, ed., *Educational Measurement.* Washington, D.C.: American Council on Education, 1951. Pp. 560-620.

Stevens, S. S. "Mathematics, Measurement, and Psychophysics." In S. S.

Stevens, ed., *Handbook of Experimental Psychology.* New York: John Wiley, 1951. Pp. 1-49.

Thorndike, R. L., and Hagen, E. *Measurement and Evaluation is Psychology and Education,* 3d ed. New York: John Wiley, 1969.

Webb, E. J., Campbell, D. T., Schwartz, R. D., and Sechrest, L. *Unobtrusive Measures: Nondirective Research in the Social Sciences.* Chicago: Rand McNally, 1966.